WESKER'S HISTORICAL PLAYS

Arnold Wesker's

HISTORICAL PLAYS

Shylock
Blood Libel
Longitude
Caritas

OBERON BOOKS
LONDON

WWW.OBERONBOOKS.COM

This collection first published in 2012 by Oberon Books Ltd
521 Caledonian Road, London N7 9RH
Tel: +44 (0) 20 7607 3637 / Fax: +44 (0) 20 7607 3629
e-mail: info@oberonbooks.com
www.oberonbooks.com

Cover photograph by Nobby Clark

Contents

SHYLOCK

a play in two acts

I do not use despair, for it is not mine,
only entrusted to me for safe-keeping.

Wislawa Szymborska, Polish poetess.

Characters

SHYLOCK KOLNER
a Jew of Venice

JESSICA
his daughter

RIVKA
his sister

TUBAL DI PONTI
his partner

ANTONIO QUERINI
a merchant of Venice

BASSANIO VISCONTI
Antonio's godson

LORENZO PISANI
Bassanio's friend

GRAZIANO SANUDO
Antonio's assistant

PORTIA CONTARINI
an heiress of Venice

NERISSA
her maid

RODERIGUES DA CUNHA
an architect

SOLOMON USQUE
a playwright

REBECCA DA MENDES
daughter of Portuguese banker

MOSES DA CASTELAZZO
a portrait painter

GIROLAMO PRIULI
Doge of Venice

Maid in Shylock's house[1]

Patricians and others at director's discretion

Time and Place

Venice 1563

---

1. Who should also be the singer at the end of the play.

This version results from a number of productions: the London workshop production directed by the author at The Riverside Studio, London in 1989, which differs from the version world-premiered in Stockholm in 1976; the English speaking version premiered on Broadway in 1977; and the version further revised for the production in Birmingham UK 1978.

Finally, some of the changes and cuts made by the author for his BBC Radio 3 adaptation in February 2005, have been incorporated into this stage version.

Act One

SCENE ONE

Venice, 1563. The Ghetto Nuovo.

SHYLOCK's study. It is strewn with books and manuscripts.

SHYLOCK a 'loan banker', with his friend, ANTONIO, a merchant, are leisurely cataloguing.

ANTONIO is by the table, writing, as SHYLOCK reads out the titles and places them on his shelves.

They are old friends, in their middle sixties.

SHYLOCK: *(Reading out.)* 'Guide to the Perplexed'. Author, Maimonides, Ram-bam, known as the Great Eagle. Cairo. Twelfth century

> *ANTONIO writes.*

Hebrew/Hebrew dictionary. Author, R. David Kimhi. England. Twelfth century. Not too fast for you, Antonio?

ANTONIO: It's not the most elegant script, but I'm speedy.

SHYLOCK: And I'm eager. I know it. But here, the last of the manuscripts and then we'll begin cataloguing my printed books. Such treasures to show you, you'll be thrilled, thrrrrrilled! You'll be – I can't wait…just one more –

ANTONIO: Do I complain?

SHYLOCK: – and then we'll rest. I promise you. I'll bring out my wines, and fuss and – the last one. I promise, promise.

ANTONIO: Shylock! Look! I'm waiting.

SHYLOCK: I have a saint for a friend.

ANTONIO: And what does the poor saint have?

SHYLOCK: An overgrown schoolboy. I know it! The worst of the deal. But –

ANTONIO: I'm waiting, Shylock.

SHYLOCK: Deed. Legal. Anglo-Jewish. Twelfth century. Author – I can't read the name. Probably drawn up by a businessman himself. *(Peering.)* What a mastery of Talmudic Law. I love them, those old men, their cleverness, their deeds, their wide-ranging talents. Feel it! Touch it!

ANTONIO: The past.

SHYLOCK: Exactly!

ANTONIO: And all past.

SHYLOCK: Antonio! You look sad.

ANTONIO: Sad?

SHYLOCK: I've overworked you. Here. Drink. Why wait till we're finished? *(Offers wine.)* Drink. It's a special day.

They drink in silence.

ANTONIO: So many books.

SHYLOCK: And all hidden for ten years. Do you know what that means for a collector? Ten years? Ha! The scheme of things! 'The Talmud and kindred Hebrew literature? Blasphemy!' they said, 'burn them!' And there they burned, on the Campo dei Fiori in Rome, the day of the burning of the books. Except mine, which I hid, all of them, even my secular works. When fever strikes them you can't trust those 'warriors of God'. With anything of learning? Never! Their spites, you see, the books revealed to them their thin minds. And do you think it's over even now? Look! *(Pushes out a secret section of his bookcase.)* The Sacred Books. The law has changed and so the others I can bring back, but still, to this day, the Talmud is forbidden.

And I have them, the greatest of them, Bomberg's edition, each of them. Aren't they beautiful?

ANTONIO: So beautiful.

SHYLOCK: *(Referring to others.)* I'm a hoarder of other men's genius. My vice. My passion. Nothing I treasure more, except my daughter. So – drink! It's a special day. Look! A present to cheer you up. One of my most treasured manuscripts, a thirteenth-century book of precepts, author Isaac of Corbeil, with additamenta made by the students. I used to do it myself, study and scribble my thoughts in the margin. We all did it. We had keen minds, Antonio, very profound we thought ourselves, commenting on the meaning of life, the rights and wrongs of the laws, offering our interpretations of the interpretations of the great scholars who interpreted the meaning of the meaning of the prophets. 'Did the prophecies of Daniel refer to the historic events or to the Messianic times, or neither? Is the soul immortal, or not? Should one or should one not ride in a gondola on the Sabbath?' Money lending was never a full-time occupation and the Ghetto rocked with argument – ha! It thrills me! *(Pause.)* There! I *have* tired you.

ANTONIO: I assure you –

SHYLOCK: Depressed you, then. I've done that.

ANTONIO: Not that either. But –

SHYLOCK: But what? What but, then?

ANTONIO: Those books. Look at them. How they remind me what I am, what I've done. Nothing! A merchant! A purchaser of this to sell there. A buyer-up and seller-off. And do you know, I hardly ever see my trade. I have an office, a room of ledgers and a table, and behind it I sit and wait till someone comes in to ask have I wool from Spain, cloth from England, cotton from Syria, wine from Crete. And I say yes, I've a ship due in a week, or a month, and I make a note, and someone goes to the dock, collects the corn, delivers it to an address, and I see nothing. I travel neither to England to check cloth, nor Syria to check cotton, or Corfu to see that the olive oil is cleanly corked, and I could steal time for myself in such places. It never worried me, this absence of curiosity for travel. Until I met you, old Jew –

SHYLOCK: Not so old *then*, old man, only just past fifty –

ANTONIO: – and I became caught up in your – your passion, your hoardings, your – your vices!

SHYLOCK: Is he complaining or thanking me?

ANTONIO: You've poisoned me, old Shylock, with restlessness and discontent..

SHYLOCK: He's complaining.

ANTONIO: A lawyer, a doctor, a diplomat, a teacher – anything but a merchant. There's no sweetness in my dealings. After the thrill of the first exchange, after the pride of paying a thousand ducats with one hand and taking fifteen hundred with the other – no skill. Just an office and some ledgers. It's such a joyless thing, a bargain. I'm so weary with trade.

SCENE TWO

Belmont.

PORTIA's estate outside Venice. The estate is in great disrepair.

PORTIA and her maid, NERISSA, both in simple, hard-wearing clothes, have just arrived to view the neglect.

PORTIA: Decided! The speculating days of the family Contarini are done. The goods warehoused in our name at Beirut and Famagusta we'll sell off cheaply to cut our losses, I shall raise what I can from the sale of our properties on Crete, Corfu and the Dalmatian towns which are too far from Venice and not worth their troubles, but –

NERISSA: – but agriculture, my lady, what does my lady Portia know of agriculture?

PORTIA: Your lady Portia will learn, Nerissa. The famines are cruel and constant visitors. We must reclaim the land.

NERISSA: – but to leave the city?

PORTIA: I love my city, Nerissa, but I hear rumours. Timber is scarce, the number of ships registered by Venice is dropping. Signs, my dear, the signs are there. It's goodbye to Venice, and into the wheat lands of my estates near Treviso and Vicenza and here, Belmont. We'll become growers! Stockbreeders! Cattle and drainage! That's where our fortunes lie.

Good God! *(Looking around.)* What a mess my father's made of my childhood! *(Pause.)* Is this the room?

NERISSA: Facing the sun at eleven o'clock. This is it.

PORTIA: And *here* we are to find the caskets?

NERISSA: *(Searching.)* Here, somewhere in all this neglect. Your father's puzzle for picking a spouse. One gold, one silver, one lead.

NERISSA reveals a dusty corner.

Found! *(Reading.)* 'By his choice shall you know him.'

PORTIA: What an inheritance! Ten estates in ruin, and a foolish philosophic whim for to find me an idiot husband. Oh father, father, father! What *were* you think of? Hear me up there. I *will* honour your wish: whom the casket chooses, I'll marry. But your rules for judging men I will forget, and these ruins will be put back again. The material things of this world count. We *have* no soul without labour, and labour I will, father, hear me.

PORTIA moves about the room pulling down tattered curtains, replacing furniture on its feet, picking up strewn books, perhaps rubbing encrusted dirt from a vase till its frieze can be seen, but moving, moving.

NERISSA: How your mother would love to be alive now, with all this possibility of work at last.

PORTIA: Perhaps that's my real inheritance, Nerissa: father's marriage to a peasant. My energy is hers.

NERISSA: And such energy, madam.

PORTIA: All stored and waiting for the poor man's death.

NERISSA: Come, be just. He didn't commit you in marriage at the age of seven as my father did. He gave you tutors.

PORTIA: Ah, thank heaven for them.

NERISSA: A very strange collection, I used to think.

PORTIA: Oh! Those caskets! Those stupid caskets! Take them out of my sight. I loved him dearly, my father, but those caskets will bring me down as his other madnesses brought down my mother, I feel it.

NERISSA: *Such* energy, madam, you tire me to watch you.

PORTIA: And you must have it too, Nerissa. I demand it. You are not only my help but my friend and I'll have you educated and protected from the miseries of an ill-chosen marriage.

NERISSA: If, that is, you can protect yourself from one.

PORTIA: True! My God, and what suitors have announced they're coming. Why, do you wonder, *is* there such interest in me?

NERISSA: Riches, madam, riches, riches, riches.

PORTIA: But my riches are potential, not realised.

NERISSA: The family name?

PORTIA: My family name is illustrious but somewhat moth-eaten.

NERISSA: Your beauty.

PORTIA: No flattery. I won't have it. My beauty is, well – it *is*, but no more than many such women of Venice I could name.

NERISSA: Why, then? *You* say.

PORTIA: I *think* I know, but I'm not certain. There are simply – mmm – pulses in my veins. I feel, I feel – I feel I-am-the-new-woman-and-they-know-me-not! For centuries the Church has kept me comfortably comforting and cooking and pleasing and patient. And now – Portia is no longer patient. Yes, she can spin, weave, sew. Give her meat and drink – she can dress them. Show her flax and wool – she can make you clothes. But – Portia reads! History and politics, logic and mathematics, she has gazed at the stars, scrutinised maps, conversed with liberal minds on the nature of the soul, the efficacy of religious freedom, the very existence of God!

NERISSA: Why! Her brain can hardly catch its breath!

PORTIA: She has observed, judged, organised and – crept out of the kitchen. The fireside chair rocks without her now, and what she will do is a mystery. Portia is a new woman, Nerissa. There is a woman on the English throne. Anything can happen and they are coming to find out.

SCENE THREE

SHYLOCK's study. He and ANTONIO have been drinking.

SHYLOCK: I gave you wine to cheer you up. It's cheered me down!

ANTONIO: Filed! Catalogued! All that knowledge. You could save the world.

SHYLOCK: When I can't be certain of saving myself?
What a thought! Not even the poor sages with all their
wisdom could save themselves. They were all poor sages.
Constantly invited to run educational establishments here
and there, and never certain whether they were running
into a massacre. From the massacre of Rouen they fled into
the massacre of London; from the massacre of London into
the massacre of York, and from the massacre of York no
one fled! *(Pause.)* Travelling wasn't very safe in those days!

ANTONIO: Are you a religious man, Shylock?

SHYLOCK: What a question. Are you *so* drunk?

ANTONIO: You *are* religious, for all your freethinking, you're a
devout man. And I love and envy you for it.

SHYLOCK: You are *so* drunk. Religious! It's the condition of
being Jewish, like pimples with adolescence, who can help
it? Even those of us who don't believe in God have dark
suspicions that he believes in us. Listen, I'll tell you how
it all happened. Ha! The scheme of things! It thrills me!
Thrills me! Imagine this tribe of Semites in the desert.
Pagan, wild, but brilliant. A sceptical race, believing only
in themselves. Loving but assertive. Full of quarrels and
questions. Who could control them? Leader after leader
was thrown up but, in a tribe where every father of his
family was a leader, who could hold them in check for
long? Until one day a son called Abraham was born, and
he grew up knowing his brethren very, very well indeed.
'I know how to control this arrogant, anarchic herd of
heathens,' he said to himself. And he taught them about
one God. Unseen! Of the spirit! That appealed to them, the
Hebrews, they had a weakness for concepts of the abstract.
An unseen God! Ha! What an inspiration. But that wasn't
all. Abraham's real statesmanship, his real stroke of genius
was to tell this tribe of exploding minds and vain souls:
'Behold! An unseen God! God of the Universe! Of all men!
and –' wait, for here it comes, '– and, of all men you are

his chosen ones!' Irresistible! In an instant they were quiet. Subdued. 'Oh! Oh! Chosen? Really? Us? To do what?' 'To bear witness to what is beautiful in creation, and just. A service, not a privilege!' 'Oh dear! Chosen to bear witness! What an honour! Ssh! No so loud. Dignity! Abraham is speaking. Respect! Listen to him. Order!' It worked! *They* had God and Abraham had *them*. But – they were now cursed. For from that day moved they into a nationhood that had to be better than any other and, poor things, all other nations found them unbearable to live with. What can I do? I'm chosen. I *must* be religious.

ANTONIO: I love you more and more, Shylock. You have a sanity I could not live without now. I'm spoiled, chosen also.

SHYLOCK: But sad, still. I can see it. I've failed to raise your spirits one tiny bit.

ANTONIO: *I'm* not a religious man. I had a letter today, from an old friend, Ansaldo Visconti of Milan, a rich merchant, and well loved in my youth. But I'd forgotten him. And in this letter he commends to me his only son, Bassanio, my godson it seems. And I'd forgotten him also. Poor young Bassanio. Probably a very noble young nobleman. His father was born in Venice, if I remember, of patrician stock, if I remember. No, he's probably a swaggering young braggart! Coming to see me in the hope I'll put trade his way, or put him in trade's way and pass on wisdom, or something. *(Pause.)* But I don't want to be wise, or to talk about trade, or to see him. Ungodly man! Doesn't that make me an ungodly man? I should never have had godsons. Not the type. Bachelor merchant. On the other hand I suppose that's just the type.

SHYLOCK: When do you expect him?

ANTONIO: Oh, tomorrow, or the next day, or is it next week? Can't remember which. Bassanio! Humph! *(Shouting out.)* I'm not a religious man, Bassanio.

SHYLOCK: Antonio, my friend, it's late. In ten minutes they lock the gates of the Ghetto and all good Christians should be outside. I have a suggestion – stay the night.

ANTONIO: *Stay* the night?

SHYLOCK: It's not permitted, risky, but with money –

ANTONIO: What about Bassanio, in search of wisdom?

SHYLOCK: We'll send a message in the morning to say where you can be found. Stay. My daughter, Jessica, will look after you – if she deigns to talk that is.

ANTONIO: Very haughty, your Jessica.

SHYLOCK: And free and fractious but – cleverer than her illiterate old father. Gave her all the tutors I couldn't have. Stay! You know how the Ghetto is constantly filled with visitors. In the morning, Solomon Usque the writer is coming with the daughter of the Portuguese banker Mendes, and in the afternoon we'll go to the synagogue to hear the sermon of a very famous rabbi from Florence. Stay. It'll be full of Venetian intelligentsia, they're always coming to attend the festivals, listen to the music. Very exotic we are. We fascinate them all, whether from England where they've expelled us, or Spain where they burn us. Stay. Risk it. *(Pause.)* He'll have to risk it, he's asleep… *(Taking the arm of the now half-asleep ANTONIO, he struggles with him towards a bedroom.)* And if the gatekeepers remember and come looking don't worry, I'll keep them happy. Happy, happy, happy. Isn't life a risk?

SCENE FOUR

SHYLOCK's main room. Next morning.

An atmosphere of activity. JESSICA, helped by SHYLOCK's old sister, RIVKA, and a MAID, is supervising the comings and goings, in preparation for the midday meal.

TUBAL, his partner, is going through accounts.

JESSICA: We shall be six to eat at midday. Yesterday it was eight, the day before seven, and tomorrow, no doubt, more again.

RIVKA: Yesterday was a very special day for him, Jessica.

JESSICA: But Aunt Rivka, he's not even awake yet. Eleven o'clock and he sleeps.

RIVKA: The books, remember, came out of hiding.

JESSICA: He dusted his dusty books! Heaven help me! I have to look at those books again. From my earliest days I remember nothing but this madness, this illness for books.

RIVKA: Your father would be ashamed to hear you talk like this.

JESSICA: My father is an intellectual snob. Every passing scholar or rabbi, or eminent physician has to dine at his table. Some men fawn before crowns, he before degrees.

RIVKA: This is not worthy of you, Jessica. Scholarship must be respected.

JESSICA: Oh, I respect scholarship, but there is a world outside the covers of a book, isn't there? Men don't *always* behave as the philosophers fear, do they?

TUBAL: Your father is a special man, Jessica. He's animated by ideas. 'Keep me moving,' he cries, 'don't let the dark overtake me, it's my only hope.' A man not afraid to have his mind changed? That's rare. I wish I had such courage.

JESSICA: But he bullies with it all, Uncle Tubal. My father's cruelty is to diminish whoever can't recall a name, a date, an event, or argument. 'Patterns! The scheme of things.' Well, I do not believe there is a scheme of things, only chaos and misery and madmen at large in the world all writing books! Men fired by this idea, that passion, full of dogma about the way other men should live, assuming moralities for us, deciding the limits of our pleasure, our endeavour, our abilities, our pain. Decreed by whom? By what right? My father is full of them and I am oppressed by them and I think my time is done for them. *(She leaves.)*

RIVKA: She exaggerates. My brother's not a tyrannical father.

TUBAL: Of course not. When their quarrels are over, Shylock makes light of it. But I fear he confuses her frustrations for her originality.

RIVKA: He wanted to prove that daughters could achieve the intellectual stature of sons.

TUBAL: A wilful thought I've always thought. But there you are, you can't discuss children with parents, you offend them where they've placed their most cherished endeavour.

> *A young man, RODERIGUES DA CUNHA, rushes in. He carries rolls of plans.*

RODERIGUES: Shylock! Shylock! The plans of the new synagogue! No Shylock?

RIVKA: Asleep still.

RODERIGUES: Asleep still? My appointment was for eleven.

TUBAL: As was mine. 'The accounts,' he cries, 'the accounts are in disorder.'

RODERIGUES: 'The plans,' he cries, 'the plans! You want me to contribute to the building of a new synagogue? Let me see the plans first.' So I stay up all night to draw a new set of plans, and he sleeps!

RIVKA: Go into the kitchen, Roderigues, Jessica is there.

RODERIGUES: All night!

RIVKA: Take mid-morning refreshment but don't complain to her, she's a little – heavy. My brother will be with us soon.

> *RODERIGUES nearly succeeds in leaving but is forced back into the room by a storming JESSICA.*

JESSICA: Did you know they were coming *now*?

RIVKA: Who, my dear, who?

JESSICA: Solomon Usque and Rebecca da Mendes.

TUBAL: But these are honours, Jessica.

JESSICA: Honours for you, work for me, and overcrowding for the Ghetto. Suddenly Venice is alive with Portuguese Anusim.

RIVKA: Fleeing the Inquisition, child, what are you saying?

JESSICA: They will be welcome, but I'm not told, I'm not told.

> *Enter SOLOMON USQUE and REBECCA DA MENDES.*

USQUE: Solomon Usque, playwright of Lisbon, otherwise known as Duarte de Pinel. May I present the Signora Rebecca da Mendes, daughter of the late Francisco Mendes, banker of Lisbon. Peace be unto you, Signor Shylock.

TUBAL: You're both known and welcome, but I'm not Shylock. Tubal di Ponti, his friend and partner, and honoured.

REBECCA: He's always greeting the wrong person –

USQUE: – pushing the wrong door –

REBECCA: – drinking from the wrong shaped glass!

USQUE: When artists aspire to elegance they end being ridiculous. Please, when will Shylock appear?

SHYLOCK enters accompanied by ANTONIO.

SHYLOCK: He appears, he appears! Friend Shylock appears! Signora Mendes, Signor Usque, I'm ashamed to have had no one waiting for you at the door. May I present my daughter Jessica; my sister Rivka; my good friend Antonio Querini, a merchant of Venice whose head is not his own this morning, and my partner, Tubal di Ponti. Oh yes, and Roderigues – er –

RODERIGUES: – da Cunha, da Cunha!

SHYLOCK: – da Cunha, architect. They're building a new synagogue for the Spanish and Portuguese refugees. Of all people you must know of the plans. Your father, Signora, renowned! Renowned! Whatever I can do –

JESSICA: I must attend to the food. Please excuse me.

RODERIGUES: I will join you. Forgive me, everyone, I'm dying of thirst.

SHYLOCK: Thirst! My goodness. Look at me! Jessica, the citronade.

JESSICA: *(Leaving.)* It's on the table, father.

SHYLOCK: Soon, dear Roderigues, I'll be with you soon.

RODERIGUES: *(Leaving.)* Beautiful! Beautiful plans!

> *They go. SHYLOCK pours drinks which he gives to RIVKA to hand out.*

SHYLOCK: Everything is beautiful to him.

RIVKA: Especially my niece.

SHYLOCK: But not he to her! Stop matchmaking! He's a sweet boy but not her match. She always match-makes. And always the wrong one. She'll marry the wrong man without your help, push not! *(To his guests.)* Now, what news do you bring?

USQUE: The news is not good.

SHYLOCK: Tell us.

Pause.

Tell us.

USQUE: In the last year the Coimbra Tribunal, which has jurisdiction over the Northern provinces of Portugal, has held thirty-five autos-da-fé drawn from different towns and villages of Trás-os-Montes and Beira alone.

REBECCA: In addition to which the Lisbon and Evora Tribunals have tried Anusim from the Eastern department of Braganza.

USQUE: Fifty people burnt at the stake.

REBECCA: Old women, young men, relatives, friends.

USQUE: Marian Fernandes, a cousin from Lisbon.

REBECCA: Maria Diez, my old aunt from Guarda.

USQUE: Sebastian Rodrigo Pinto, a friend from Lamego.

REBECCA: Diego Della Rogna, his wife Isabelle Nones, their four daughters and two sons.

USQUE: An entire family burnt.

REBECCA: Facing each other.

Silence.

But there are survivors. It's to those we must attend. Signor Shylock, we are among friends?

SHYLOCK: Everyone, inseparable.

REBECCA: I have been told that you are a courageous man –

SHYLOCK: Please! A fool with my chances, perhaps –

REBECCA: During the next months, a steady stream of the Portuguese community will be making their way to Ancona before leaving for Salonika. Though not easy, Venice is the least dangerous place for them to stop en route and rest. We would like you to arrange places for them to stay, families who would put them up, and a fund started to assist their journey.

RIVKA: And who else but my brother!

SHYLOCK: Who else! I'd have been offended had anyone else been approached. You knew who to come to, didn't you?

REBECCA: We've been told.

SHYLOCK: They talk, you see, Antonio! I'm a name in my community. From nobody to somebody, a name! Now, you'll stay for food, you must eat with us.

RIVKA: Of course they'll stay and eat with us. You imagine I wouldn't ask them to stay and eat?

SHYLOCK: Say you'll stay, please, please, I insist.

RIVKA: We all insist.

SHYLOCK: We all insist. And you must allow me to show you my collection of manuscripts, come.

USQUE: Signora Mendes is the collector, I only write them.

SHYLOCK: You must persuade him to sign one of his books for me.

USQUE: Ha! They hardly perform me let alone print me.

REBECCA: Fortunately he has other skills.

USQUE: Self-appointed plenipotentiary for refugees.

REBECCA: A constant occupation but one giving him great opportunity for travel – from Constantinople to London.

SHYLOCK: To London?

RIVKA: Are there still Jews in England?

REBECCA: Hardly any. A clandestine existence. But we go back and forth for trade.

SHYLOCK: Then you must look out for a rare manuscript for me – 'The Fox's Fables'.

REBECCA: What's your special interest?

SHYLOCK: There's an edition in the library of Exeter Cathedral written by the author *himself* in which he complains about his life in England and the indifference of its wealthy Jews to intellectual and literary activities.

USQUE: Perhaps *that* accounts for the massacre of London.

SHYLOCK, REBECCA and RIVKA prepare to leave.

REBECCA: *(To SHYLOCK as they're leaving.)* I shall never understand this habit of using our misery to feed our wit.

USQUE: *(Parting shot as they go off.)* What else is left to feed it, Signora?

SHYLOCK: And the plans for the synagogue! We simply must look at the plans for the new Spanish synagogue together.

SHYLOCK exists with REBECCA and RIVKA.

USQUE: Is that how it is every day?

TUBAL: Every day! A house never still.

ANTONIO: When he's not negotiating loans, he's dispatching men around the world to buy him books, or opening the sights of the Ghetto to visiting dignitaries.

TUBAL: Though in time you'll find he's a very melancholy man, will you agree, Signor Antonio?

ANTONIO: In my warehouse is a young man, Graziano Sanudo, in charge of the import of spices. Now *he's* a happy man, no melancholy in him, and I don't know that I can stand him around. He has no real opinions, simply bends with the wind, quickly rushing to agree with the next speaker. He's a survivor, not defiantly, which is honourable, but creepily, like a chameleon, blending with everyone to avoid anyone's sting. He laughs when

every idiot farts out thin wit, fawns on the tyrannical,
is reverential before the papal, and manifests the most
depressingly boisterous happiness I know. Give me
Shylock's melancholy, gentlemen, and take away my man's
smiles.

TUBAL: But Jessica is right. Shylock's kind of intelligence *is* an
illness.

ANTONIO: Aye! You die from it in the end.

USQUE: I see he has an eternal friend in you, Signor Antonio.

ANTONIO: And I in him. Now, gentlemen, excuse me. I've
been expecting a young man to call for me here in search
of wisdom, and I fear he's lost.

TUBAL: The message went to your offices, Antonio, first thing
this morning. Come at once to the Ghetto Nuovo between
the German Synagogue and the Association for the Jewish
Poor. Ground floor, ask if lost.

ANTONIO: Thank you, but I've no knowing what kind of soul
he is, simple or bright. And in case the former, I'd better
go out in search. I think I need the air, besides.

ANTONIO leaves.

USQUE: Your community lives well, I see. You can build your
synagogues and depend upon Gentile friends.

TUBAL: Personally I depend upon no Gentile but, misery is
difficult to wear all weathers. We survive from contract to
contract, not knowing if after five years it will be renewed,
and if renewed whether it will be for another five, or ten or
three but –

USQUE: – trade is trade –

TUBAL: – trade is trade and they know it also, and we pay!
An annual tribute of twenty thousand ducats; another
twenty thousand for renting these squalid walls, another
hundred for the upkeep of the canals, which stink! And,
on top of all that, ten thousand more in time of war which,

since our beloved and righteous republic seems constantly fighting with someone or other, ensures that sum too as a regular payment. Why, sometimes there's barely pennies in the Ghetto. For days we're all borrowing off each other, till new funds flow in. Only fourteen hundred souls, remember, trapped in an oppressive circus with three water wells and a proclivity for fires.

SHYLOCK enters.

SHYLOCK: *(Calling)* Roderigues! In here! Bring the plans in here, the light's better.

RODERIGUES struggles in with rolls of plans.

The entrance, why so plain? Why no wrought-iron gates? They're Spanish, come from a highly cultured background! Signor Usque, *you* must look at these plans for the Spanish synagogue.

ANTONIO and BASSANIO enter at this point but hold back to watch and listen.

TUBAL: *(Continuing to USQUE.)* And I make no mention of special demands in times of 'special distress', nor of the unreturned 'loans' to the treasury which bring in no more than a four per cent rate of interest. And did I leave out the cost of up-keeping our own community services and our own streets? I did, I did!

RODERIGUES: And did you leave out the bribes demanded by petty officials?

TUBAL: I did! I did!

RODERIGUES: And payments to the local church? the local police?

SHYLOCK: He did! He did! But never mind about politics. Why is the façade so dull? Is the new mint dull? Or the library and museum of antiquities? And the windows! There's no light!

RODERIGUES: Give me the taxes of Venice and I'll give you light!

SHYLOCK: You don't need money to be bold. You need boldness! Take them away and think again. Bolder! Be bolder!

ANTONIO: *(Finally making himself known.)* Gentlemen, allow me to introduce my godson, Bassanio Visconti.

SHYLOCK: Ah, Antonio. You found him. Welcome, young man, welcome. You'll stay to eat with us, won't you? Do you know anything about architecture? We're building a new synagogue, look. We don't have a Palladio to build us a San Giorgio Maggiore, but with our modest funds …

ANTONIO: I don't think Bassanio plans to stay, but we would like to talk together, and if –

SHYLOCK: Of course, the first time godfather and Godson meet is a special and private time.

> *To TUBAL as he and SHYLOCK prepare to leave.*

Tubal, you *should* look at these plans for the new synagogue before they're folded away. It's your money too, you know.

TUBAL: I'm plan-blind, Shylock. They mean nothing to me. *You* spend my money.

> *SHYLOCK and TUBAL leave.*

BASSANIO: And *that* is a Jew?

ANTONIO: *(Reprimanding.) He* is a Jew.

BASSANIO: I don't think I know what to say.

ANTONIO: Have you never met one before?

BASSANIO: Talked of, describes, imagined, but –

ANTONIO: Shylock is my special friend.

BASSANIO: Then, sir, he must be a special man.

ANTONIO: *(Suspicious and changing the subject.)* Your father speaks highly of you and begs me to help where I can.

BASSANIO: My lord Antonio –

ANTONIO: I'm not a lord, I'm a patrician – lapsed and indifferent to their politicking but a patrician nonetheless.

BASSANIO: Lord, patrician – you are my godfather, and my father talked of you and your goodness and your good time together, but –

ANTONIO: There were good times together, were there?

BASSANIO: He spoke of little else. What he shared with you, I shared. What happened between you, I saw happen. If I did wrong he'd say, your godfather would not approve of that. And as I grew I did what I did, thought what I thought, saying to myself – what would the good Antonio do now, how would the wise Antonio decide?

ANTONIO: Ah, wisdom! I feared it.

BASSANIO: You must surely have experienced this yourself, sir, that in your mind there is always one person, a vivid critic, whose tone of voice and special use of words is there in your brain constantly.

ANTONIO: They call him God, Bassanio.

BASSANIO: I think you're mocking me. Have I come at a wrong time? Perhaps I shouldn't have come at all. To be honest, I hate arriving behind letters of recommendation. What can the poor host do but be courteous, obliging. Forgive me, sir. You know nothing of me. I'll go. But I'll find ways of making myself known to you, and useful, and in the coming months I'll try to earn your trust. Goodbye, sir.

ANTONIO: No, no, no. Don't go, young man. I've been rude and discourteous, forgive me. Bachelors have special dreads. Old age, loneliness, too much noise, too many requests; we fear opportunists and women. Forgive me.

> Sit and talk about yourself and what you want of me.
> Of course I remember your father. We were good for
> one another in lean years. Talk. I'll help his son. Tell me
> what you want. Trade? Tricks of the trade? Contracts? To
> represent me?

BASSANIO: In Belmont, sir, there is a lady.

ANTONIO: Ah, love!

BASSANIO: Her father's family goes back to the time when
Venetians were fishermen, and –

ANTONIO: And would now prefer to forget it!

BASSANIO: – and, like all of those ancient families, became
wealthy. These, the Contarinis, had their wealth reduced
by my lady's father with – with – what shall I call it? – not
madness, but – unorthodoxy. The father of my lady, whose
name is Portia, was – well – odd! A philosopher.

ANTONIO: Oh, very odd.

BASSANIO: He evolved, it seems, a strange theory that
men's character could be learned by tests, and to this
end he devised a huge chart divided into the most
important aspects of a man's character. Honour, common
sense, loyalty, stamina and so on. His entire estates
became manned by men he'd chosen based upon these
philosophically evolved tests. All, with one exception, fell
into ruin.

ANTONIO: What an incredibly sad story.

BASSANIO: There is a happy side. The daughter –

ANTONIO: Beautiful?

BASSANIO: Well, not beautiful perhaps, but – striking, vivid.
Intelligent eyes, mobile features – handsome. In fact, if
I must be blunt, determination and strength of will give
her face a masculine aspect. She's feminine to the extent

that she doesn't deny her sex, yet misleading because she doesn't cultivate, exploit, abuse it.

ANTONIO: Just such a woman I'd like to have met in *my* youth.

BASSANIO: You'll understand, then, the reason for my agitation.

ANTONIO: But not yet how it concerns me.

BASSANIO: Three caskets rest at Belmont. One gold, one silver, one lead. Who chooses the correct casket wins the daughter.

ANTONIO: Aha! The final test. And my role in this?

BASSANIO: I've lived a stupid wasting life, Signor Antonio. I possess nothing and can lay my hands on nothing. I had hoped to marry wealth but instead I fell in love with ruins. I mean to choose the right casket, marry that extraordinary woman and work to restore her property to profit. But I'm without means either to dress myself or reach her.

ANTONIO: It will cost?

BASSANIO: To present myself without insult? Three thousand ducats.

ANTONIO: Three thousand ducats!

BASSANIO: I believe no claim was ever made on your godfather-ship before.

ANTONIO: Bassanio, you come at a bad time. I've ships to sea but no cash to hand. More, I plan retirement, and all my wealth lies in their cargoes. The small change I need for daily living is easily got on credit from friendly traders, but the eyes of the Rialto are on me and I know no one who'll lend me so large a sum except –

BASSANIO: Who?

SHYLOCK: Shylock.

BASSANIO: The Jew?

ANTONIO: I've told you, young man, the Jew is my special friend.

BASSANIO: Of course. Forgive me, sir. And now, I'll go. If there's anything I can do for you in the city?

ANTONIO: Yes, take a message to my assistant, Graziano Sanudo. Tell him I won't be in today, but to arrange for dinner on Wednesday. I'm entertaining my friend, Shylock, so no pork. Join us, Bassanio, I keep a good wine cellar.

BASSANIO: With the greatest of pleasure, and honoured. May I bring with me an old friend I've recently met again? A sort of philosopher.

ANTONIO: 'Sort of'?

BASSANIO: Writes poetry occasionally.

ANTONIO: A 'sort of philosopher' who 'writes poetry occasionally'! Good! Old Shylock might enjoy that. What's his name?

BASSANIO: Lorenzo Pisani.

ANTONIO: Ah! The silk manufacturers.

BASSANIO: You know them?

ANTONIO: The fabric, not the family.

BASSANIO: You won't regret this trust, signor.

ANTONIO: I hope to God I do not, Bassanio.

> *BASSANIO leaving, meets SHYLOCK on the way out. SHYLOCK bows but is ignored.*

I hope to God.

SHYLOCK: And what was that like?

ANTONIO: I'm not certain. He'd not met a Jew before.

> *SHYLOCK goes into fits of laughter.*

What is so funny?

SHYLOCK: There are a hundred million people in China who've not met a Jew before!

ANTONIO: Still he worries me for other reasons. There was too much calculation in him. You'll be meeting him on Wednesday and can judge for yourself. I've invited him for dinner. With a friend of his, Lorenzo Pisani.

SHYLOCK: Pisani?

ANTONIO: You know him?

SHYLOCK: I know him. He wrote a poem once: 'The Ruin of the Nation's Heart'. A murky thing, full of other people's philosophy. Jessica showed it to me. Too long! She seemed impressed because it called for a return to simplicity...

ANTONIO: Of course! My assistant Graziano showed it to *me*. It had a sense of doom, which the poet seemed to enjoy rather more than he was anxious to warn of.

SHYLOCK: He's the one!

> *He calls.*

Children! Children! Let's eat.

> *To ANTONIO.*

You must be starving, and the Portuguese must be bored to death with my books by now, and we must be finished eating in time for a sitting. I'm having our portrait painted. A great painter, old now but exquisite, Moses da Castelazzo. Renowned!

ANTONIO: Shylock?

SHYLOCK: My friend!

ANTONIO: I have a favour to ask of you.

SHYLOCK: At last! A favour! Antonio of Shylock!

ANTONIO: To borrow three thousand ducats.

SHYLOCK: Not four? Five? Ten?

ANTONIO: I'm not making jokes, Shylock.

SHYLOCK: And why do you think I make jokes?

ANTONIO: For three months?

SHYLOCK: Your city borrows forever, why not three months for you?

ANTONIO: You know my position?

SHYLOCK: I know your position. Your fortune in one voyage, insane. Still.

ANTONIO: You're a good man, old man.

SHYLOCK: Old man – forever! Good – not always. I'm a friend.

ANTONIO: What shall you want as a surety in the contract?

SHYLOCK: The *what?*

ANTONIO: The contract, Shylock. We must draw up a bond.

SHYLOCK: A bond? Between friends? What nonsense are you talking, Antonio?

ANTONIO: The law demands it: no dealings may be made with Jews unless covered by a legal bond.

SHYLOCK: That law was made for enemies, not friends.

ANTONIO: Shylock! The law says, in these very words, 'It is forbidden to enter into dealings with a Jew without sign and sealing of a bond, which bond must name the sums borrowed, specify the collateral, name the day, the hour to be paid, and –

TOGETHER: – and be witnessed by three Venetians, two patricians and one citizen, and then registered.'

ANTONIO: Shylock! We are a nervous Empire with a jealous law. No man may bend it. Be sensible!

SHYLOCK: Sensible! Sensible! I follow my heart, *my* laws. What could be more sensible? The Deuteronomic code says 'Thou shalt not lend upon usury to thy brother'. Let us interpret that law as free men, neither Christian nor Jew. I love you, therefore you are my brother. And since you are my brother my laws say I may not lend upon usury to you. Take the ducats.

ANTONIO: But law in Venice is sacrosanct, dear Shylock, dear brother.

SHYLOCK: My dealings with you are sacrosanct.

ANTONIO: The city's reputation thrives on its laws being trusted.

SHYLOCK: I thrive on my reputation being trusted.

ANTONIO: I would trust you with my life but you must not bend the law of Venice.

SHYLOCK: *(Angry with the law.)* You can have three thousand ducats but there will be no bond, for no collateral, and for no time-limit whatsoever.

ANTONIO: I understand. And it brings me closer to you than ever. But the deeper I feel our friendship the more compelled I feel to press my point, and protect you. You are a Jew, Shylock. Not only is your race a minority, it is despised. Your existence here in Venice, your pleasures, your very freedom to be sardonic or bitter is a privilege which has to be negotiated every five or seven or ten years. It is not a right. Your lives depend upon contract. Do you want the city councillors to respect *their* contract? Then you of all people must respect their *laws* behind contract. The law, Shylock, the law! For you and your people, the bond-in-law must be honoured.

SHYLOCK: Oh, you have really brought me down. That's earth I feel now. Solid.

Pause, not losing his good humour.

We'll cheat them yet.

ANTONIO: You mean you're still not persuaded?

SHYLOCK: I'm persuaded, oh yes, I'm very persuaded. We'll have a bond.

ANTONIO: Good!

SHYLOCK: A nonsense bond.

ANTONIO: A nonsense bond?

SHYLOCK: A lovely, loving nonsense bond. To mock the law.

ANTONIO: To mock?

SHYLOCK: Barbaric laws? Barbaric bonds! Three thousand ducats against a pound of your flesh.

ANTONIO: My flesh?

SHYLOCK: You're like an idiot child suddenly. (Mocking) 'A nonsense bond? My flesh?' Yes. If I am not repaid by you, upon the day, the hour, I'll have a pound of your old flesh, Antonio, from near the part of your body which pleases me most – your heart. Your heart, dear heart, and I'd take that, too, if I could, I'm so fond of it.

> *Pause as SHYLOCK waits to see if ANTONIO accepts.*

ANTONIO: Barbaric laws, barbaric bonds?

SHYLOCK: Madness for the mad.

ANTONIO: Idiocies for the idiots.

SHYLOCK: Contempt for the contemptuous.

ANTONIO: They mock our friendship –

SHYLOCK: – we mock their laws.

ANTONIO: *(Pinching himself.)* Do I have a pound of flesh? I don't even have a pound of flesh.

SHYLOCK: *(Pinching him.)* Here, and here, and here, one, two, three pounds of flesh!

He's tickling him; ANTONIO responds. Like children they're goosing each other and giggling, upon which note –

JESSICA and RIVKA enter with food, RODERIGUES also.

TUBAL, REBECCA and USQUE enter deep in animated conversation. A meal is to be eaten, the sounds and pleasures of hospitality are in the air.

SCENE FIVE

ANTONIO's warehouse. Bales of coloured cloth, some from PISANI factories. Sacks of spices.

GRAZIANO, throwing cloth over BASSANIO to see which suits him. He tends to have conversations with himself, ignoring what others are saying.

LORENZO, plunging his hand in a sack drawing spice pebbles which run back through his fingers.

BASSANIO: I was amazed. 'And *that* is a Jew?' I asked. '*He* is a Jew,' my godfather corrected.

LORENZO: I don't like it. A world turned upside down.

GRAZIANO: Quite right, Lorenzo, a world turned upside down.

BASSANIO: You should have heard them, discussing Venice as though the city *cared* for their voice, existed for their *judgement!*

LORENZO: Money is a dead thing, with no seed, it's not fit to engender.

GRAZIANO: Well said.

LORENZO: Shylock dares play God with a dead thing, and Venice has only a tired language to answer him with. Of course his usury flourishes. A nation that confuses timidity for tolerance is a nation without principle.

GRAZIANO: A nation turned upside down.

BASSANIO: *(To LORENZO.)* Do you know Shylock well?

LORENZO: *(Moving from sack to sack, the spices trickling through his hands.)* I know him.

GRAZIANO: *(Pursuing his own conversation with BASSANIO while winding cloth around him.)* Who do you know asserts authority?

LORENZO: A loud, enthusiastic man.

GRAZIANO: Men fear earning hatreds! No leadership!

LORENZO: I've stood by him in the Ghetto when he's showing visitors its sights.

GRAZIANO: Not even the priests have time for God, and our painters paint their Virgin Marys like whores.

LORENZO: Thin achievements in stone which he magnifies with a loud voice.

GRAZIANO: The aged are in control of Venice, my friends.

LORENZO: There's hysteria in his description of things. His tone is urgent –

GRAZIANO: A burning issue.

LORENZO: – excited –

GRAZIANO: I burn whenever it comes up.

LORENZO: – excited, ornate and proudly erudite.

GRAZIANO: It comes up burning and I burn.

LORENZO: His sin? Intellectual pride. His daughter can't bear it.

BASSANIO: You know Shylock's daughter?

GRAZIANO: A friend of yours?

LORENZO: You'd not think they're of the same blood. He's proud, she's modest. He imagines knowledge is all, she lives in the world. His voice is metallic with contempt, hers is sweet with reason. And she listens to music.

BASSANIO: And poetry perhaps?

LORENZO: And poetry, perhaps.

BASSANIO: Even praised some?

LORENZO: Even that.

BASSANIO: Good God, Lorenzo, are you in love?

LORENZO: Love? Who knows about love? She admired my poetry, and those who admire us must have merit we think. Can that be love? Respect perhaps.

BASSANIO: What an uncertain young man!

LORENZO: It's true! My nature can't decide itself. I despise power yet so much offends me that I want power to wipe out the offence. And where does power lie? In trade or moral principle? The spirit of the trader is in me as in every Venetian but there is such a frenzy of avarice and unbridled ambition that I feel the end of the world must be near, a world which one moment I want to renounce, the next help save from itself.

BASSANIO: Beware, young man, beware. Help the poor world save itself? The trap is that preachers intoxicate themselves, abuse their powers and weary men by perpetual admonitions. Beware, young man, beware.

GRAZIANO: Beware, nothing! Lorenzo's right. Horrible times. There's little for young men of character here.

BASSANIO: Nonsense! Everywhere I turn I hear of young patricians being schooled for trade, diplomacy, the Council's work.

LORENZO: But can those young patricians vote for the Doge if they're under thirty, or become senators before forty? Power doesn't reside in principle but in the hands of a few families.

BASSANIO: Who trade with the world! Come, what are you saying? Venice is a free city. Her doors are open, open!

LORENZO: Her legs are open, open! Venice – brothel of the Mediterranean. And all so that we can boast to everyone of a freedom which tolerates corruption.

BASSANIO: Steady there, Lorenzo. The toleration of Jews may be *unpalatable* to us, but trade, I sometimes think that men in trade have kept our mad world sane, preserved us from destructive politicians. Venice built its glory on its ancient trading families, after all.

GRAZIANO: And that's where the power lies, in the long ancient families who trade. I should know, coming as I do from one of them.

BASSANIO: You, Graziano?

GRAZIANO: Don't be surprised, my friends, not all Venetian aristocracy is bright. Least of all I. Me. Least of all me. Or is it 'I'? I'm what they call an academic failure. My family is wealthy but not illustrious. They hoped I'd rise to be a statesman and add honour to their fortune, but I've neither tact nor memory, and in shame my family apprenticed me to trade. Personal assistant and happy!

BASSANIO: But what is a 'long family'?

GRAZIANO: A long family it is us, listed in the chronicles as one of the twenty-four families. Of old. Who began it all. Or rather, there are twelve, from which I come, who claim the greatest nobility because they go back before 762, or is it 726? When the first Doge was elected, whose name was Orso, a military man, or was that Anafesto? Because some say the first Doge was elected in 679, or was it 697? And that *his* name was Anafesto, or was *his* name Orso? Whoever, my family goes back beyond then.

BASSANIO: And all were fishermen?

GRAZIANO: No! I mean, yes! I mean, the point is we're – old. Go back a long way. The Roman Empire. Venice as a second Rome. Ancient.

BASSANIO: So if you're ancient you're noble?

GRAZIANO: Exactly!

BASSANIO: So, a peasant family if it had the memory of a long past would be noble too?

GRAZIANO: Ah, no.

BASSANIO: So that's *not* exactly what you're trying to say?

GRAZIANO: That's what I'm saying, not exactly.

BASSANIO: Something more is needed to be a noble family?

GRAZIANO: Power!

BASSANIO: Which comes from where?

GRAZIANO: Stop teasing me, Bassanio. The question of Venetian nobility is an anxious one, my family quibble about it constantly.

LORENZO: And pointlessly. The question remains. Does power lie in trade or moral principle?

BASSANIO: Trade! Power resides in trade. See this pebble of pepper – it's this has the power to push men across seas. Three million pounds passed through Venice this year. Do you know what amount of gold that represents? *Kings* monopolise the spice trade for themselves.

LORENZO: But religious principle is constant, trade is not. A Portuguese sailor circumnavigates the Cape? The spice trade of the Mediterranean dies!

BASSANIO: And who takes over? The Portuguese! Another Catholic nation! And where is religious principle then?

LORENZO: More reason to defend it! For it would then have power to bind the trade of nations who would otherwise fight.

BASSANIO: Precisely! As I said! Trade keeps the world sane while the wild men rant on about their principles. Gentlemen, it's my time to go. I must cut my suits and sharpen my wits for Belmont. I chase a woman there they say has intellect.

LORENZO: And what is *her* inheritance? Ruins!

BASSANIO: Which she will rebuild.

LORENZO: If she has cunning and connections and the facility to fawn.

BASSANIO: She will, she will! Rebuild! As youth does, ignoring the evil within, defying the past. We're young, Lorenzo! Don't be so solemn. We'll meet at Antonio's for dinner and talk more. Perhaps we'll get to know you better, Graziano.

GRAZIANO: You'll love me I promise you.

BASSANIO: And old Shylock too. What more will be discovered of him, I wonder?

LORENZO: Nothing much for loving there.

GRAZIANO: I know what he means, I know what he means.

SCENE SIX

SHYLOCK's main room.

Chairs and easel are being set up for a portrait sitting.

SHYLOCK enters with USQUE, followed by a bustling RIVKA, and RODERIGUES who is planning to do his own sketch of JESSICA.

The old Jewish portrait painter MOSES DA CASTELAZZO arrives.

SHYLOCK: Ah! Moses, you're here!

MOSES: No! I'm not here!

SHYLOCK: Signor Usque, playwright, allow me to introduce you to the renowned Moses da Castelazzo, painter!

MOSES: *(Ignoring the niceties of introduction and going straight to the easel.)* Renowned! Renowned! Who cares about renown at eighty!

SHYLOCK and RIVKA take up positions.

RODERIGUES: And where's Jessica? How can I draw a subject who's not there?

MOSES: *(Mocking.)* And where's Jessica? How can I draw a subject who's not there! Look at him! If you must be in love don't show it! If you must show it don't draw it! Let me see.

Snatches sketch book.

You can't draw! Why are you trying to draw when you can't draw? Suddenly everybody imagines he's an artist!

RODERIGUES: The very old like him should be kept apart from the very young like me. I can see it now.

SHYLOCK: Stop squabbling. Moses can begin without Jessica, and Signor Usque has promised to tell us about his new play.

MOSES: Another one! Suddenly! Everyone! An artist!

USQUE: It will be a debate.

SHYLOCK: Between whom?

USQUE: Between rabbis who were interpreting –

SHYLOCK: – the interpretations of the interpretations of the great scholars who interpreted the meaning of the meaning –

JESSICA enters and takes up her pose the other side of SHYLOCK.

SHYLOCK: You're late.

JESSICA: This is the last time I sit, father.

SHYLOCK: Don't you understand how insulting it is to be late for an appointment?

JESSICA: Signor Castelazzo was not held up by me.

SHYLOCK: This is my house, and while under my roof –

JESSICA: *(Challengingly.)* While under your roof, *what?*

SHYLOCK: An appointment is sacred.

JESSICA: You exaggerate.

SHYLOCK: To keep another waiting is to say to him you don't care for him.

JESSICA: Or that you care more for what you've left. Or that what you've left presented problems unanticipated. Or that what you've left was a dying man, you were needed, or you were compelled, or forced – really! Father! You're so full of tight, restricting little codes.

SHYLOCK: An appointment is a bond. Between two people. They depend upon each other honouring it, and if it's broken – lives can be affected, deals fall through, hearts broken, disappointment –

JESSICA: The scheme of things! The scheme of things! Stop lecturing me with your scheme of things.

MOSES: Enough! I have a painting to paint. Please.

USQUE: You've not answered my question, Signor Shylock.

SHYLOCK: Ask my daughter. She's the clever one.

USQUE: My new play, about a quarrel between rabbis, some interpreting Deuteronomy on behalf of the Papacy, others Leviticus on behalf of Henry the Eighth. The positions were this –

JESSICA: With respect, Signor Usque, I don't need to have their relative positions described. The idea is offensive. To scurry backwards and forwards in and out of the Bible's pages for such an obscene quarrel – the rabbis should have been ashamed of themselves helping an English king to divorce his wife. The cause doesn't interest me.

USQUE: The cause doesn't interest me, either, but the nature of interpretation does.

SHYLOCK: *(But proud.)* Forgive her. She's had good tutors to exercise her mind but no mother to shape her manners.

RODERIGUES: *(Sketching furiously.)* But keep her angry, she look beautiful when she's angry. Beautiful!

MOSES: Idiot!

JESSICA: *(Topping her.)* This is the last time I pose, father.

SHYLOCK: You've told me already.

JESSICA: As you've told me a thousand times that this is your house and your roof.

SHYLOCK: Under which you are deprived of nothing.

JESSICA: Except the sweetness of feeling that it is *my* house and *my* roof also. You want a debate for your play, Signor Usque? Then debate this question: to whom does a house belong? Only the father? Not even the mother? And if not the children and the mother, then how must their relationship be described? As temporary occupants? As long-standing visitors? At what point is the *child's* right of movement and taste taken into consideration? Does she only become whole when taken from the possession of her father to the possession of her husband? Look how my father swells with pride at his daughter's intellect. He's given me teachers to nourish and exercise my mind, while he continues to exercise control.

SHYLOCK: If she is talking about control and the child's right it can only mean she wants to go out again one day soon.

JESSICA: He talks as though the world elected him.

SHYLOCK: *She* talks as though the tutors' fees were well spent!

JESSICA: Tell him his daughter must be taken seriously.

SHYLOCK: Tell her she should not be neglecting her music studies.

JESSICA: Tell him you can be oppressed by study.

SHYLOCK: Dancing, singing, the instruments I bought for her – tell her.

JESSICA: Tell him not everyone wants to perform, some are content to listen.

SHYLOCK: Tell her –

JESSICA: Tell her, tell her! Tell her nothing more –

JESSICA storms out.

SHYLOCK is shocked.

RIVKA: Mean! Mean! To withhold praise from your daughter, mean. From your own daughter.

SHYLOCK: The Talmud says: praise not a man more than ten per cent of his worth.

USQUE: Forgive me, Signor Shylock, I do not think you've judged well. You'll drive her into a hasty marriage.

RIVKA: He doesn't *want* her to marry.

USQUE turns to SHYLOCK for a response.

SHYLOCK: The *Pope* calls for the vows of chastity, but *God* only ever ordained matrimony. To whom should I listen?

But SHYLOCK is thinking of other things.

SCENE SEVEN

ANTONIO's house.

Present are BASSANIO, LORENZO and GRAZIANO. They have just eaten.

SHYLOCK has been with them but is out of the room, unwell, accompanied by ANTONIO.

Contented pause of men who've eaten, drunk and conversed well.

GRAZIANO: Well, the poor Jew is very sick, for sure. He's been gone a quarter of an hour.

BASSANIO: The food was too rich for him.

GRAZIANO: Or you gave him too much wine.

LORENZO: Neither! He eats, drinks and talks at the same time. There's no grace in the man.

BASSANIO: I find him most interesting. *You* see many Jews in Venice – at least ten thousand, I'd say –

GRAZIANO: Fourteen hundred.

BASSANIO: Really? Well, they *seem* more.

SHYLOCK and ANTONIO enter.

SHYLOCK: Oh, I love Venice.

GRAZIANO: A noble city, Signor Shylock, you're right.

LORENZO: *(Nastily implying he wasn't.)* You were born here, of course.

SHYLOCK: Yes, I was born here, of course.

LORENZO: I ask because so many of you come from here, there and everywhere.

SHYLOCK: I know why you ask.

LORENZO: It must be very difficult for your tribe to produce much of art or thought, as civilised nations do who have roots in territory.

SHYLOCK: Very.

LORENZO: Would you not agree that – ?

> *SHYLOCK, bored and despising LORENZO, turns aside to talk with his friend, ANTONIO. He's still a little drunk.*

SHYLOCK: Oh, Antonio, I love Venice. A city full of busy living, and men passing through freely as a right, not as a favour.

ANTONIO: Venice is distorted through your gratitude, Shylock, you've forgotten your yellow hat.

SHYLOCK: Damned yellow hat! If I'd been a physician, I'd not have to wear this damned yellow hat every time I took a walk. Physician! Now *there* was a profession to belong to instead of my own seedy lineage. Failures! (Pause) I descended from German Jews, you know. My grandparents. Grubby little things from Cologne. Came to Venice as small-time moneylenders for the poor. But my parents – they tried a new profession. Very brave. Second-hand clothing! My mother went blind patching up smelly old clothes and my father became famous for reconditioning old mattresses. On the other hand they were bringers of sleep – not a dishonourable trade don't you think, gentlemen? Mattresses: bringers of sweet sleep.

LORENZO: And sweet plagues.

SHYLOCK: *(Hisses.)* Yes! I know! Better than you, I know! *(Relaxing again.)* But he was not an ambitious man, my father. Had no confidence in himself. Not like the really big pawnbrokers, men who built up huge stores of carvings, furniture, paintings. For their banquets the Doges could always be certain of hiring a dazzling tapestry in the Ghetto. Except from my father. Verminous vests you could get from him.

LORENZO: The Ghetto is indeed notorious for its smells.

ANTONIO: I will not have discourtesies in my house.

LORENZO: You must forgive me, Signor Antonio. But I too
am a guest. You ask me to respect your Jewish friend
but what respect has he shown for me? Disputation is a
sacred right in our city. On several occasions this evening
I've attempted to engage Signor Shylock in a theological
discussion. He's turned away, and –

SHYLOCK: Perhaps I'm too frightened to dispute with you,
friend Lorenzo. Yours is a university-trained mind. Mine is
the Ghetto's.

BASSANIO: You must not be surprised if with such scorn you
attract hostility.

LORENZO: *(With evangelistic fervour.)* 'They are not humbled
even unto this day, neither have they feared, nor walked in
my law, nor in my statutes, that I have set before you and
before your fathers.' Thus sayeth Ezekiel.

SHYLOCK: It was Jeremiah. Oh dear. You want theological
discussion? Consider this. You have us for life, gentlemen,
for life. Learn to live with us. The Jew is the Christian's
parent. Difficult, I know. Parent-children relationships,
always difficult, and even worse when murder is involved
within the family.

LORENZO: You dare reduce the crucifixion to 'murder within
the family'?

SHYLOCK: What can we do? It *is* the family! Not only *would* I
be your friend I *have* to be your friend. Don't scowl, Signor
sweet Christian. For life. Old Shylock, Jew of Venice. For
ever!

Long embarrassed pause.

GRAZIANO: Yes. Well. A very noble city. You are absolutely
right, Shylock. We were discussing nobility and poweer
only the other night.

SHYLOCK: Nobility and power?

GRAZIANO: What *is* the nature of nobility and in what does power reside? Bassanio here believes that power resides in our ability to trade.

BASSANIO: Lorenzo-the-silent on the other hand believes power resides in the strength of moral superiority, while Graziano here believes power resides in ancient families.

GRAZIANO: Which power in turn gives the family nobility, and is why Venice can be compared to Rome.

ANTONIO: Compared to Rome? Nonsense! We're a commercial enterprise and no more.

BASSANIO: Come, Antonio, that's cynicism. What about Venetian rule of law? Her Christian pride and fervour? All vital organs of the Empire.

ANTONIO: The most vital organs of our Empire are warehouses, ships' holds, barges and pack-horses. We're not even honest industrialists, we're simply importers and exporters, rich because the commerce of other people flows through us, not because we produce it ourselves. And as for Venice's sense of justice, it's to retain for her patricians the best opportunities for long-distance trade. Our motives are opportunist and our power rests on a geographical accident.

SHYLOCK: No, no, friend Antonio. Forgive me, I must quarrel with you as well. Oh, this is terrible. You defend me and I contradict you. You both miss the point of Venice, of all Italy. Venice as Rome or not, as a commercial enterprise or not is irrelevant. There is a scheme of things much grander.

GRAZIANO: Grander?

BASSANIO: Explain yourself.

SHYLOCK: I will, I will! Let me remind you of three distinct developments affecting the history of this extraordinary land of yours and let's see where real power resides.

LORENZO: Are we now to be given a history lesson about our own lands by a German Jew?

SHYLOCK: Don't be offended, Lorenzo-the-silent. Remember, the synagogue existed in Rome before the Papacy.

GRAZIANO: *(Incredulous.)* The rabbi before the Pope?

SHYLOCK: The Roman wars. Jewish slaves. The captured princes of Israel. Now ssssh! And listen. It's a very thrilling story. Three developments! But first, who said: 'We cannot enforce acceptance of a creed since no one can be compelled to believe against his will?

GRAZIANO: 'Religionem imperare non possumus quia nemo cogitur ut credat invitus'?

SHYLOCK: Excellent, Graziano, bravo!

GRAZIANO: Had to learn it by heart at school.

SHYLOCK: But who said it?

> *Pause.*

ANTONIO: Cassiodorus!

SHYLOCK: Correct, Antonio! Cassiodorus! The last and lovely link between Imperial Rome and Gothic Italy. A sweet and intellectual man. A statesman! A scholar! And for what is this man remembered most? His administrations on behalf of monarchs? Never! During his life he'd succeeded in preserving through all the devastations of civil wars and foreign invasions a great collection of Greek and Roman manuscripts, and – here is development one.

> *SHYLOCK tells his story with mounting excitement and theatricality, using whatever is around him for props, moving furniture, food, perhaps even people, like men on his chessboard of history.*
>
> *ANTONIO is singled out to be 'Cassiodorus'.*

At sixty he retires to Brutti taking with him his library of classics which he makes certain are scrupulously copied by the monks. *What* a work! What a faith! But why? Why should he have bothered? What makes one man so cherish the work of others that he lovingly guards it, copies, preserves it? And a Christian, too, preserving the works of pagans! From monastery to monastery the monks were busy, busy, scribbling, for centuries, until the book trade creeps from the monasteries into the universities. The scholars take over from the monks. The pattern takes shape.

Development number two: the destruction of the Roman Empire! Italy breaks into three pieces. The north goes to the German Holy Roman Empire, the centre becomes dominated by the Papacy, and the French house of Anjou takes over the South. Look how fortunes change, rearrange themselves.

LORENZO: Your pleasure in history is superficial, Signor – playful. Its *patterns* please you but not its *meanings*. You'd have us believe there was no cause and effect.

SHYLOCK: Aha! Spirit! I might even come to respect you, young man, but –

LORENZO: Don't patronise me, Signor.

SHYLOCK: But – you read me wrong if you believe I read history so carelessly. I'm perfectly aware how causes work their effects – but *within* their time. The line *I* stretch joins together men and moments who could never possibly have forecast one another's acts. Did old Cassiodorus working a thousand years ago see how Italy's development would shape a thousand years later? Hear me out. It's thrilling, thrilling – believe me.

The land in three pieces, then. But does everything stand still? Impossible! Watch in the north how the German Holy Roman Empire disintegrates; in the centre how the families of Rome brawl among themselves; in the south how the French house of Anjou fights the Spanish house of Aragon.

Nothing stands still! And as the dust of war and madness settles what, gentlemen, is revealed? What? City States! The magnificent City States of Milan –

BASSANIO: Genoa!

GRAZIANO: Florence!

ANTONIO: Venice!

SHYLOCK: Precisely! And every one of them is left to its own government. What can it do? How *does* one govern? Industry and trade grows. Can't help itself. What! The centre of the Mediterranean basin and *not* trade? So, as you know, you Italians invent partnership agreements, holding companies, marine insurance, credit transfers –

GRAZIANO: Don't forget double-entry book-keeping!

SHYLOCK: Double-entry book-keeping! Progress! But what else happened? Don't forget old Cassiodorus lurking away patiently down there in the sixth century. More business meant more complex agreements, which meant more law, which complicated the business of government, which meant men of greater education were needed, which meant a *new* kind of education, more practical, more – ah! worldly! And where, where I ask you, could that worldly, new education come from to produce that new law, that new government? Tell me. *(Pause.)* Why, from books! Where else? And where *were* the books? Old Cassiodorus! In the monasteries! He'd preserved the ancient manuscripts of Rome and Greece, hallelujah! Praise be to wise old men! Aren't you enjoying it? Admit it, doesn't it thrill you to watch it take shape! Be generous. Let yourselves go, for here comes development three.

The year 1450. Two beautiful births: a wily old German from Mayence named –

BASSANIO: Gutenberg?

SHYLOCK: Gutenberg, gives birth to an extraordinary invention called – ?

GRAZIANO: The printing press?

SHYLOCK: – and a great classical scholar named Aldus Manutius is born. Here! In our very own city of Venice, at the age of forty-five, less than a hundred years ago, the great Manutius sets up his divine press and produces the incredible Aldine Editions. Suddenly – everybody can possess a book! And what books! The works of – Plato, Homer, Pindar and Aristophanes, Xenophon, Seneca, Plutarch and Sophocles, Aristotle, Lysias, Euripides, Demosthenes, Thucydides, Herodotus, and all printed from manuscripts kept and preserved in monasteries as far apart as Sweden and Constantinople which Italians were now bringing back home. Amazing! Knowledge, like underground springs, fresh and constantly there, till one day – up! Bubbling! For dying men to drink, for survivors from dark and terrible times. It thrills me! When generals imagine their vain glory is all, and demagogues smile with sweet benevolence as they tighten their screws of power – up! Up bubbles the little spring. Bubble, bubble, bubble! A little, little lost spring, full of blinding questions and succulent doubts. The word! Unsuspected! Written! Printed! Indestructible! Boom! It thrills me!

> *Bells ring.*

SHYLOCK: Ah! Time to return to the Ghetto.

> *LORENZO gives SHYLOCK his yellow hat.*

LORENZO: And don't forget your yellow hat, Signor Shylock.

SHYLOCK: Thank you, young man.

> *SHYLOCK looks at ANTONIO and shrugs sadly, as though the hat is evidence to refute all he's said.*

ANTONIO: What little lost spring can help you now?

And yet ...SHYLOCK defiantly places it on his head, embraces ANTONIO, bows to the other three and goes off chuckling and mumbling...

SHYLOCK: Bubble! Bubble! Bubble, bubble, bubble! Bubble, bubble, bubble! Bubble! Bubble! Bubble...

Act Two

SCENE ONE

A room in Belmont.

Time has passed. Some order is restored.

PORTIA and BASSANIO in conversation.

NERISSA reading.

BASSANIO: Wrong, madam, wrong! It may be true that trade in spices and the old wares is less profitable and safe these days, but land and agriculture are not where the fortunes lie. Precious metals! Trade in those. Gold! A bank! The bank of Contarini! – doesn't that thought dazzle you?

PORTIA: All possibilities are there. But now dear friend, you must choose. Choose wisely. None of the others did. Take your place and take your time. I'll talk with Nerissa. She's reading the letters of Seneca and I've asked her to select a favourite one. I think I know which one it will be.

> *BASSANIO takes up his place by the caskets.*
>
> *NERISSA approaches PORTIA.*

NERISSA: This one, my lady, letter forty-seven. *(She begins to read.)* 'I'm glad to hear, from these people who've been visiting you, that you live on friendly terms with your slaves. It is just what one expects of an enlightened, cultivated person like yourself...'

> *NERISSA lowers her voice as the main melody takes over. Attention must be focused upon BASSANIO.*

BASSANIO: What an eccentric test of love. Whose mind constructed this? 'By his choice shall you know him.'

> *His tone of 'reasoning' is dismissive, arrogant and cunning throughout.*

What shall you know of him? That if he chooses gold he
will be a man without a soul, with a purse where his heart
should be? But a man without a soul may have cunning,
surely? Or he may love gold but be plagued with guilt for
doing so. Now there's a man who'd shy away from the
shiny stuff. No, I don't see the point of such a simple trick.

And silver? What's one supposed to think of that, stuck
between gold and lead? Oh, here's the mediocre man?
Here's the man plays safe with life and neither dares much
nor achieves? Or is silver the test of the temperate man,
the sober man? Perhaps the *diplomat* is being looked for
here! The statesman! Judge? Not unworthy men! Yet I
hardly riot in those qualities. Still, if such a man is wanted
for that extraordinary lady, and that extraordinary lady
is what I want, then perhaps the statesman, diplomat and
judge in me had *better* blossom. Hm! Not such a simple test
after all. Come on now, Bassanio, use your wits. You've
not survived this far without an arsenal of guile. Think!
What father, wanting his daughter to marry a statesman,
diplomat or judge would devise such a scheme? More to
the point – does Portia look the kind of a daughter who'd
have the kind of father who would *want* her to marry a
statesman, diplomat or judge? *(Pause.)* I will go mad.

The wrong approach! These caskets are more a test for a
sort, a kind, a spirit. The question then is: what kind, what
sort, what spirit would such a woman's father want for
her? The father! Look to the father. He's the key. Good!
That's something. So. The father descends from a ruling
aristocracy whose blood by the time it reached her father,
had been watered down to the blood of a philosopher. And
now, abundant though the estates' possibilities are, yet
they're in ruin. Very decorous ruin, but – ruin. What metal
would a ruined ruinous philosopher choose?

> *Long pause, smile, he's seen through the strategy, but
> at first cunningly misleads.*

There can only be one answer. Simple! The end of philosophy is despair. He looked around him, saw the constant battles being fought, the waste, disintegration and decay, and he concluded: for my daughter, none of that! Gold! The hard, determined, merciless pursuit of gain, security and comfort. Gold! With gold is bought beauty, art, obedience, the power for good. Gold! For my daughter shall be trapped a man of gold. The sun is golden, the harvest too – energy and sustenance. These things I will, for my only child, these things which I with my engagement in philosophy neglected to provide. Gold! *(Pause.)* And then he changed his mind! For who can change the habits of a foolish lifetime?

To PORTIA.

Lead, my lady. Lead I choose. My brain has battled. There's its choice.

PORTIA: Your brain, Bassanio? Not your heart? Still, heart or brain, you've chosen as my father wished.

BASSANIO: Not you?

PORTIA: I? You must forgive me. It *is* possible for eyes to meet and feel their love at once, I know. But I'm not made that way. Love grows with me. My mother taught love ripens on the mind, is made of passions, laughter, all the minutiae of living *shared* rather than surmised. Is that pedantic, you think? Would you rather I embrace you now and say, with routine ardour, that *your* choice decides? You'd rather have my love relaxed and confident, Bassanio? Be patient. We will live together. All I have is yours, you know that. Settle here. Rehearse the role of husband. We'll work together, find each other carefully. We *may* be born for one another, part of me believes we are. I want my *all* to know it though. See, I'm trembling as I talk. I think you must embrace me after all.

They embrace.

Now leave. I must arrange and scheme for you.

BASSANIO: *(Facilely.)* I have no words.

PORTIA: *(Catching the tone, cools.)* I'm touched.

BASSANIO leaves.

'*No* words'? Perhaps I should be his mistress only. That gives him no holds over me then. As his wife the State chains me. *There's* something to exercise your logic on, Nerissa.

NERISSA: You're uncertain?

PORTIA: Oh, I am that.

NERISSA: You should not love someone you don't like.

PORTIA: What a ridiculous carrier of passion – a casket. I'm uncertain all right. What if I should tire of him? God forbid a woman should tire of a man. Of his vanities and little faults which always, always magnify with time. He has such a blindness for his image, such an incredible satisfaction with his long-considered thimbleful of thoughts, his firm decisive manner over that which should be racked with doubts, his silly coloured feathers which he feels to be his masculinity. Oh! his masculinity!

NERISSA: Have you watched the way a man walks? Careful that the width of him is seen? As though his shoulders balanced cannon balls?

PORTIA: Such presumption! What else could woman be but his rib, a mere bone of his body? After all, my dear, men have won battles with a bone missing!

NERISSA: *(Lasciviously.)* And lost them even with one there!

Great laughter between them.

PORTIA: Heaven help us, but there are so few poets among them!

NERISSA: Such dull and clumsy things.

PORTIA: And worse at wooing-time! Note that collapse of features they imagine tenderness? That slow softening of the eyes into a milky melancholy they confuse for lovesick helplessness?

NERISSA: That sudden clenching of the jaw and fist which struggles to be passion?

PORTIA: What feeble and pathetic arts they have. And we must pretend! Poor gimcrack men! Oh! There are such stirrings in me. Such untried intellect. Such marvellous loves and wisdom. I could found cities with my strengths, Nerissa, cities undreamed of by any man.

> *Bells peal out as we change to –*

SCENE TWO

> *The 'loggetta' beneath the campanile of St Mark's. Normally a meeting-place for patricians.*
>
> *TUBAL and RODERIGUES approach from different parts. It is night.*

TUBAL: Nothing?

RODERIGUES: Nothing!

TUBAL: You've asked discreetly?

RODERIGUES: Discreetly and indiscreetly. What do I care now!

TUBAL: The entire Ghetto is out looking for her, taking risks. Foolish girl.

RODERIGUES: 'I know your daughter,' I told him, I warned him.

TUBAL: Who didn't warn?!

RODERIGUES: 'She's too intelligent to be constrained, too old to be teased and too hot to be predictable,' I told him.

TUBAL: Foolish girl!

RODERIGUES: But he understands nothing. 'If I'd beaten her, been a drunkard, gambled my money away playing cards and dice...but we loved one another!' As if loving helps!

TUBAL: Nor is that his only tribulation. There are other calamities in the wind. The sea's wind. Your clever patron signed a bond with his best friend, Antonio. It was to be a joke, to mock the laws of Venice: a loan of three thousand ducats with a pound of flesh as bond if, within three months, the loan was not repaid. And now –

RODERIGUES: A pound of flesh?

TUBAL: And now his ships are threatened.

RODERIGUES: A pound of flesh?

TUBAL: A pound of flesh, his ships in threat, the Ghetto penniless, and the time is up at six the evening after tomorrow.

RODERIGUES: A pound of *human* flesh?

TUBAL: Yes, yes, yes, YES!

RODERIGUES: But, of course, the ships are not sunk.

TUBAL: No! Captured only! By pirates. The market is buzzing with the news.

RODERIGUES: And the bond is a joke.

TUBAL: There are no more jokes left in this world, Roderigues. The next, perhaps – ach! I am so loath to lend and deal in this trade any more.

Enter GRAZIANO.

GRAZIANO: Ah, Signor Tubal, if anyone knows where Antonio is, it will be you.

RODERIGUES: Here comes everyman's everything and I'm in no mood for him.

TUBAL: What's the news of Antonio's ships?

GRAZIANO: Bad, bad, bad, oh bad.

TUBAL: Bad, we know. Facts we want.

GRAZIANO: *(Cheekily.)* The facts are that the news is bad.

TUBAL: *(With powerful anger.)* No courtesies and games. Tell us the news.

GRAZIANO: *(Portentously.)* Grave. The news is grave. In view of how huge the cargo is the maritime office has ordered armed ships to the rescue.

TUBAL: Good, that's news worth taking back. Come, Roderigues.

GRAZIANO: But the damn winds are not helping, they fear a storm. The armed ships are paralysed.

TUBAL: Oh, Abraham! Abraham! Someone's God is angry. I'm too old for all this, too old, too old...

> *TUBAL and RODERIGUES leave.*

GRAZIANO: *(Mocking as he, too, leaves.)* Oh Abraham, Abraham! I'm too old for all this, too old, too old...

> *LORENZO and JESSICA who have been looking for each other now meet, clutch one another in relief.*
>
> *She is agitated.*

LORENZO: You're trembling.

JESSICA: I'm frightened and I'm ashamed, so I'm trembling.

LORENZO: Oh, those eyes. Those sad, sad eyes.

JESSICA: Forget my eyes, Lorenzo, and tell me what is to happen next.

LORENZO: First be calm, if for no other reason than not to command the staring of others.

JESSICA: It's cost so much, you see.

LORENZO: I know, I know.

JESSICA: The decision to break away. You can't imagine. To be cut off.

LORENZO: I know.

JESSICA: So I'm drained. I'll be all right soon but for the next hours my reason is numb and you must do it all.

LORENZO: Trust me.

JESSICA: Kiss me?

> *He hesitates.*

Why do you hesitate? All these months of meetings and you've not kissed me.

> *He hesitates again.*

Haven't you kissed a woman before?

LORENZO: A hand, a cheek.

JESSICA: Not lips?

LORENZO: Not lips.

JESSICA: Then mine will be the first for you.

LORENZO: And mine?

JESSICA: Will be the first for me.

> *They kiss.*

Oh, I have known that kiss all my life.

LORENZO: *(Lifting her and whirling her around.)* Now, I would like to nail your name, proclaim you, claim you!

JESSICA: And say this is mine, and this, and here I've been before, and that skin, that smell, that touch so belongs, belongs, belongs that surely I was born the twin to it.

LORENZO: Nail your name and claim your strength!

> *They kiss as SHYLOCK's voice is heard.*

SCENE THREE

SHYLOCK's study.

He's trying to read a letter from his daughter.

SHYLOCK: 'Dear Father. I am not what you would like me to be, and what I am, brings me to this. To write more will urge upon me the necessity to think more. I have thought and reassured enough, not conclusively, but sufficient to drive me out. Reflect on our quarrels. They have said all. Your daughter, Jessica.'

RIVKA enters.

RIVKA: And where has your joking got you?

SHYLOCK: I have a letter from my daughter, now be silent, Rivka.

RIVKA: Have you asked yourself why she's gone?

SHYLOCK: I'm trying to find out, don't nag at me.

RIVKA: Are you certain there was no wrong in *you*?

SHYLOCK: You're the only person I know who *asks* accusations.

RIVKA: Please, Shylock, I beg you. Be a kind man, be a considerate brother. I've no health for laughter. Be finished with joking.

SHYLOCK: I have a letter from my daughter.

RIVKA: You've read it seven times, already. Talk with me. I'm not a fool.

SHYLOCK: What would you have me talk about, sister?

RIVKA: The meaning of your bond.

SHYLOCK: It has meanings? Clauses, perhaps, but meanings?

RIVKA: Clauses, meanings, meanings, clauses! If *you* won't read the meanings like a man, then this old woman will.

What you wanted to mock now mocks you! That's what
your bond means.

SHYLOCK: I don't see what meaning that meaning means.

RIVKA: Oh yes you do.

SHYLOCK: I see problems. I see possibilities. I see maybes and
perhapses. The *problem* of Antonio's ships captured, the
possibility of rescue, though *maybe* the wind will delay it or
perhaps Antonio's creditors will advance him more money
and there'll be no *problem* because he'll have the *possibility*
to repay me in time.

RIVKA: In time? What time? The clocks will soon strike six
and that will leave only one day.

SHYLOCK: I must hear this nonsense through, I suppose.

RIVKA: Don't be rude to me, Shylock! You have a friend.
Good. A Gentile and gentle man. Good. You made some
peace for yourself. I was happy for you. Good. But could
you leave it like that, my wise man, always throwing
his voice, his ideas about, on this, on that, here, there,
to anyone, could you leave it well alone like that? Oh
Shylock, my young brother. It made me ache to watch
you, looking for moral problems to sharpen your mind, for
disputations – as if there weren't enough troubles inside
these peeling walls. But you *can't* pretend you're educated,
just as you can't pretend you're not an alien or that this
Ghetto has no walls. Pretend, pretend, pretend! All your
life! Wanting to be what you're not. Imagining the world
as you want. And now, again, as always, against all reason,
this mad pretence that Antonio's ships will come in safe.

> *Pause.*

You've mocked the law.

SHYLOCK: Which mocked at us.

RIVKA: A hero! Shylock to the defence of his people. Can't
you see what you've done?

SHYLOCK: Asserted dignity, that's what I've done.

RIVKA: That? That's what you've done? Nothing else?

Pause.

To assert the dignity of your mocked people you have
chained your friend's life to a mocking bond, *that's* what
you've done.

SHYLOCK: Go to your room, Rivka, you're becoming excited.

RIVKA: Shylock! Go and find the money! Knock on every
Ghetto door, beg, plead, bully – but get it. Now. Before it's
too late.

SHYLOCK: Foolish woman. Do you think I haven't tried? The
Ghetto is drained. The last tax emptied every purse.

RIVKA: Then let him borrow from his friends.

SHYLOCK: They don't trust his future now.

RIVKA: Then plead with the court to bend the law and relieve
you of your bond.

SHYLOCK: Tomorrow. Tomorrow we'll talk about it.

RIVKA: But not everyone in the Ghetto will agree to the
bending of the law, will they?

SHYLOCK: Please, Rivka.

RIVKA: Having bent the law for us, they'll say, how often will
the Venetians bend it for themselves, and then we'll live in
even greater uncertainties than before. They'll be divided,
as you are, my clever brother. Who to save – your poor
people or your poor friend?

SHYLOCK: We'll talk about it tomorrow.

RIVKA: You want moral problems to sharpen your mind?

SHYLOCK: Tomorrow, tomorrow.

RIVKA: Then sharpen your mind on this: who *will* you save? The Christian friend you love or the families of your blood?

> *Beat.*

Well, am I a fool or not? Are there to be jokes or not? Have you a problem or not?

SHYLOCK: Tomorrow, tomorrow. We'll talk about it tomorrow.

RIVKA: Tomorrow! Tomorrow! *What* tomorrow? The clocks will soon strike six and it will *be* tomorrow.

> *Long pause. RIVKA rises to leave.*

Me you can get out of the way, your problem – not!

> *RIVKA leaves.*

> *SHYLOCK returns to his letter.*

SHYLOCK: *(Aloud.)* 'Reflect on our quarrels. They have said all. Your daughter, Jessica.'

> *It is as though he has not understood.*

'Our quarrels.' What quarrels? How could she have called them quarrels? *Enemies* quarrel. 'I am not what you would like me to be.' What did I want you to be, Jessica? My prop, my friend, my love, my pride? Not painful things, those. Are they?

Oh, Jessica. What wretched, alien philosophy has taken up your mind, muddied it with strange fervours? Where are you now? Oh, vulnerable youth. You must be so lonely. So lost and lonely. So amazed and lost and lonely. Oh daughter, daughter, daughter.

> *ANTONIO enters. He too appears burdened with worries. They confront each other in silent and all-knowing commiseration, then embrace.*

> *SHYLOCK at once begins to fuss over his friend, sitting him down, pouring wine.*

SHYLOCK: It'll be all right. Your ships will find their harbour and my daughter will find her home.

ANTONIO: But whose harbour and whose home and when?

SHYLOCK: Ah! I see you're gloomy.

ANTONIO: And I see you pretend you're not.

SHYLOCK: And supposing you lose your ships, what? You've no credit, no friends? What?

ANTONIO: I'm in debt to all Venice.

SHYLOCK: No skills to start again?

ANTONIO: You're evading the implications.

SHYLOCK: Drink! I think we both need a little helpful drink.

ANTONIO: The implications must be faced and talked about.

SHYLOCK: Nothing presses, nothing threatens – drink.

ANTONIO: We've signed a foolish bond.

SHYLOCK: The bond will not be called upon – drink.

ANTONIO: It's known the ships were attacked, and my entire fortune staked in a single convoy. We've signed a foolish bond.

SHYLOCK: The storm will drop.

ANTONIO: We've signed a foolish bond, whose forfeiture is due.

SHYLOCK: The maritime office's fleet will sail – drink.

ANTONIO: At six o'clock there will be only twenty-four more hours to go.

SHYLOCK: Perhaps the days have been miscounted.

ANTONIO: SHYLOCK!

Beat.

What will you do with a knife in your hand and my flesh to weigh?

Long pause.

SOLOMON, USQUE and REBECCA arrive.

REBECCA: Signor Shylock, is it true? We heard that your daughter is missing.

SHYLOCK: No commiserations, please. You're welcome. I love my friends around me, but there's been no death in my family, simply – a holiday. Every young person must have a holiday from home. Sit. I'll pour drink for you. Are you hungry? Tell me news.

REBECCA: Little change, families wanting passage to Constantinople, old men waiting for our funds for their voyage to Jerusalem, but your daughter, Signor.

SHYLOCK: Who can write plays in such misery, eh, Signor Usque.

USQUE: Who is there *great* enough to write plays in such misery!

SHYLOCK: Ah ha! Who is there great enough to write plays in such misery!

TUBAL and a crestfallen RODERIGUES arrive. SHYLOCK looks to them expectantly.

RODERIGUES: I told you! I warned!

TUBAL stays him.

TUBAL: She has joined the man called Pisani.

SHYLOCK: Pisani?

TUBAL: They left last night for an estate named Belmont.

SHYLOCK: Lorenzo Pisani? A nothing! A sour, silly young man with little talent but that of envy, who confuses complaint for protestation. Jessica! you have been grabbed by air!

GRAZIANO enters. Everyone knows what he has come to announce. They wait. He's terrified both of such an audience and the news he brings. He wants to hand the list to ANTONIO.

ANTONIO: Read me the list. *(Pause.)* Yes, here.

GRAZIANO: A ship carrying raisins from the Island of Zante, olive oil from Corfu and the cotton from Syria. Another with wine, corn, and cheese from Crete. The Danish ship you chartered for the English cloth and the Spanish wool. The assignment of timber and, the last, from –

ANTONIO: – from the sugar estates of Cyprus. All lost. They have taken or sunk the consignment I swore would be my last. I do not possess one ducat, Shylock.

A clock strikes six. TUBAL motions to the others that they should leave the two friends alone.

ANTONIO: I cannot raise the money now.

SHYLOCK: I know.

ANTONIO: Nor can you lend it me again.

SHYLOCK: The Ghetto's drained, I know.

Long pause.

They'll let us drop the bond.

ANTONIO: We cannot, must not.

SHYLOCK: You understand?

ANTONIO: I understand.

SHYLOCK: I'm frightened that you don't.

ANTONIO: I do.

SHYLOCK: I will not bend the law.

ANTONIO: I understand.

SHYLOCK: I must not set a precedent.

ANTONIO: I know.

SHYLOCK: *You* said. *You* taught.

ANTONIO: Shylock, Shylock! I'm not afraid.

SHYLOCK: Oh friend! What have I done to you?

> *Pause.*

ANTONIO: Your yellow hat belongs to both of us. We both
shall be put to death.

SHYLOCK: I know.

ANTONIO: I by you. You by them.

SHYLOCK: I know, I know.

ANTONIO: We know, we know! We keep saying we know so
much.

SHYLOCK: Gently, gently, dear friend. I'm not afraid either.

> *Beat.*

Just promise me silence in the trial.

ANTONIO: Will we make no explanations? The court must
understand.

SHYLOCK: Understanding is beyond them. I protect my
people and my people's contract. I could not bear
the honour would be accorded me if I pleaded such
explanations. 'He saved his people!' It would be grotesque.
Just promise me silence at the trial.

ANTONIO: No one will understand.

SHYLOCK: You must let my pride have its silence.

ANTONIO: They won't think it is pride, they will mistake your
silence for contempt.

SHYLOCK: Perhaps they will be right. I am sometimes
appalled by my contempt for men. Can I so lack pity for
their stupidities, compassion for their frailties, excuses

for their cruelties? The massacres by kings, the deathly little spites of serfs, the oppressive jealousies and hurts of scholars who had more learning than wisdom. Seeing what men have done, I know the pattern of what they will do, and I have such contempt, such contempt it bewilders me. Surely, I say to myself, there is much to be loved and cherished. Surely. I force myself to remember. Sometimes I succeed and then, ha! I'm a good man to know, such a good man. Children warm to me in the streets. They don't cry out 'Shylock Old Jew' then. No, they skip at my side and hold my hand, and on those days I walk so upright, like a young man, and I feel myself respected and loved. And love I myself also. Why, you ask, if joy comes through praising men, why do we not praise them all the time? The balance, dear friend, the balance! Take those books, one by one, place on one side those which record men's terrible deeds, and on the other their magnificence. Deed for deed! Healing beside slaughter, building beside destruction, truth beside lie.

> *Beat.*

My contempt, sometimes, knows no bounds. And it has destroyed me.

ANTONIO: Ah, Shylock, Shylock, why didn't we know one another when young?

SHYLOCK: *(Smiling.)* I'd have been wiser you mean?

ANTONIO: No, fool! It was myself I was thinking of.

SHYLOCK: I love thee, Antonio.

ANTONIO: And I thee, old man.

SCENE FOUR

Belmont. The garden. PORTIA.

BASSANIO enters with LORENZO and JESSICA.

BASSANIO: Greetings, dear friends. What a pleasure to meet people you love in new places. Lorenzo, here she is. You've heard her described, now you see her in the flesh. Here, Portia, is the man I spoke to you about – poet, philosopher, prophet, and he who may one day lead Venice – Lorenzo Pisani.

PORTIA: I hope, Signor Lorenzo, you are not as intimidated by what is expected of you as I feel stripped by the words describing me! Nevertheless, says flesh to prophet: welcome!

BASSANIO: And Jessica welcome too. We've not met before and so both Portia and I have this pleasure together.

PORTIA: Oh those sad eyes.

LORENZO: We're honoured and grateful for your hospitality but those sad eyes carry sad news.

BASSANIO: Whose sad news?

LORENZO: Antonio's sad news. The ships are gone. The wreck of one was found and it's assumed the others either shared the same fate or have been taken off for use by the pirates.

PORTIA: But I don't understand the problem. Antonio owes Shylock three thousand ducats. What's that? I'm able to raise that sum and more besides to set him up in trade again.

LORENZO: No good! The hour is up and the Jew has turned mad. 'My people! My bond! My people! My bond!' as though the Jewish population were in threat instead of a poor, beguiled friend of the Jew who must now have the skin of his breast scraped from his bones.

JESSICA: Lorenzo!

LORENZO: The dilemma for the Doge is unprecedented.

JESSICA: Forgive me, Lorenzo...but...

LORENZO: You're right. My anger's made me indelicate.

JESSICA: It's not simply that –

BASSANIO: I warned him! A Jew to be trusted?

JESSICA: *Please*! Gentlemen! Remember me! I'm raw. My rhythms still belong to the Ghetto. I can't slip so quickly from God to God like a whore.

LORENZO: Jessica!

JESSICA: Yes, I'm also angry. You misrepresent the bond. Whatever else my father's flaws you know the bond had mockery not malice in it.

PORTIA: And that I understand. There's not enough of mockery in Venice. We're a city boasting very little of intelligent self-scrutiny or ridicule. But to mock the law is one thing, to squeeze it of its last punitive drop is another.

JESSICA: He must have his reasons.

PORTIA: *(Warmly.)* And you must be hungry. Nerissa and I have prepared a light meal. Nothing too heavy.

BASSANIO: And I must prepare my luggage. Antonio will expect me to be near him while the court conducts its inquiries.

LORENZO: I'll join you, there's a principle affecting the future of Venice tied up in this case. Someone must air it.

BASSANIO: *(Leaving.)* Forgive me?

PORTIA: The decision is yours.

To LORENZO.

I'll be happy to look after your Jessica for you. It's a tragic affair but there's nothing we can do in it.

PORTIA follows BASSANIO off.

LORENZO: 'Those sad eyes.' They tell me I'm unworthy of you, that I don't appreciate your sacrifice. I do. Have courage. You've joined the world now.

JESSICA: *(Sardonically.)* Is that what I've joined?

LORENZO: Come, lie in my arms these last minutes. You're shocked still. Let me tell you about yourself.

JESSICA: *(Trying to relax.)* Oh do, Lorenzo, do tell me about myself, what I've done. Make sense of my actions for me. It seemed such a natural, inevitable thing to do. And now this bond, this wretched, stupid bond threatens.

LORENZO: Hush, then.

JESSICA: I feel so full of discontent.

LORENZO: Quiet, then.

JESSICA: As though it's not in me ever to be happy.

LORENZO: Sssssssh!

JESSICA: I'm frightened and…

LORENZO: Sssssssh!

JESSICA: All right. I'm quiet. Look. Start.

LORENZO: *(After a pause, portentously.)* Some families are doomed.

JESSICA: That's not a very joyful start.

LORENZO: You should find all truths joyful.

JESSICA: Oh dear.

LORENZO: Even unhappy ones.

JESSICA: Oh dear, dear.

        He wants to be solemn. She tries to be gay.

So, some families are doomed.

LORENZO: Parents have ill chosen one another.

JESSICA: Parents have ill chosen one another, so?

LORENZO: So, as parents can ill-choose one another, similarly can men ill-choose their gods.

> *JESSICA, slowly realising with disgust his meaning, rises angrily, and backs away.*

JESSICA: I see.

LORENZO: Not with those reproachful eyes, Jessica. You know that is the truth about yourself. The sadness Portia saw was also of a forsaken race, married to a God they thought had chosen them. Doomed!

JESSICA: *(Icily.)* You think so?

LORENZO: But there are always survivors. I will make you a wife, a woman and a Christian.

JESSICA: *(With controlled fury.)* Sometimes I think the sadness in my eyes comes from the knowledge that we draw from men their desperate hates. Poisons rise in our presence, idiocies blossom, and angers, and incredible lapses of humanity. That is my doom! To know that secret: that at any time, for any reason, men are capable of such demented acts. So I regard a stranger with dread, reproach, fear. Forever vigilant. That's difficult for him to bear, to be looked at like that, for no reason, to be thought guilty before the act, to be known for the beast in one, the devil in the making. Who can forgive eyes that have such knowledge in them?

LORENZO: I see there's a great deal of unthreading to do.

JESSICA: Yes, I see there is.

> *NERISSA enters.*

NERISSA: Signor Lorenzo, you must leave at once. The wind is right. I've prepared food for your journey.

LORENZO: There's no better place to be left, Jessica.

He embraces her. She cannot respond.

Trust me, please.

LORENZO leaves.

JESSICA looks very much alone.

PORTIA enters. At once, women together, they relax.

PORTIA: Good, the three of us alone. Talk to me, Jessica. Tell me about the Ghetto. My tutor in Hebrew studies was a strange man called Abraham Cardoso. *He* came from the Ghetto.

JESSICA: We knew him.

PORTIA: You did? What a coincidence.

JESSICA: Hardly a coincidence, madam, the quarter is so small.

PORTIA can see something is not right for JESSICA. After a moment –

PORTIA: Tell me what you love in him.

JESSICA: I loved his questioning the wisdom of age, his clamouring to give youth its voice, his contempt for what men wrote in books. His strength, his seriousness, his devotion. I loved, I suppose, escape from oppressive expectations.

PORTIA: And now?

JESSICA: Now, I'm feeling his strength is arrogance, his seriousness is pedantry, his devotion is frenzy, and I am confused and drained.

PORTIA: And the truth about the bond?

JESSICA: Antonio asked my father for the loan, which he would have given ten times over without a contract.

PORTIA: Shylock didn't want a contract?

JESSICA: Not with his dear friend, no. They almost quarrelled, till Antonio finally persuaded him – the Jews have need of the laws of Venice to remain in Venice, therefore the law must be respected, and so, if there must be a bond, my father wanted a bond that asserted his love of Antonio, and mocked the law of Venice that mocked their friendship.

PORTIA: I see. A difficult contract to explain to Venetian Senators.

NERISSA: Why don't *you* attend the court in Venice, madam?

PORTIA: To do what?

NERISSA: A word, a thought, have faith in that 'untried intellect'.

PORTIA: Faith in that 'untried intellect' I have, but knowledge of the law I have none.

NERISSA: Perhaps it isn't law that's needed.

PORTIA: But there's so much work to do here.

NERISSA: Two men's lives are at stake.

PORTIA: But not men I know.

NERISSA: One, her father.

PORTIA: What can I do? I pity men their mad moments but a bond is a bond. The law demands its forfeitures. A pound of flesh is a satanic price to conceive, even as a joke but –

> *She is struck by revelation. She can't believe the thought, rejects it but it persists.*

Holy Mary mother of Christ! I have it! But no. No! No, no, no, no, it's too simple. The law is complex, devious. This is commonsense, justice. The law is not to do with justice. No. It *can't* be applicable. And yet – who could possibly deny... Then surely...dare I? I'm no advocate. My temper's not for public places...and yet...a wrong is a wrong...

JESSICA: To whom is she speaking?

PORTIA: *(Triumphantly.)* Why don't we all three go to Venice and attend the court? There is a contract I must scrutinise and a father with whom you should be.

JESSICA: Are women granted entry to the courts?

PORTIA: They'll grant these women entry to the courts!

> *The scene immediately becomes the Courtroom of the Doge's Palace.*

SCENE FIVE

> *The women turn and sweep into the Courtroom of the Doge's Palace, Venice.*

> *PORTIA and NERISSA walk straight up to ask the DOGE permission to enter. He grants it. PORTIA whispers to him. They leave together.*

> *JESSICA is embraced by RIVKA and TUBAL,*

> *NERISSA moves to the Christian side where are BASSANIO, LORENZO and GRAZIANO.*

> *Present are USQUE, REBECCA, RODERIGUES and SENATORS.*

> *The YOUNG MEN are surprised.*

BASSANIO: Portia!

LORENZO: Jessica!

BASSANIO: Did the women say they were coming?

LORENZO: On the contrary, Portia felt there was nothing to be done.

BASSANIO: Nor is there. Silence! For two hours this court of inquiry has had nothing but silence from him. Shylock! Will you speak?

> *No response.*

He says nothing, offers no explanation, simply claims the bond.

JESSICA: Explain it to them, father, explain!

SHYLOCK: Do not speak to me.

> *SHYLOCK hates scorning her, but can't help himself.*
>
> *She retires in distress to the Christian side.*

BASSANIO: Look at that scowl.

> *To SHYLOCK.*

He was your friend! You boasted a Gentile for a friend!

GRAZIANO: What did you say, old Jew? Not only would I be your friend, but I have to be your friend. Friendship? Ha!.

BASSANIO: But why hasn't Antonio said something?

GRAZIANO: Well, of course, he wouldn't. Bewitched, wasn't he? Forced into the bond.

BASSANIO: Shylock, will you speak?

LORENZO: Perhaps it's not Shylock who should speak but some of our own city councillors. Why have they been silent? What Jewish money do they owe? It must be huge if they're prepared to let a fellow citizen be skinned alive.

> *Calling out.*

Fellow Venetians, is this city so far gone in its quest for profit and trade that there's no morality left? Usury is a sin against charity. When God had finished his creation he said unto man, beasts, and fishes, increase and multiply, but did he ever say increase and multiply unto money?

ANTONIO: Profit is the fruit of skill, young man!

JESSICA: And this bond was the fruit of friendship, Lorenzo, not usury, you know it!

LORENZO: I promise you, fellow Venetians, that when the young patricians take their seats there'll be more God than Mammon on our statute books. Usury is a sin against charity. The –

TUBAL: To deprive the people of an opportunity to obtain help is a sin against humanity!

LORENZO: *(Ignoring him.)* Usury is a sin against charity, and the people suffer from it!

ANTONIO: The people suffer from ignorance, Lorenzo, believe me. To deprive them of knowledge is the sin.

LORENZO: Knowledge! Knowledge! How Shylock's books have muddied your mind. A man can be strong and happy with *no* knowledge, *no* art. Turn to the shepherd and the tiller and the sailor who know of the evils of usury, without books, without art. Real knowledge, simple knowledge is in the wind and seasons and the labouring men do.

ANTONIO: You say a man is happy with no knowledge or art? There is wisdom in the wind, you say? The seasons tell all there is to know of living and dying? I wonder. Is it really understanding we see in the shepherd's eye? Is the tiller told more than the thinker? I used to think so, sitting with sailors roughened by salt, listening to their intelligence. They perceive much, I'd say to myself. But as I sat a day here, a day there, through the years, their intelligence wearied me. It repeated itself, spent itself upon the same complaints, but with no real curiosity. How alive is a man with muscles but no curiosity? You wonder why I bind my fate to Shylock, what I see in him? Curiosity! *There* is a driven man. Exhilarating! I thank the shepherd for my clothes and the tiller for my food, good men. Blessed. Let them be paid well and honoured. But they know, I, we know: there is a *variousness* to be had in life. Why else does the labourer send his sons to schools when he can? He knows what self-respect knowledge commands. All men do, wanting for their children what fate denied *them*, living without meat and keeping warm with mere sticks to do it. I'd have died before now if no man had kindled my soul with his music or wasn't there with his bright thoughts keeping me turning and taught about myself. Yes. Even at such an hour, I remember these things. Don't talk to me about the simple wisdom of people, Lorenzo. Their simple wisdom is no more than the ignorance we choose to keep them in.

> *Silence.*

GRAZIANO: As I thought. Bewitched. A knife hangs over him and he defends the man who holds it.

LORENZO: Be quiet, Graziano.

GRAZIANO: Lorenzo!

LORENZO: Stop meddling. You're a fool! The situation is too complex for you and I've no time for your tavern tattle.

BASSANIO: Quiet now. The Doge is ready.

> *The DOGE returns to the official proceeding leaving PORTIA to continue perusing papers.*

DOGE: Antonio Querini?

ANTONIO: *(Stepping forward.)* Most serene Prince.

DOGE: Shylock Kolner?

SHYLOCK: Most serene Prince.

DOGE: This court has never had before it such a case. The issue's clear, the resolution not. We must retrace and nag at it again. Signor Shylock, are you fully aware that the court is prepared to release both parties from the need to see this contract through?

SHYLOCK: I am, Excellency.

DOGE: Yet you refuse, and state no reason?

SHYLOCK: I refuse and state no reason. Yes.

DOGE: And do you know this man may bleed to death?

SHYLOCK: I have our greatest doctors standing by.

DOGE: To do what? What can even Jewish doctors do to stem such awful draining of a man's life-blood? You, Querini, dear fellow patrician, we beg you break your silence. You once enjoyed running the affairs of our city. Tell the court. Don't be afraid. What has happened?

ANTONIO: *(Impatiently.)* Nothing has happened, Excellency, more than I've lost my appetite for the intrigues and boredom of administration.

DOGE: Then at least explain why you shared the madness of a bond, which twice endangers you: from a man insisting that you pay a forfeiture of flesh, and from the law which must punish you for mocking it.

> *No response.*

Your silence does not help.

GRAZIANO: I knew it! I warned it!

ANTONIO: Graziano, be quiet!

GRAZIANO: A plot! A plot! A Jewish plot!

ANTONIO: Be quiet, I say.

GRAZIANO: I can't be quiet, I love you.

ANTONIO: You love no one and nothing but a safe place with the multitude. Now be quiet.

DOGE: Why do you attack your friends, Antonio? These men who've come to speak for you? And why are you not speaking for yourself?

> *Silence.*

LORENZO: Incredible! The Jew has even chained his victim to silence. Most serene Prince, I beg you –

DOGE: Be careful!

LORENZO: – there are principles involved that go beyond this case.

DOGE: Do not attempt to make capital!

LORENZO: We should not be inquiring into silence but questioning if Jews and usury, no matter what the bond, should be permitted to pollute the fabric of our city's life. The real question is –

TUBAL: Do you think we enjoy lending to your poor at the high rate your city imposes…?

LORENZO: …the real question is…

RODERIGUES: Collect for your poor among yourselves!

LORENZO: …the real question is…

USQUE: You have pious fraternities, collect from them for your poor!

TUBAL: Or use taxes!

LORENZO: …THE REAL QUESTION IS…

DOGE: The question of the city's contracts with the Jews is a matter for the Council. The laws of Venice are very clear and precise and cannot be twisted this way and that for political significance or gain, nor denied to foreigners, otherwise justice will not obtain. And the principal foundation of our city is justice. The people of Venice must have justice.

ANTONIO: *(Finally angry.)* Justice? For the people of Venice? The people? When political power rests quite firmly in the hands of two hundred families? That, though he talks of principle, is what Lorenzo is impatient for, to share that power. He uses the people's name for through their grievances he'll come to power. One of their grievances is what he calls usury. The usurer's a Jew, and the Jew the people's favourite villain. Convenient! Easy! But usury *must* exist in our city. We have many poor and our economy can't turn without it. The Jew practises what he hates because we have forbidden him rights to practise other professions. *He* relieves *us* of the sin. Do we condemn

90

the Jew for doing what our system has *required* him to do?
Then if we do, let's swear, upon the cross, that among us
we know of no Christian, no patrician, no duke, bishop
or merchant who, in his secret chambers, does not lend at
interest, for that is what usury is. Swear it! On the cross! No
one, we know no one!

Pause.

Who's silent now?

Pause.

You will inflame the people's grievances in order to
achieve power, Lorenzo, but once there you'll sing such
different songs I think.

DOGE: You do not make inquiry easy for the court, Signor.

BASSANIO: How can you make inquiries into silence, most
serene Prince, the inhuman silence of an arrogant chosen
people? Heretical! They still refuse to acknowledge that
they are no *longer* the chosen people.

SHYLOCK: Oh horror of horrors! Oh heresy of heresies! Oh
sweat! Oh flutter! Oh butterflies, gooseflesh, hair-on-end!
Oh windbag of windbags! And *you* I suppose, have been
chosen instead?

LORENZO: *(Flooding the proceedings with conciliatory warmth
and charm.)* Most serene Prince, Signor Shylock is not
here because he is a Jew. Come now, the patricians of
Venice are good men and justly fear being accused of such
prejudice. No! What is on trial in this court is, I insist,
the principle of usury whose evil this bond so tragically
exemplifies, and from whose consideration we should not
be distracted. The *bond* is inhuman, not the man.

No one doubts the Jew is human. After all, has not a Jew
eyes?

SHYLOCK: What is *that* fool attempting now?

LORENZO: Has not a Jew hands?

SHYLOCK: Is he presuming explanations on *my* behalf?

LORENZO: Has not a Jew organs, dimensions, senses, affections, passions?

SHYLOCK: *(With incredulity.)* Oh no!

LORENZO: Is not the Jew fed with the same food, hurt with the same weapons, subject to the same diseases, healed by the same means, warmed and cooled by the same winter and summer as a Christian is?

SHYLOCK: No, no!

LORENZO: If you prick him, does he not bleed?

SHYLOCK: No, no, NO! I will not have it. *(Outraged but controlled.)* I do not want apologies for my humanity. Plead for me no special pleas. I will not have my humanity mocked and apologised for. If I am unexceptionally like any man then I need no exceptional portraiture. I merit no special pleas, no special cautions, no special gratitudes. My humanity is my right, not your bestowed and gracious privilege.

GRAZIANO: See how ungrateful the Jew is? I knew it! I warned it! The Jew was silent because he knew that the moment he opened his mouth he'd hang himself with his arrogance. The Jew...

SHYLOCK: *(Furious but low and dangerous, building.)* Jew! Jew, Jew, Jew! I hear the name around and everywhere. Your wars go wrong, the Jew must be the cause of it; your economic systems crumble, there the Jew must be; your wives get sick of you – a Jew will be an easy target for your sour frustrations. Failed university, professional blunderings, self-loathing – the Jew, the Jew, the cause the Jew. And when will you cease? When, when, when will your hatreds dry up? There's nothing we can do is right. Admit it! You will have us all ways won't you?

For our prophecies, our belief in universal morality, our scholarship, our command of trade, even our ability to survive. If we are silent we must be scheming, if we talk we are insolent. When we come we are strangers, when we go we are traitors. In tolerating persecution we are despised, but were we to take up arms we'd be the world's marauders, for sure. Nothing will please you. Well, damn you then!

Drawing a knife.

I *will* have my pound of flesh and not feel obliged to explain my whys and wherefores. Think what you will, you will think that in any case. I'll say it is my bond. The law is the law. You need no other reason, nor shall you get it – from me.

SHYLOCK turns to the DOGE, justice must be done.

ANTONIO joins him on the other side of the DOGE. They turn to face one another – doomed friends.

Though no Jew must take another's life yet SHYLOCK has made the decision to damn his soul for the community that he feels is threatened.

PORTIA: Most serene Prince, I have read the documents.

Pause.

Your Excellency, forgive my presumption, I know nothing of the law, but I cannot see that there is sufficient detail in this contract to make it legally valid.

Murmurs in court.

And if not valid, then not binding.

Excitement grows.

But I'm anxious in case my intelligence is merely foolish faith in little more than a hair of the law.

DOGE: The courts of Venice are open to justice no matter how tenuous a hair binds it to the law.

PORTIA: Then it seems to me this contract contains nothing but contradictions.

Tense silence.

There is in this bond a call for flesh but none for blood.

Noise in court.

There is in this bond a call for a precise pound weight but none for more or less.

Growing noise.

It cannot be executed because torn flesh draws blood.

Still growing noise.

It cannot be executed because precise weight cannot be achieved.

Yet more noise.

This contract is not binding because – impossible.

A swift silence in court.

SHYLOCK: *(Stunned moves first to embrace ANTONIO.)* Thank God! Thank God! Of course! Idiots! Cut flesh draws blood. No blood, no flesh. Oh, Antonio, how could such a simple fact escape us? Pedants of the law! Shame on you, Shylock a disgrace to your tribe. Down to the bottom of the class. Oh, Tubal, what a fool you've had for a partner. No wonder we never owned the really big warehouses.

Offering knife to the three men.

There! For you! *You* need it. You've no wit to draw blood with your brains or tongue, take this. Cruder, but guaranteed. Ha ha! No blood, no flesh. I love the lady. Young lady I love you. You have a future, I see it, a great future.

PORTIA: *(Sadly.)* But not you, old Shylock.

SHYLOCK: Not I? Are you mad? I've been delivered of
murder – I have a clean and honest life to continue. Oh,
not for a hundred years, I know, and it's a pity because
today, TODAY I feel I want to go on living for ever and
ever. There's such wisdom in the world, such beauty in this
life. Ha! Not I, young lady? Oh yes, I! I, I, I! A great future,
also. Back to my books.

DOGE: No, Shylock, no books.

SHYLOCK: No books? Will you take my books?

ANTONIO: You take his life when you take his books.

SHYLOCK: What nonsense now?

DOGE: No nonsense, I'm afraid, Shylock. An old Venetian law
condemns to death and confiscation of his goods the alien
who plots against the life of a citizen of Venice.

SHYLOCK: I? Plot? Against a citizen of Venice? Who?
Antonio?

DOGE: You pursued that which would end a man's life.

SHYLOCK: But was 'that' which I pursued 'plot'? Plot? Malice
aforethought?

DOGE: Malice aforethought or not, the end was a citizen's
death.

ANTONIO: However –

SHYLOCK: But there's no perception, no wisdom there –

ANTONIO: However –

SHYLOCK: – no pity there.

GRAZIANO: Pity's called for now!

ANTONIO: HOWEVER! The law also says the offender's life
is at the mercy of the Doge –

DOGE: Which mercy I make no delay in offering him. But the State must take his goods. The people of Venice would not understand it if –

SHYLOCK: Oh! The people of Venice, of course.

LORENZO: See what contempt he has.

SHYLOCK: The people again. Ah, Lorenzo, what strange things happen behind the poor people's name.

ANTONIO: And I? What punishment do the people of Venice exact of me?

DOGE: Your foolishness, Signor, was punished by the pain of threatened death. Enough!

ANTONIO: The wisdom of patrician privilege, of course.

DOGE: But do not strain it, friend. Do not.

ANTONIO: *(Bowing.)* I thank you.

> *The DOGE and all leave, except SHYLOCK, ANTONIO, PORTIA, JESSICA.*

JESSICA: Father?

SHYLOCK: Go! Leave me!

JESSICA: I *will* go, but I will never leave you.

> *JESSICA leaves in tears. SHYLOCK reaches out to her. Too late.*

SHYLOCK: *(Turning to PORTIA.)* And the lady, where is the lovely lady, what does she say to all this?

PORTIA: *(Raging at the departed DOGE.)* I would not carry a sword in one hand and scales in the other. That image always seemed to me ambiguous. Is my sword held high to defend the justice my left hand weighs? Or is it poised threateningly to enforce my left hand's obduracy?

SHYLOCK: *(Ironically.)* Impartial justice, lovely lady, impartial justice.

PORTIA: Impartial? How? *I* am not a thing of the wind, but
an intelligence informed by other men informed by other
men informed! *I* grow. Why can't they? What I thought
yesterday might be wrong today. What should I do? Stand
by my yesterdays because *I* have made them? I made
today as well! And tomorrow, that I'll make too, and all
my days, as my intelligence demands. I was born in a city
built upon the wisdom of Solon, Numa Pompilius, Moses!

They exchange sad smiles.

SHYLOCK: *(With sad pleasure, taking her hand, still as to a
daughter.)* You have a future, young lady, I tell you, a great
future.

> *JESSICA finds this tender moment between her father
> and another young woman unbearable and flees.*

ANTONIO: Shylock! Explain to the court you did not want to
set a precedent in law. You'll save your books.

SHYLOCK: *(Sardonically and with finality.)* No. Take my books.
The law must be observed. We have need of the law, what
need do we have of books? Distressing, disturbing things,
besides. Why, dear friend, books might even make us
question laws. Ha! And who in his right mind would want
to do that? Certainly not old Shylock. Take my books. Take
everything. I do not want the law departed from, not one
letter departed from.

> *We hear the distant sad singing of a woman. The
> song is 'Adiós querida', a Sephardic song.[1]*

SHYLOCK: Perhaps now is the time to make that journey
to Jerusalem. Join those other old men on the quayside,
waiting to make a pilgrimage, to be buried there – ach!
What do I care! My heart will not follow me, wherever it
is. My appetites are dying, dear friend, for anything in this
world. I am so tired of men.

---

1. See EMI label ASD2649, sung by Victoria de los
Angeles.

SHYLOCK moves away, a bitter man.

Everyone has left except PORTIA. The scene has changed to Belmont.

The singing carries over into the next scene.

SCENE SIX

Belmont. The garden. A warm, heavy, melancholy evening.

PORTIA strolling.

JESSICA stands aside.

The woman singing in the distance. The air is broken by the sound of raucous laughter.

BASSANIO, LORENZO and GRAZIANO enter carrying food.

NERISSA follows them. A picnic is prepared. They talk, NERISSA spreads a rug, light candles, and leaves.

BASSANIO: A farewell supper! Our friends are leaving, Portia. Tonight must be made memorable. *(Calling.)* Drinks, Nerissa, drinks for the heroes.

NERISSA: *(Off.)* Coming, my heroes, coming!)

LORENZO: Jessica! Food!

But PORTIA and JESSICA seem reluctant to join the three young men. LORENZO alone notes the indifference, especially of JESSICA who cannot bear him.

GRAZIANO: It's a splendid house, Signorina Contarini, splendid. The most beautiful I've seen. And what a library! It made me pick up a book for the first time in years.

LORENZO: *(Acidly.)* Which book?

GRAZIANO: No, no, Lorenzo. You can't keep getting at me. We've been through a lot together now and you know me to be your faithful admirer. I know my limitations and I'm happy to be factotum to your cause. Or causes. Name them, I'll follow. Plot them, I'll execute them. Don't be ungracious. There's a lot to be said for a sycophant.

ANTONIO appears.

PORTIA: I'm so grateful you stayed, Signor Querini. These two weeks have been made bearable, and I've found a new friend.

ANTONIO: While I've found a woman who's made me mourn my youth. What mixed blessings in these last years of my life: to meet an acerbic old Jew who disturbed my dull complacency, and you, blossoming with purpose, reminding me of a barren life.

Pause.

He will haunt me, that man.

Silence but for the singing.

What will you do?

PORTIA: Honour my father's wishes, marry the man who chose lead, look to what must be grown. And you?

ANTONIO: Sort out what has been salvaged from my ships. See my friend off to the Holy Land. Visit him, once, perhaps, before I die, and you often, if I may, before I die.

PORTIA: Oh please!

LORENZO: *(Calling her to eat.)* Jessica! Food, I say.

JESSICA ignores him.

LORENZO waits throughout the next exchange for her to turn to him. She does turn, contemptuously, then turns away.

ANTONIO: But what will happen to her?

PORTIA: I'll look after Jessica. My marriage is a parent's will, not hers, though. Mine can't be held back, hers, I will see, never takes place.

ANTONIO: But *which* place will she take? There's no father's house to return to.

PORTIA: But there is a Jerusalem, where he can be followed.

ANTONIO: I don't think I really fear for Jessica, but you...

PORTIA: Nor fear for me. I'll fill my house with poets and philosophers, and politicians who are poets and philosophers. Bassanio will come to know his place, accept it, or leave it. I am to be reckoned with, you know, not merely dutiful. Although, something in me has died struggling to grow up.

> *LORENZO turns angrily away from looking at JESSICA, finally understanding that he's lost her.*

LORENZO: I don't think I shall ever lose the image of that man's scowl from my mind.

BASSANIO: 'And you I suppose have been chosen instead!' How he spat the words out.

> *PORTIA and ANTONIO move away to different corners of the garden.*
>
> *They, with JESSICA, are three lonely points of a triangle, which encircles the grating sounds of an inane conversation.*

LORENZO: Perhaps now they will learn, the elders. Virtue consists in simplicity, suffering, renunciation!

GRAZIANO: But we forget Portia, his wife...

BASSANIO: Not yet, not yet!

GRAZIANO: His wife to *be.* Now there's a mind to be careful of. Should we envy him or fear for him?

BASSANIO: It was in my stars to make such a match for my bed.

GRAZIANO: You're mad to think only of bed with an intellect like that at your side.

BASSANIO: It shall be cherished but not spoilt. I shall turn to it but not let it rule! Ah! Here comes Nerissa with drink for the heroes.

NERISSA: *(Piercing mockery.)* And heroes you are, sirs, true. No denying it. True, true, heroes indeed. Heroes!

> *Only the singing now and a fading, warm and sad evening.*
>
> *The End.*

BLOOD LIBEL

(Commissioned for the opening of the new Norwich Playhouse)

A man may start by wishing for truth without going the right way to arrive at it, and may end by embracing falsehood till he cannot bear to part with it.

> Augustus Jessopp D.D.,
> from the introduction to his
> translation, together with
> Montague Rhodes James,
> from the Latin of
> *The Life and Miracles of St.*
> *William of Norwich.* 1896.

Characters

HERBERT DE LOSINGA – Bishop, founder of Church of Norwich – 60

WILLIAM – a skinner's apprentice – 12

STRANGER – 35

THOMAS OF MONMOUTH – Monk of Norwich – 48

ELVIVA – mother of William – 28

WENSTAN – farmer, father of William – 32

WULLWARD – priest, father of Elviva – 50

HETHEL – sister of Elviva – 29

GODWIN – priest, husband of Hethel – 35

MATHILDA– daughter of Hethel – 16

PENITENT – 50

PRIEST OF HAVERINGLAND

SKINNER – William's employer – 35

JOHN DE CHEYNEY – Sheriff of Norwich – 50

ELIAS – Prior of Church of Norwich – 60

DOM AIMAR – Prior of St Pancras – 50

MAUDE – Maidservant to Jewish household – 50

AELWARD DED – Citizen of Norwich – 50

THEOBALD – Monk, Jewish convert – 35

1ST VOICE

2ND VOICE

3RD VOICE

1ST MONK

2ND MONK

3RD MONK – rabble rouser

Those upon whom miracles were worked

EDMUND

CLARICIA

MURIEL

RADULFUS

STEPHEN

OLD WOMAN

WALTER

COLOBERN

ANSFRIDA

Note

Although there are 34 characters only 11 actors are needed. It may even be possible to perform the play with 10 actors. Of course the more actors used the greater will be the impact of the crowd scenes.

Suggested groupings: *[Thomas and Elias cannot be doubled with any other character]*

Actor A   Bishop Herbert de Losinga
               Theobald
               Penitent

Actor B   Stranger
               Wenstan
               3rd Monk
               Stephen

Actor C   Wullward
               Priest of Haveringland
               Skinner
               2nd Monk
               Radulfus

Actor D   Godwin
               1st Voice
               1st Monk
               Edmund

Actor E   Sheriff John
               Dom Aimar
               Aelward Ded
               Colobern

Actor F   William
               Walter

Actress A Elviva
               Old Woman
               Claricia

Actress B Hethel   **Actress C** Mathilda
               Maude   2nd Voice
               3rd Voice   Ansfrida
               Muriel

Production Note

There is no interval.

All actors are on stage throughout as though they have assembled to listen to one another tell the story – a familiar theatrical device but one belonging to the nature of the play, attempting to piece together the story of a crime about which there are only a few inconclusive facts. It is as though they, the actors, are witnesses and jury both.

Only one scene they do not watch: the rape scene. When this occurs they turn their backs on it.

From Scene 3 onwards **Thomas of Monmouth** takes control of the play. He is on stage continuously – sometimes writing in his cell, sometimes haranguing, sometimes watching and urging, driving, driving the play forward to its 'hosanna' finale like a latter-day preacher at a revivalist meeting.

Music

The *Hymn to St. William,* needs to be specially composed.

I suggest 'religious music' based on traditional church music should also be specially composed for scene-linking, background and ceremonial moments.

Although there is no interval the play is divided into **four parts.**

Part One – the story as it was told, with a few added suppositions.

Part Two – the first witnesses present their evidence and are countered by Prior Elias

Part Three – Brother Thomas of Monmouth presents new witnesses with additional evidence.

Part Four – we hear of the miracles and rejoice.

Part One

The story as it was told, with a few added suppositions.

SCENE ONE

Pulpit, Church of Norwich Circa 1110 A.D.

Bishop HERBERT DE LOSINGA is delivering a sermon.

HERBERT: ...Like a stream of brimstone are the fiery troubles of this present life; but Christ is with you; the Virgin is with you; the holy angels are with you; and he who fights before such witnesses as these may fix his thoughts only on victory.

I will relate to you a circumstance, brethren, which I learned from a faithful report, and which I believe – especially in this very year of our Lord, eleven hundred and ten – is still of relevance to thee, my humble flock, and me, thy humble Bishop de Losinga. There was a certain city of the Greeks in which Christians and Jews dwelt mingled with one another. Thence sprang familiarity and common dealings. The language of both was the same, while their religion differed. The children of the Jews were taught the learning of the Christians, and thus the sap of truth was by degrees distilled into the tender minds of the Jews, whence it came to pass that on the holy Day of Easter, a Hebrew boy among his fellows and those of his own age approached to the Altar and received the Holy Communion. When the rites of the sacred solemnity had been performed, the Hebrew boy returned home and with childish simplicity disclosed to his mother that he had received a sacred portion from the Christian Altar.

Then the mother, stirred with a woman's fury went to her husband, declared to him what had passed, and kindled in the father of the child madness and cruelty. Whereupon this most unnatural father heated a furnace, and threw his son into the midst of it, into the live coals and raging flames, and in his madness sealed up the mouth of the furnace with stones and cement. The mother's bowels of compassion were moved, and she yearned over her dying child; she cried out in her rage, ran to the Christians, and disclosed that cruel and horrible tale to the ears of mourning friends. The Christians fly to the furnace, and more quickly than it takes to say it, break open the mouth thereof, and drag out the boy alive and safe whom they had supposed to have been burned within. They wonder and rejoice and render due thanks to the Divine Presence. They ask the boy how he had escaped, and by whose protection he had overcome the flames of the furnace. To which he replied; The Lady who sitteth above the Altar of the Christians, and the Little One Whom she cherishes in her bosom, stood around me, and stretching forth their hands hedged my body round, and protected me from the flames and fiery coals, so that I felt no burning but only the refreshment and comfort of a frame which could take no harm. By His fostering care therefore I escape unharmed from the furnace, Whose most sacred Body I received at the Altar of the Christians.

Forthwith there followed a most just vengeance on the heads of the Jews; and they who would not believe in the Incarnate Word were all alike burned in the aforesaid furnace.

Behold, brethren, Christ everywhere protects His own fellow-soldiers, and suffers no one to perish whom He hath foreknown and predestined to be a partaker of His Heavenly Kingdom. He calls those whom He hath predestinated; He predestinates those whom He hath foreknown; and in the foreknowledge of God no change or alteration can be made.

Let us be born again unto our Saviour, Who was on this day born; and walking in the newness of life let us forget those things which are behind and reach forth unto those which are before, cleaving to Christ, abiding in Christ, enjoying Christ, Who with the Father and the Holy Ghost liveth and reigneth, God for ever and ever. Amen.

SCENE TWO

Thorpe Wood on the edge of Norwich. 1144.

WILLIAM, a skinner's apprentice, is walking alongside a malevolent-looking STRANGER who seems to be accompanying him somewhere.

The STRANGER has become agitated. He stops. Confronts a surprised WILLIAM. Begins to rape him.

The boy screams, is gagged and dragged off.

From the direction the boy has been taken there grows a glow into an intensely bright, ethereal light.

As the light grows there grows with it a swelling sound of mob voices.

VOICES: The Jews! The Jews! The Jews! The Jews! The Jews! The Jews! The Jews! THE JEWS!

The rape, the light, 'the Jews, the Jews':

This sequence will be repeated every so often throughout the play.

NOTE: *The rape must be distressing but not graphic, it's impact made with the simplest of actions and sounds rather than long, drawn-out visual violence.*

SCENE THREE

THOMAS's cell.

He writes at his table.

THOMAS: 'April 27 in the year of our Lord 1172. Twenty-eight years after the event, twenty-eight years of argument against those who would deny his martyrdom, twenty-eight years of miracles which prove his sainthood, I, Thomas of Monmouth, the least of your monks, sendeth greeting and all due obedient service to His Holiness the Reverend Father and Lord, William de Turba, by the grace of God, Bishop of Norwich.

Here beginneth the Prologue concerning the Life and Passion of Saint William the Martyr of Norwich.

> *He stands to harangue an imaginary adversary, using those who sit around, listening.*

But before I offer my testimony hear me you wordy gabblers driven against me by malice or envy; you who with saucy insolence and insolent sauciness contradict all that which I know to be true and is here proved to be true. I pierce you with the spear of satire and restrain you with the curb of reason because I can no longer put up with it. I cannot! I have testimony! It has been written down and it shall be known.

SCENE FOUR

> *The house of ELVIVA and WENSTAN, WILLIAM's parents.*

> *ELVIVA is pregnant and in the company of her husband and her father, WULLWARD, a priest.*

ELVIVA: The dream were about you, father, you an' a fish. I were standin' in a road, you by my side, an' I saw at my feet, there as I bent my eyes, a fish, a luce it were. An' it hed twelve fins on each side, all red, like they were splashed with blood. An' I say to you, surprised wi' wonder, I say, 'father, I see a fish, but how do it come here and how do it live in so dry a spot?' An' you say to me, you say, 'take up the fish, Elviva, take it up and put it on thy bosom. An' I do just that. Like you say I should. An' that fish lay there an' you know what? That grew! That moved and grew and grew till I couldn't hold it on me no more, an' suddenly – an' this were what were really strange, father – suddenly it slipped out through my sleeve and it grew wings. Yes, it did! The fish grew wings and flew away, up and up, passing through the clouds and into heaven which open to receive it.

Weren't that a strange dream? That *were* a strange dream. So now, father, you've always told me what my dreams mean. Since I bin a gal, look, you told me. Tell me now.

WULLWARD: That dream mean you'll give birth to a child what'll be special by the time he come of twelve years old.

ELVIVA: How so, 'special'?

WULLWARD: Special. Special. I can't be no more precise'n that.

ELVIVA: Special handsome? Special strong? Special brave? Special clever?

WULLWARD: Special holy. You talked of heaven in your dream, didn't you?

ELVIVA: Well?

WULLWARD: About a fish that flew from your bosom up into heaven?

ELVIVA: Heaven, well?

WULLWARD: Well, your child will be honoured in heaven.

ELVIVA: Honoured in heaven!

WULLWARD: Twelve fins mean twelve years.

ELVIVA: My son?

WULLWARD: Up there with the highest.

ELVIVA: Honoured in heaven.

WULLWARD: Rejoice, daughter, that your son, my grandson, is goin' to be raised to this pitch of glory

SCENE FIVE

Candlemas Day, 1132.

House of ELVIVA and WENSTAN.

ELVIVA gives birth.

A feast! In celebration! Music!

Guests: HETHEL, GODWIN, WULLWARD, a PRIEST, OTHERS.

In the midst of the festivities enters a PENITENT, his arms shackled in chains, begging for alms.

He's given a drink and food.

While eating he notices ELVIVA nursing her child and stretches out his arms to be allowed to cradle the baby.

WENSTAN: Give William to the man doing penance – a holy child to a holy state.

ELVIVA: *(Holding back.)* What's your penance for, old man?

PENITENT: The worst a man can do. Struck my son in anger.

WENSTAN: Narthin' wrong wi' a trashin' now and then.

PENITENT: Crippled him.

ELVIVA: For doin' what? What could a son hev done was so awful?

PENITENT: If I'd've thought on it hard and wise – narthin'.

ELVIVA: Narthin's not much to do so much penance for.

PENITENT: For disagreein' wi' me – struck him for that! For my son using his own head which I asked him to do since time, look, an' when he did I struck him. Don't reckon you'll let me hold that babe now, will you?

WENSTAN: Any man big enough to own up guilt can hold my child.

> *The infant, WILLIAM, is handed to the PENITENT.*
>
> *Soon, after some rocking, his chains fall off.*
>
> *The GUESTS are amazed.*
>
> *The PRIEST steps forward to pick up the chains.*

PRIEST: Glory be to God, he's given us a sign. I'll hang these holy chains in our church here in Haveringland. A memory for those now and those to come. William – a holy child!

> *ELVIVA takes back her child.*

PENITENT: William – a holy child.

> *The PENITENT falls to his knees before her.*
>
> *Other GUESTS follow, crying out –*

GUESTS: William – a holy child.

> *Even her husband falls to his knees.*

ELVIVA: Don't do that. No, don't do that. Thaas a daft thing to do. Don't do that –

SCENE SIX

> *A SKINNER's yard.*
>
> *WILLIAM, aged 12, is an apprentice of four years standing.*
>
> *SKINNER and WILLIAM stand before a table on which lay a pile of skins.*

SKINNER: Now listen to me, William – a warnin'. The Jews hev a good nose for a skin and a good nose for a bargain, an' they like you. They respect skill an' learnin', an' they know a craftsman when they see one, I'll give 'em that. But you bin seen goin' in an' out too often an' that ent safe. They beint normal like us Christians, they be Jews. Remember!

WILLIAM: They be Jews but they spoil me well enough.

SKINNER: More'n any other I've sent to deal wi' 'em they spoil you rotten.

WILLIAM: Well ent that good?

SKINNER: Thaas very good, bor. For you thaas good, for me thaas good, an' because you're the skilled o' the lot thaas good for them. But them's strange, wi' their prayers and loud goings on at festival-times, an' the secretive way they keep theirselves to theirselves. People what hide hev secrets to hide. So heed you my warnin', visit them on business but no more'n that.

WILLIAM: They tell me I'm their friend.

SKINNER: Thaas cos they need all the friends they can get 'cos no one don't much like them. But you're too good-natured and too trusting which it don't do no good to be in this life. Specially with Jews around.

Now, smell them skins. Run your hand over them.

> *WILLIAM runs his hands over the skins – sensuously.*

WILLIAM: Good for patchin' up an' rough work but no more.

> *SKINNER ruffles the boy's hair.*

> *WILLIAM smiles the most charming of flirtatious smiles at his employer.*

SKINNER: You smile too much, bor. You worry me.

> *WILLIAM takes off his apron, puts on his jacket. Packs tools in his satchel.*

> *He's ready to leave for his lodgings and friends.*

SCENE SEVEN

Outside the SKINNER's workplace.

WILLIAM is confronted by a STRANGER, nervous and agitated.

STRANGER: There you be. I bin searchin' for you here there and everywhere.

WILLIAM: Who are you, mister?

STRANGER: I bin sent for you.

WILLIAM: Sent? Who sent you for me? I ent never seen *you* these parts.

STRANGER: But I've seen *you*. Many a time. I was told, see, to make enquiries 'bout you, to follow you an' to watch you. An' I done all that.

WILLIAM: Watch me? Follow me? What for?

STRANGER: For good things, that's what for. Boy like you? Only good things.

WILLIAM: What good things?

STRANGER: To take you off into the service of William, Archdeacon of Norwich.

WILLIAM: Archdeacon of Norwich? You're hevin' me on a lead.

STRANGER: *(Angry.)* Listen! I don't make jests. *(Quieter.)* I'm his cook, see. I need the help of a youngun' what's got sense an' good legs 'cos there's a lot of standing around to do in a kitchen. An' you've got good legs, I can see that. Fine legs.

He squeezes WILLIAM's thighs and calves.

WILLIAM: But I got a job. Skinner's apprentice.

STRANGER: An' thaas all you'll ever be! But wi' me? In the Archdeacon's service? There's a ladder there, do you see a ladder in the skinner's yard?

WILLIAM hesitates.

He's waitin'. The Archdeacon said bring him at once. The boy's bin talked about. Soon everyone will want his skills an' intelligence an' sweet nature. Oh, I see it! Sweet nature. Sweet, sweet, sweet! Come –

He puts his arm round the boy's shoulders.

WILLIAM draws away.

WILLIAM: You must ask my mother first, though.

STRANGER: Straight way! We'll go now. 'Bring him at once,' the Archdeacon said, or they'll all be after him.' But I'm first. Ha! Got here before the lot on 'em!

SCENE EIGHT

ELVIVA's house.

ELVIVA, WILLIAM, and STRANGER.

ELVIVA: But he've a job already. 'Prentice to the skinner.

WILLIAM: Skins smell.

STRANGER: Listen to him.

ELVIVA: Skins've served you up till this day.

WILLIAM: Skins've served the skinner.

STRANGER: Listen to him.

WILLIAM: Him's rich, not me.

ELVIVA: One day you'll be skinner, you'll be the richun'.

WILLIAM: Who needs so many skins?

STRANGER: Listen to him, listen to him!

ELVIVA: Skins'll always be needed – gloves, jackets, hats, boots. An' look at all the patchin' up the Jews call on you to do for the stuff them unfortunates hev to pledge 'gainst loans.

WILLIAM: The Jews have a good nose for a skin an' a good nose for a bargain. There's no future there.

STRANGER: Right, bor! There's never any future with the Jews. Stay away from them. Your mother's right – they live rich lives off the lives of unfortunates. Stay away from the Jews.

ELVIVA: Now's the time I need your father. *(To STRANGER.)* Died when the boy was three. Brought up three on 'em alone, look, an' hed to make all the decisions meself.

STRANGER: Then let me help you decide this time, woman. First – cook's help. Then – a cook! Next – a clerk to buy and stock up. Then – a steward. Then Chamberlain p'raps. An' then, if he save prudently, he can purchase his own appointment.

ELVIVA: That do sound like a good future for you, boy.

STRANGER: Now I see where his brains come from as well as his pretty looks.

ELVIVA: I got neither o' those but I do know about preparing for the future. I see to it that he can read an' write for the future; an' I worked hard on the land so's all our sons had a future.

STRANGER: An' here's more for your future.

> *He takes coins from a purse. Attempts to press them into her hand.*

ELVIVA: No, I can't take them.

STRANGER: For the future.

ELVIVA: Wait till after Easter.

STRANGER: Not for thirty pieces of silver!

ELVIVA: I won't decide till Easter's passed.

He again offers the coins.

STRANGER: For the future. Some shillings from the
Archdeacon who tell me: she'll be anxious for him, his
mother, cos she be a good an' anxious mother.

ELVIVA: Well you go, son, an' you look an' work a little,
an' if that beint anythin' you're happy with, you leave.
Remember the dream I hed what your grandfather give
meanin' to. You're blessed. An' that mean you can turn
your hand to anythin'.

STRANGER: Blessed! Blessed! Indeed blessed. Come.

SCENE NINE

The rape.

The light.

'The Jews! The Jews!'

SCENE TEN

GODWIN's house.

But first, THOMAS from his cell.

THOMAS: And you out there who don't believe the testimonies
I've assembled, who doubt the signs I've recorded, who
don't believe the witnesses I believe, you who don't believe
me, call me presumptuous – I know you! You're those who
delight in other's misfortune, you're those saddened by
success. Disappointed with no evidence for slander, aren't
you? Eager to find fault, unwilling to praise, prompt to
disparage – I know you! Well hear me: your idle barking
wearies the air! You claim religion but have none. You
deny divine mystery because it's happening *now*! Only that

which is past are you able to accommodate. Only what *age* sanctifies do you sanctify. Well hear me – I have testimony!

GODWIN relates his story to a stunned HETHEL.

GODWIN: The first to see it was the nun, Lady Legarda, she what lives like a beggar an' tends the sick for the good o' her soul. She see this light, 'like a ladder to heaven' she say, two shafts from the ground up, an' it make her wonder. 'What did the Lord want me to know?' she ask herself. So she walk with her attendants towards it prayin' that he'd direct her in the right direction. An' he did! An' there he were, William, at the root of an oak, dressed in narthin' but his jacket an' shoes, his head shaved, an' full o' stab wounds which ravens was a peckin' of. She didn't knowed that were Elviva's boy, but she knew she was lookin' at a boy what was special. 'A person o' merit' she say, an' she go home rejoicing an' she tell others.

HETHEL: I knowed something dreadful were goin' to happen.

GODWIN: Next come the Bishop's forester, Henry o' Sprowston. He see the light, too, an' he was making towards it when a peasant stop him an' say to come look quick 'cos he'd seen the body of a boy.

HETHEL: I just knowed it!

GODWIN: 'Brutally slain,' Henry tell his wife. 'Stripped an' stabbed an' gagged an' bruised' He call a priest to bury him but the priest say to wait till Easter is passed.

HETHEL: I knowed somethin' dreadful were goin' to happen cos I hed this dream last night.

GODWIN: But no one could stop the rumour spreadin' –

HETHEL: About Jews.

GODWIN: – an' crowds an' lads went looking cos it's one o' the sad things o' this life that a dead body is like a side-show at a fair. An' they see him, the dead boy, their friend,

William. An' they tell his brother, Robert, an' you know
the rest.

HETHEL: The dream were about Jews.

GODWIN: We go to verify an' we verify: their friend an' our
nephew.

HETHEL: I knowed somethin' dreadful were goin' to happen
cos I hed this dream last night – about Jews.

GODWIN: *(Suddenly interested.)* Narthin' more?

HETHEL: They were chasin' me.

GODWIN: More, woman, more. You know dreams is important
for knowin' the truth.

HETHEL: An' *you* know I can't never remember my dreams,
only the sensation o' them – happy, sad, fearful. I wake up
laughin', cryin' or terrified but I don't ever remember why.

GODWIN: Someone must tell his mother.

HETHEL: Me, I suppose.

GODWIN: You're her sister.

SCENE ELEVEN

ELVIVA's house.

HETHEL with her.

HETHEL: An' the nun, Legarda, see these ravens tryin' to settle
on his body but they couldn't settle.

ELVIVA: Oh, William.

HETHEL: They kept tryin' to peck at his head but they couldn't
peck.

ELVIVA: My best beloved.

HETHEL: They kept tryin' to settle an' peck at his poor ole
head but they kept slidin' off.

ELVIVA: Oh, William, my best beloved.

HETHEL: An' when she see that, the nun knew! She *knew*, look. This was a special boy. Your son William was no ordinary boy, he was special.

ELVIVA: My best, best beloved –

HETHEL: Well let me tell you my dream the other night –

ELVIVA: Loved by everyone.

HETHEL: Saturday before Palm Sunday the Lord see fit to give me – an ignorant woman – a forewarning of all what was to come, cos he tell me, I heard him say in this dream, that soon I'd lose one o' my dear ones.

ELVIVA: Justice!

HETHEL: One I loved more'n any o' the others.

ELVIVA: Justice!

HETHEL: It were a dream about Jews.

ELVIVA: I want justice for my boy's dyin'.

HETHEL: They were chasing me.

ELVIVA: Who'll gi' me justice for my boy's dyin'?

HETHEL: I was standing in the high street of the market place and suddenly the Jews come upon me from all sides an' surround me an' – but I can't remember narthin' more.

SCENE TWELVE

ELVIVA in Norwich Market Place.

CROWDS around her.

ELVIVA: An' she try to flee, my sister. In this dream – which she remember from beginnin' to end it were so vivid – she try to flee from the Jews, but they seize her an' break her right leg with a club, an' tear it away from the rest on her

body, an' off they run, carrying it away wi' them. True!
A true vision!

1ST VOICE: An omen!

ELVIVA: Justice!

1ST VOICE: That were an omen, woman.

ELVIVA: Who'll give me justice 'gainst the Jews?

1ST VOICE: An omen 'bout your poor son, William.

ELVIVA: They seduced him wi' false promises o' gain in high
places. A man come an' he tell me he were cook to the
Archdeacon who wanted my son to work for him.

2ND VOICE: What work?

3RD VOICE: Dyin' work!

1ST VOICE: Jews' work!

> The CROWD *huddle and exchange inventions and
> exaggerations.*

2ND VOICE: Did you hear the story how he was found? A
heavenly light directed a holy woman to the place.

3RD VOICE: Thorpe Wood. They find him in Thorpe Wood.

1ST VOICE: Ravens peckin' at his head.

3RD VOICE: Tryin' to peck, *tryin'!*

1ST VOICE: But she see a light over the body an' out of it come
a figure with thorns on his head, an' he speak to her an' he
say: this boy do I want at my side in Heaven.

2ND VOICE: An' here's a thing – when his family went to dig
him up the earth move, look! It move!

3RD VOICE: He were alive!

2ND VOICE: No, he were dead but it were a spirit in him sayin'
'be comforted! I be goin' to heaven in peace.'

3RD VOICE: An' here's somethin' else – his poor body should've smelt o' the dead but it didn't! Instead there come the perfume o' spring flowers. Spring flowers an' fragrant herbs, look!

ELVIVA: An' did I tell you? When I were pregnant wi' him I hed this vision of a fish with 12 fins either side? splashed wi' blood? which I suckled at my breast till it grew wings and flew to heaven? Twelve fins! All bloody! Like my blood-splashed boy were only twelve year old.

1ST VOICE: An omen!

ELVIVA: Justice! Who'll give me justice 'gainst the Jews?

> *3RD MONK who has been part of THE CROWD stands upon a barrow, orator/rabble-rouser.*

3RD MONK: Hear me! Who are the hereditary enemies of the church?

CROWD: The Jews!

3RD MONK: Who are the money-lenders?

CROWD: The Jews!

3RD MONK: Who dwells in stone houses while we live in wattle, wood and mud?

CROWD: The Jews!

3RD MONK: Christian doctors use herbs for their medicine but which doctors use blood?

CROWD: Jewish doctors, doctors of the Jews!

3RD MONK: Who challenges Christian doctrines, who chastises us for our trust in miracles, who are the clever-tongues, the know-alls, the richest of them all?

CROWD: Jews! Jews! Arrogant Jews!

3RD MONK: Who condemned our Lord to the cross?

CROWD: The Jews! The Jews! The Jews! The Jews! The Jews!

The Jews! The Jews! THE JEWS!

SHERIFF, JOHN DE CHEYNEY appears.

SHERIFF: No! Who touches the Jews answers to me. The Jews are the property of King Stephen and I'm King Stephen's man. Go to your homes and pour sense over your senseless tempers. There'll be no blood-letting while I'm Sheriff of Norwich.

THOMAS takes over.

THOMAS: And who was this Sheriff of Norwich? John de Cheyney. Sheriff John, who, when the Synod called for the Jews to come and answer the accusations made against them advised them not to attend and hid them in his castle till the just wrath of the people settled into Christian peace and reason. But oh he was punished. By his own testament, which I obtained from his servants after he had passed away, at the very moment when he protected the Jews, the very moment when he opposed Christian law – at that very moment, look! he began to suffer from internal haemorrhage. The Vengeance of God!

And let that be a warning! To those hard and slow of heart to believe that the Jews perpetrated this crime in scorn of the Lord's Passion and the Christian law – let Sheriff John's bleeding be a warning. There will be blood for blood!

Part Two

The first witnesses present their evidence and are countered.

SCENE THIRTEEN

The Synod – an ecclesiastical council-meeting presided over by PRIOR ELIAS.

Among those present are ecclesiastical functionaries including the priest, GODWIN; DOM AIMAR – Prior of St Pancras, visiting; ELVIVA, HETHEL, MATHILDA.

GODWIN rises to address the assembly.

Easter 1144.

GODWIN: Very Reverend Lord an' Father, Prior Elias. May that goodness of your'n which everyone here abouts know, make you bend your ears to what t'is I, your humble priest, Godwin, have to say by way o' complaint and accusation. May the reverend assembly also o' my brethren an' fellow priests, who I see before me attending this present synod also bend their ears. For what I hev to say is sad an' bitter an' I'm angry, so all must forgive me my simple an' direct words.

Your fathership know, an' I don't 'spect t'is a secret to most o' the rest on you, that a certain boy, a very little boy, a harmless innocent little boy were treated in the most horrible manner in Passion Week an' found dead in Thorpe Wood, an' up to this day, look! he've hed no Christian burial. He were a cousin to my own children an' because of kindred ties he were very dear to me. So what I relate will p'raps make a fond uncle cry. You'll hev to forgive that, too.

His name were William. He were only twelve. He'd been
stripped, his head shaved, stab wounds in his side, his
skin scolded wi' boiling water, an' his mouth gagged wi'
a wooden gag which, very reverend brother, I hev in my
hand, look. A gag! To stop him from screaming. To gag up
his poor ole cries. The cries of an innocent lamb. William.
Twelve year old.

Now, brethren, who could do this? Who do you know
among the good towns-folk of Norwich could carry out
such a terrible crime? An' which other crime in history do
it remind you of? A bloody head, from a crown of thorns?
A stab wound in the side? Is there any *Christian* you know
could carry out such a bloody thing? Who did it once? An'
who've done it agin and agin in mockery o' the first time
they did it? You'll know which crime I'm thinkin' of. That
don't need me to name it. Eleven hundred an' forty-four
years ago – once. Eleven hundred an' forty-four years later
– once again!

The Jews! I accuse the Jews! Enemies of the Christian
name. Shedders of innocent blood. An' I can prove their
guilt. Facts! so's you can judge for yourselves, so's you can
add to what you know 'bout Jews an' their practices an'
what they must carry out on days specified.

An' because that do concern me when my neighbour's
house go up in flames therefore I dare bend your ears and
lay before you my complaint, sure that you'll find justice
for the sister o' my wife, the mother o' the boy, William.

ELVIVA steps forward.

ELVIVA: An' he says 'I'm cook to the Archdeacon, and his
reverend sir wants your boy William in his kitchen to
work for him, look.' 'No!' I say. 'He've got a job' I say.
But William argue 'cos he weren't so happy sellin' skins
to Jews. An' this mysterious stranger wooed me like the
cunning serpent make Eve eat the apple, an' I'm a woman
alone, sirs, wi' no man to help me make decisions, an'

poor wi' it. So's when this devil, sent by the Jews, offer
me money, my resolve weaken. I let my son go, a poor
innocent – an' don't I regret that, Oh! I do so regret that.
But he were supposed to hev gone to the Archdeacon,
look, an' blame-fool, me, I listen to him!

HETHEL steps forward.

HETHEL: An' in this dream which come to me like a vision,
the Jews seize me an' tear off me leg an' run wi' it an' I
hear this voice say to me, it say: 'through the Jews will you
lose a part o' your family that you love dearly.' 'Cos I lost
me leg, see. They ran off wi' me leg like they ran off wi' me
nephew. True! Well, thaas what dreams is for, ent they, to
tell you the truth?

MATHILDA steps forward.

MATHILDA: So, after this mysterious stranger persuade my
aunt to let him take William to work for the Archdeacon's
kitchen, they visit us. The stranger an' my cousin. They
don't stay long 'cos he were in a hurry, weren't he, the
stranger? 'We be goin' off to work at the Archdeacon's
kitchen,' say cousin William to me. 'Wish me luck and gi'
me blessin's.' Which 'corse we did 'cos he were a lovely
boy an' we love 'im. But we don't trust *him*. Him! The
stranger. He look evil an' ugly, an' so my mother tell me to
follow them. 'Follow them,' she say to me, 'follow them an'
see where they go.' An' I did. An' they went into a Jew's
house an' shut the door an' I don't see my cousin not ever
agin'.

ELIAS stands to question them.

ELIAS: Young woman –

MATHILDA: Mathilda.

ELIAS: Mathilda. This mysterious stranger. Could you tell us –
was he a Jew or a Christian?

MATHILDA: Like I say, he were evil-lookin' an' ugly, sir. He must've been a Jew.

ELIAS: Must he? Look around you, Mathilda. Look. Some forty faces. Carefully. Is every face you see, beautiful?

MATHILDA is fearful and hesitant.

Answer me, young woman. Look at every face and tell me, is every face you see a sweet and saintly face?

She is silent.

And you followed them, you say? That's not an easy thing, to follow someone without them seeing you. Is it something you do often? Follow people?

She is silent.

Something you do well? You're an expert follower?

Silent still.

And did he look back, this mysterious stranger? This man who was on such a cruel errand, an errand that he knew would bring great punishment upon himself and his people, did you observe him taking every precaution to ensure no one was following him to see where he was going?

Silent still

Or was this a stupid Jew who imagined there was no danger and so he walked boldly forward with not a glance back, thus making your difficult task of following him easier?

Silent still.

And the house, the Jew's house. Could you say exactly which one it is?

Silent still

If we took you to the street could you point with absolute certainty and say – in there they went, Prior Elias. That one! The mysterious stranger and my cousin William. That one. Without a doubt, that one. Could you?

She is silent still, and moves away.

He turns to HETHEL.

And you, woman, with your dreams. Do you dream often?

HETHEL: Every night, reverend, sir.

ELIAS: Every night. And what did you dream last night?

HETHEL: Oh I can't remember that, reverend sir.

ELIAS: I understand. I, too, often dream but can rarely remember my dreams. What about the night before, can you remember that?

HETHEL: Oh no, sir. That I can't. The truth is I dream every night but I remember narthin'. I only ever remember the sensation o' them – happy, sad, fearful. I wake up laughin', cryin' or terrified but I don't ever remember why.

ELIAS: But this dream, about the Jews seizing you and wrenching your leg from your body and running off with it down The High Street by the Market Place, this one you remember in every vivid detail?

HETHEL: Oh yes, sir, I do, I do! Every vivid detail.

ELIAS: Remarkable. Possible, I suppose, but remarkable.

HETHEL: It come from God, see, sir?

ELIAS: Ah. Yes. God. But I have a question has been nagging at me ever since I heard the story. Perhaps you can help me answer it. This mysterious stranger – his was a terrible errand.

HETHEL: Terrible indeed, sir.

ELIAS: Planned, calculated, evil.

HETHEL: Evil indeed, sir.

ELIAS: First he found the boy and seduced him.

HETHEL: Like the serpent seduced Eve, sir.

ELIAS: But the boy being well brought up and responsible insisted that his mother be asked for her permission first.

HETHEL: An' that were the right and proper thing to do, sir.

ELIAS: And so they went to his mother and the mysterious stranger bribed and seduced her.

HETHEL: Like the serpent seduced Eve, sir.

ELIAS: And that was that.

HETHEL: That was that, sir.

ELIAS: He hed his boy for the Jews.

HETHEL: Had 'im, sir.

ELIAS: Evil.

HETHEL: Evil indeed, sir.

ELIAS: And he took him straight there. To the Jews house.

HETHEL: Oh no, sir. He bring the boy first to me.

ELIAS: I forgot. He brought the boy to you.

HETHEL: My nephew wanted my blessing.

ELIAS: A blessing to work in a kitchen?

> *She is silent.*

Does a nephew require an aunt's blessing to work in a kitchen?

> *She is silent.*

And the mysterious stranger, a Jew perhaps, commissioned to bring a Christian child to be ritually slaughtered, agreed to let himself be seen a second time and run the risk of being followed just in order to allow his victim to get an aunt's blessing? Why would such a scheming, evil messenger do that, I wonder?

She is silent, and moves away.

ELIAS turns to ELVIVA.

And you, mother of the poor boy, you allowed your precious son, in return for money, to go off with a man *he* did not know, *you* did not know, and now of whom no trace can be found?

She is silent, and moves away.

One by one everyone in the assembly has moved away leaving only three: GODWIN, ELIAS and DOM AIMAR

(To GODWIN.) And did you actually *see* a crown of thorns?

GODWIN realises he is not believed. He moves away, angry, vengeful-looking.

AIMAR confronts ELIAS.

AIMAR: That was an engaging but unfair spectacle, brother Elias.

ELIAS: I know it, brother Aimar. I don't know how you administer *your* priory at St. Pancras but I will not have superstition replace true faith in mine.

AIMAR: What you call 'superstition' many of us would argue is the honest faith of a simple flock.

ELIAS: I have heard such arguments.

AIMAR: Do I detect contempt in you, brother Elias?

ELIAS: I have heard that said, too. Yes, I do not confuse a duty to care with a need to admire those I must care for.

AIMAR: Since, then, you doubt there exists conclusive evidence of Jewish culpability I have, as prior to prior, a proposition. Sell me the body of the boy.

ELIAS: That's not a holy thing either for you to propose or me to consider, Brother Dom Aimar.

AIMAR: Everything that enables the church to survive and carry out its work is holy.

ELIAS: A dubious ethic and one I don't really think you believe. Besides, the body is not the possession of the church.

AIMAR: Not yet.

ELIAS: Nor ever will be while I'm prior.

AIMAR: Ah, Brother Elias, you may have contempt for those in your care but you're a wily church administrator and know full *well* whats in your possession. God's placed a martyr in your hands and you know his value. Had I been in your place I'd not have sold a martyr either.

ELIAS: You and my bishop, both. Ebolard also argues that the boy be named a martyr. 'It'll bring pilgrims!' he cries.

AIMAR: He cries wisely.

ELIAS: He cries shamelessly.

AIMAR: He knows pilgrims bring money in the hope of miracles.

ELIAS: A shameless fool!

AIMAR: I see that like me you too quarrel with your bishop. Good with souls, inept with accounts. But mark me, Elias, you have a treasure on your doorstep.

ELIAS: A martyr is not a martyr unless he die for his religion. Not suffering but *why* he suffered is what lays claim to martyrdom.

AIMAR: Precisely!

ELIAS: Precisely what? The boy William was murdered I strongly suspect by a mad and cruel stranger for cruel obscene desires of the flesh.

AIMAR: But prove it was the Jews, you prove a martyr.

ELIAS: It cannot be proven. Besides, such spilling of blood goes against their teachings.

AIMAR: That is not what the Christian world knows.

ELIAS: Then the Christian world is ill-informed.

AIMAR: Humility, Elias, humility.

ELIAS: It goes against all reason. The Jews have no normal freedoms here. They're the property of the King, who taxes them at a whim. They're clever and rich for both of which they're hated and resented. They're small in number –

AIMAR: Thirty thousand.

ELIAS: – *three* thousand. Why should they risk such crimes?

AIMAR: Your priest, Godwin, thinks he was murdered by the Jews in mockery of our Lord's suffering.

ELIAS: My priest, Godwin, is a greedy, ignorant and superstitious man who has made mischief before. He thinks wrong!

AIMAR: But supposing that for once in his life he thinks right?

ELIAS is a sick but passionate man.

ELIAS: Somewhere you will read that to drink dried menstrual blood will induce the menstrual cycle; that to eat three lice between bread will cure colic; that to prevent the bursting of a dam a child must be buried alive; that to immure a human being in its foundations will ensure the building stands.

And if you read the books of early Christian sects you will find *them* full of blood rituals, the sacrifice of babes and the eating of their parts. Whereas turn to Leviticus, turn to Deuteronomy and you will find such sacrifice most strictly forbidden to the Israelites.

The ecumenical councils pass edict after edict declaring such belief in Jewish slaughter false, yet such belief persists.

I am tired of the ignorance and stupidity of the simple
flock. The simple flock chooses superstition for which it
needs no learning. I am tired, yes, and full of contempt.
Jesus was a Jew steeped in the knowledge of the wisest
laws. Law, learning, mercy, wisdom – these are the pillars
of the Christian faith. They represent all that I cherish in
this damned existence, they are the only hope for hopeless
mankind, they are what formed my life and what in life
I informed. I will not bow to the fevered intoxications of
illiterate monks who love more their image before God
than God's meaning to the world.

> *AIMAR is not impressed. A cynic, he ignores ELIAS's
> words.*

AIMAR: Think on it. A precious treasure on your door-step,
Elias. I would guard it most diligently.

> *ELIAS is troubled.*

Murdered by the Jews. *(Pause.)* In mockery of our Lord's
suffering. *(Pause.)* As an insult to Christ. *(Pause.)* Think on
it.

> *AIMAR leaves.*

> *Three MONKS approach ELIAS.*

1ST MONK: Bishop Eboard has granted us permission to
transfer the blessed boy's body to our cemetery.

ELIAS: *(Angered.)* So, you appealed to the Bishop, a man
terrified of his own shadow, when you knew I was against
the translation?

2ND MONK: We don't think you understand how strongly we
feel about the martyred child, Brother Elias.

ELIAS: I understand your feelings only too well – you want to
bask in the unholy light of an unholy relic.

3RD MONK: We want to bring glory to our church, Brother
Elias.

ELIAS: You'll bring shame instead.

1ST MONK: We respect and venerate you, Brother Elias –

ELIAS: *(Mocking.)* Brother Elias! Brother Elias!

1ST MONK: – but many of us believe the boy to be a martyr to our faith.

ELIAS: And there are many, thank God, who believe him to be a poor murdered child.

2ND MONK: The signs cannot be denied, Brother Elias.

ELIAS: Signs! Signs! What signs?

3RD MONK: The signs of a ritual murder as it is known the Jews commit in mockery of our Lord.

The sounds of a requiem mass.

ELIAS: And would the Jews strip and batter and then hang a child in the open to be gawped upon by every and any passer by?

> *The MONKS leave to pick up a coffin which they take in procession round and round the stage followed by crowd carrying lighted candles.*

(Over the singing.) It is presumptuous to maintain that which the church universal does not accept.

> *He is ignored.*

I will not allow you to honour upon earth him whom it is not yet certain that God has glorified in heaven.

> *He is ignored.*

There is much mischief and foolishness in this church and I...

> *But ELIAS is a sick man. He cannot sustain his anger.*

> *As the procession and singing continue THOMAS steps forward with his book.*

THOMAS: And still they slur his name and fame. Let them listen, then, those who slur the fame of the most gloriously named martyr. Let them listen those who persecute him by making light of him, who deny his sanctity, who do all they can to stop the spread of his renown. Let them listen, those who say we are mad – for we have testimony! We have certain testimony that he was slain by Jews as is their custom on the day of Passover. The nature of his wounds prove it. We have testimony that the Jews perpetrated this crime in scorn of Christian law and the Lord's Passion. And it is testimony unknown by Elias or Godwin or Elviva or Hethel all those eight and twenty years ago. Incontrovertible.

SCENE FOURTEEN

The rape.

The light.

'The Jews! The Jews!'

Part Three

BROTHER THOMAS OF MONMOUTH presents new witnesses with additional evidence.

SCENE FIFTEEN

An old maidservant, MAUDE, sits carding wool, talking to THOMAS as he writes.

THOMAS: Listen.

MAUDE: They called me Maudie the Maidservant an' I worked long an' I worked hard for the Jews, cleanin' an' serving an' mendin' an' runnin' their errands on days their religion forbad *them* do it. I can't say they was good to me nor can't I say they was bad. But this I can tell you – they was strange.

First they treated the boy kindly. Fed 'im an' fussed 'im like they always did, for they'd taken a shine to his sweet nature. Then things change. From bein' angels one minute they become devils the next. Strange. Like I say, strange.

They'd come back from their synagogue, Passover-time that were, an' they was still singin' what hymns they hev to sing in that strange language o' their's, when suddenly they seize hold o' the bor as he were eatin', an' some hold him from behind while others push into his jaws what they call a teazle – a kind o' gag which they tie round the back o' his neck as tight as they can.

Next they git a rope an' make four knots in it. Round his head it go an' under his chin an' round his neck tight as ever it can be so's the knots press into his forehead an' temples an' his poor ole throat.

But that weren't enough for them, no, that it weren't! They hev to shave his head, look, then they hev to prick it, prick his poor ole scalp wi' thorns so's the blood come horribly

out an' then – an' this is what git to me, what really upset
me – they tie him to a cross an' nail one foot an' one
hand, the right one I think that were, an' then they push a
knife into his side so's there was even more blood all over
the place an' you should've seen their hands. Covered
in blood! An' they was crying out these very words, I
remember them word for word: 'Even as we condemned
the Christ to a shameful death so let us also condemn the
Christian. Lord an' servant in like punishment so's they
can feel the pain of *our* reproach as we feel the pain of *their*
reproach.' Word for word! As God is my witness.

Oh, there was a commotion in that room I can tell you.
Every Jew fighting with the other tryin' to do the worst
they could to the poor ole thing. But they got frightened,
see. Blood all over the place. They got scared.

'Bring boilin' water!' they yell at me. 'Quick, boilin' water.'
So I rush up an' rush down to boil them the water they ask
for, thinkin' they wanna clean up the mess they was makin'
so's no one would notice the horrible things they bin doin',
but no! That *ent* what they wanted boilin' water for. Know
what t'were? To throw over the bor to stop the bleeding!
Scalding water! To stop the bleedin'! Well, that fair upset
me. It did. But what could I say to anyone? The Jews was
my livin'. An' what they pay were poor 'nough, but *I* were
poor, too!

You ask me how I know all this? I'll tell you how I know
all this. 'Cos when I bring them water an' they hev to open
the door a little, I see wi' one eye through the chink in the
door. Didn't last long. They open an' close the door in a
small second 'cos they was afeared I might see the terrible
things they done, but I see all I need to see. In that small
second. Through the chink in the door. All what I tell you.

THOMAS rises.

THOMAS: *(Reading from his book.)* 'Thus then the glorious boy
and martyr of Christ, William, dying the death of time in

reproach of the Lord's death but crowned with the blood
of a glorious martyrdom entered into the kingdom of glory
on high to live for ever.'

Looks up at his listeners.

Presumption? Am I to be accused of presumption for
keeping up the memory of a saint whom the world does
not know and the church does not celebrate? Then who
is *not* presumptuous? Of few saints can it be said that the
whole Christian world knows them. Whom Rome honours,
does Gaul and Britain equally accept? Or is the famous
name of our most blessed King and Martyr Eadmund, or
the glorious Confessor Cuthbert, equally well known to the
people of Greece or Palestine?

The next scene of the death of AELWARD DED fades in.

DED: Not all my wealth…

THOMAS: Listen.

DED: …nor all the respect given me as a worthy citizen of
Norwich…

THOMAS: It continues.

DED: …could help relieve my pain.

THOMAS: Our testimony.

DED: So I thought…

THOMAS: Listen.

SCENE SIXTEEN

AELWARD DED is dying.

From his death-bed he tells his story to a Monk.

It is the year 1149.

THOMAS is at his desk, writing.

DED: …Aelward Ded, you must visit the holy churches of the city. Pray there. Do what good deeds you can. Perhaps the Lord will hear you and take pity and ease the pain of your last years. I took my servant one evening. A pilgrimage through the night. I walked from one church to the next, asking God to forgive my sins and distributing alms to the sick and the poor who were sheltering in God's houses.

And as I was making my way from the Church of St Mary Magdalene to St Leonards Church, along the edge of Thorpe Wood, I came across two Jews known to me, riding their horses deeper into the wood. Why? And more, it was the holy day of the Adoration of the Cross, a day when Jews usually dare not leave their houses. And more, across the neck of one horse was a sack. On such a day where could they be going?

I was curious. So I dismounted and walked up to them and touched their sack with my right hand. Inside was a human form. Well, they fled! It was obvious I'd surprised them because they fled in terror. Into the thick of the wood.

But I did nothing. My suspicions were aroused but my pain and my devotional task pressed upon me and I alerted no one, nor to my shame did I myself take action.

THOMAS: *(Reading from his book.)* But the enemies of the Christians, being alarmed and in despair determined to make advance to John the Sheriff who had been their refuge and one and only protector. 'Look you' they said, 'we are placed in a position of great anxiety, and if you can help us out of it we promise you a hundred marcs.' And John the Sheriff was well pleased with so many marcs.

DED: The next I knew I was summoned by the King's Sheriff, John de Cheyney. Upon oath he made me swear never to divulge in my life-time, or at least not until the point of death, what I knew against the Jews. And I *had* to. I had to swear it. He forced me.

> *Pause.*

I am upon the point of death.

MONK: But John de Cheyney died three years ago. Why did you not tell us then?

> *DED rises in his bed in anger, able only to make the gurgling sounds of a dying man.*
>
> *Dies.*

THOMAS: Whoever attributes to me the sin of presumption, whoever charges me with rashness let him come forward with his babble and jabber and I will answer him.

And what is his babble and jabber? It is this, look you. *(Mocking voice.)* 'It is very presumptuous to maintain that which the church universal does not accept, it is rash to honour so magnificently upon earth him whom it is not yet certain that God has glorified in heaven.' Babble and jabber!

Lo! by the sling of my lips I will crash through the shameless forehead with the smooth stone of the word – for I have testimony! Listen – the testimony of testimonies. Brother Theobald. Once a Jew now a convert to the army of the Lord.

SCENE SEVENTEEN

> *THEOBALD, monk of Norwich, talks and sews a church vestment meanwhile.*
>
> *THOMAS writes.*

THEOBALD: For that I was once a Jew – no! For that I was *born* a Jew. Distinctions. Important to make distinctions. I was born a Jew but in my *heart* I could never have been one because I came so easily to Christ. No! Not easily. I cannot say that. Hard. I struggled. For what can be worthy that comes easily? So, for that I was born a Jew and therefore grew up with Jews, I am familiar with their teaching, with their laws, and with their holy rituals. Not a scholar, I must add. It would not be true to say I was a scholar – to my regret and shame, for I was scorned harshly for being slow in the school where Talmud was taught and argued over. I learned poorly and argued feebly and was laughed at for that. So, though not a scholar I was privy to their teaching, to their laws, and to their holy rituals and – oh, I've already said that, forgive me, I repeat myself. It is a failing. Yet another which they scorned me for. No! Not scorned. Mocked. Scorn can be ignored. Mockery is withering. Distinctions. Important to make distinctions. I try hard to make distinctions in this life. And fail. Mostly.

So. The Jews' teachings.

It is laid down in the writings of our fathers, *their* fathers, that the Jews, unless they regularly shed, each year, the blood of a Christian child in some part of the world in scorn and contempt of Christ – no! in *mocking* contempt of Christ, then they will never obtain their freedom nor could ever return to the land of their fathers. Christ's death had shut them out from their own country and made them slaves in foreign lands, therefore must they avenge their sufferings on him.

So, the chief Rabbis, who live in Spain where they are held in high esteem, assemble every year in the city of Narbonne and cast lots for all the countries which the Jews inhabit; and whichever country the lot falls upon then the chief Jews of that country's capital city must cast lots again for the city in which the fulfilment of this terrible duty must be imposed.

THEOBALD knows this to be a lie.

He speaks faster, as though to get it over with quickly.

So. In that year when William, God's glorious martyr,
was slain, the lot fell upon the Norwich Jews, and all
the synagogues in England signified consent that the
wickedness should be carried out here. I know all this
because at the time I lived in Cambridge, a Jew among
Jews. The commission of the crime was no secret to me.

> *THEOBALD suddenly and abruptly becomes exultant,
> in the grip of religious ecstasy. An escape from his
> sense of guilt.*

But oh, oh, oh! In the process of time…the glorious display
of miracles…divine power…through the merits of the
blessed martyr…I became afraid…afraid, afraid, afraid!
My conscience…burned guilt…like coals of hell…I forsook
Judaism…turned to the Christian faith. To the Christian
faith, brothers, to the love of the Lord Jesus Christ. To the
lovely love of the Lord Jesus Christ.

> *He swoons away.*

SCENE EIGHTEEN

*A sick ELIAS wearily listens to a haranguing
THOMAS who at first is writing in his book*

THOMAS: *(Writing.)* But the struggle to raise our martyr to his
rightful place in the minds of many was long. And as so
often in the history of our faith it is those who should know
better who are the prevaricators.

ELIAS: You are referring to me, Brother Thomas.

> *THOMAS rises to him.*

THOMAS: Sometimes I think we are weighed down by too
much learning –

ELIAS: There cannot be too much learning.

THOMAS: – too much thought –

ELIAS: There cannot be too much thought.

THOMAS: – too much learning and too much thought lead to doubt –

ELIAS: To wisdom.

THOMAS: – leaving no room for faith.

ELIAS: Faith without wisdom is superstition. I will not have superstition in my church.

THOMAS: And revelation? What place has revelation in your church?

ELIAS: What is revealed to you this time, Brother Thomas?

THOMAS: Testimonies! By the grace of God! I have testimonies of a wondrous revelation given me by the grace of God.

ELIAS: And who am I to deny God's grace?

THOMAS: Oh you confuse me, Brother Elias.

ELIAS: But with God's grace all will be wondrously revealed. I'm waiting.

THOMAS: With the blessing of the late Bishop Eboard, may he rest in peace, who sanctioned it, the holy body of our martyr was transferred from Thorpe Wood to the Monks' cemetery.

ELIAS: Where it should have remained.

THOMAS: A poor resting place for so great a martyr.

ELIAS: His martyrdom is not proved.

THOMAS: *(Pressing ahead.)* But heaven was not satisfied or happy with so poor a resting place for so glorious a martyr.

ELIAS: His martyrdom is not proved.

THOMAS: And so the body was permitted burial in the Chapter House.

ELIAS: Where I believe it should remain.

THOMAS: The resting place of Saint William of Norwich
should be by the high altar of the Church of Norwich.

ELIAS: His martyrdom is not proved and sainthood cannot be
conferred.

> *This is a battle of wills between a relentlessly fervent*
> *monk with a cause and an ailing, weary sceptic.*

THOMAS: Listen to me, brother Elias, listen how in a dream
I saw standing beside me a venerable old man with grey
hair clothed in Episcopal robes who roused me with his
Episcopal staff saying: 'Arise, brother! and make haste to
bid my beloved son, Elias, Prior to the Church of Norwich,
that he must announce to your new Bishop William from
me: remove that precious treasure which the brethren
keep hidden away in their Chapter House. Obey not my
paternal order and they will lose that treasure to the great
harm of their Church. For those relics, unless soon placed
safely by my high altar, will be carried off by a thief who
now stands on the threshold of a deliberation, led on by
hope of gain. Wherefore, brother, when thou risest in the
morning neglect thou not to carry my paternal orders to
those my sons whom I have named.'

Then, as I inquired who was making this announcement,
he answered: 'I am that Bishop Herbert who, by God's
grace, founded this Church of Norwich.'

> *THOMAS awaits a response as one who has dealt an*
> *unbeatable trump.*

ELIAS: I believe not one word you utter, Brother Thomas,
but I am a dying man and the clamour for this poor boy
to be declared martyr and named saint grows beyond my
control. As Prior my responsibility is order. If I deny the
claim, the clamour will become conflict. Therefore let his
body be transferred into the church –

> *THOMAS is triumphant, jubilant, and rudely*
> *interrupts.*

THOMAS: – beside the tomb of Blessed Herbert himself! Oh yes! It will be done. God has blessed you with wisdom, Brother Elias. It will be done! To be buried in the church is the glorious Martyr's rightful place. The sweet Saint has found his home. It will be done! And you mark, Brother Elias, you mark how all of England will travel to his tomb. Mark! His fame will spread far and wide. It will be difficult to hold back all the pilgrims. Swarms of them! Tides of them! Knights will compete with one another to endow the church.

ELIAS: Ah – endowment!

THOMAS: And miracles!

ELIAS: Endowment and riches.

THOMAS: To serve God.

ELIAS: To serve pride.

THOMAS: To serve Christ.

ELIAS: To serve your self-intoxicating fervour.

> *Music!*
>
> *The air is thick with jubilation.*
>
> *Four MONKS, including THOMAS, carry a coffin to the centre of what has now become the interior of the Church of Norwich.*

Part Four

We hear of the miracles and rejoice.

SCENE NINETEEN

The interior of the Church of Norwich.

Over the coffin is placed a sepulchre which dominates our attention.

'CROWDS' of PILGRIMS form a queue.

Each has a different ailment.

The sounds of ailing and religious fervour mix with the music.

With THOMAS urging them, guiding them, saluting them, they one by one list and enact before the sepulchre their miraculous cures.

THOMAS: Mighty works and miracles!

EDMUND: I, Edmund, monk of Norwich, troubled with a most terrible toothache, I touched the sepulchre with my suffering face and straightway the swelling disappeared. Glory be to God and the blessed Martyr!

CLARICIA: I, Claricia, wife of Gaufridus de Marc, for years kept pain in my knees till the fame of the excellent Martyr reached me and with the support of my husband and sons I approached his holy sepulchre with my bare knees and immediately I felt soundness through the bones of my body. Glory be to God and the Blessed Martyr!

THOMAS: Mighty works and miracles!

RADULFUS: I, Radulfus, nephew to Prior Elias, had an infant son sick to death. Advice was given to my wife that we should cause to be made a candle the length and breadth of our little boy –

THOMAS: The blessed saint was born on Candlemas Day and he loved candles. Everyone had to bring a candle –

RADULFUS: – the length and breadth of our little boy to be offered to Saint William for the restoration of our little boy's health. Which we did, straightway, and laid it at the sepulchre of the holy Martyr. And when we returned, lo! he was well. Our boy was safe and well. Glory be to God and the blessed Martyr!

MURIEL: I, Muriel de Setchy, bled without pause till I offered two candles covered with my tears, knelt, prayed and kissed the sepulchre of the Martyr and then O then the Grace of the Lord's pity came down upon me and I ceased to flow. Glory be to God and the Blessed martyr!

STEPHEN: [a very old man] Stephen, me. Old Stephen. Oldest of the Norwich monks. I couldn't sleep. Closed my eyes but stayed awake till my head rocked and throbbed and I was fit for nothing but howling. So I upped and supplicated and devoted and prayed and this here is what I said:

He kneels before the sepulchre.

'Oh holy Lord William! grant me thy servant some rest that I may recover the power of sleeping which I have lost.' And it happened. There and then. My eyes became heavy. My head lost its neck. My rocking, my throbbing, my howling stopped. I slept! They tell me – like a child. Not a snore! Glory be to God and the blessed Martyr.

THOMAS: Glory be! My William's fame spread! Who came with coin and candle was not denied his miracle.

SCENE TWENTY

GODWIN's house.

A bowl of holy water on the floor.

An OLD WOMAN has come for a miracle cure.

OLD WOMAN: And is it true, you dip it in holy water an' you drink it an' you get better?

GODWIN: This is the martyr's gag, old woman. Wi' this they plugged up his cries for help. You won't find no more holy relic than this.

OLD WOMAN: You've helped many, they say,

GODWIN: They keep a comin' for help an' I'm a man o' pity.

OLD WOMAN: Then gi' me your pity.and help this poor old'un, for I've pains and aches fit to kill me they've bin wi' me so long.

GODWIN: And what d'you bring for offerin's?

OLD WOMAN: You see I'm poor.

GODWIN: You're not so poor you can't bring me a hen.

OLD WOMAN: From where in heaven's name?

GODWIN: In heaven's name no one's *that* poor.

OLD WOMAN: Believe me, reverent Godwin. *That* poor.

GODWIN: You 'spect me to heal you for narthin'?

OLD WOMAN: Narthin's all I got, look, you can see.

GODWIN: I'm lookin' and I can see clothes on your body, shoes on your feet, an' flesh what's bin fed on your bones.

OLD WOMAN: You and the blessed martyr are my only hope.

GODWIN: Did the tailor gi' you clothes for narthin'? Did the cobbler shoe you for narthin'? Did you get your bread for narthin'? Did you?

OLD WOMAN: All what I had left I spent on doctors what do me no good.

GODWIN: Then nor can't the martyr heal you for narthin'.

OLD WOMAN: But I'm in pain.

GODWIN: Well you listen to me, woman: he that gives not what he prizes gets not what he asks. So if you want your pain eased you go get me a hen.

OLD WOMAN: May God judge between us.

GODWIN: He will, I can assure you.

OLD WOMAN: An' may the merciful martyr Saint William treat you as you've treated me.

GODWIN: He were my nephew. Him and me understand one another well 'nough so don't you be worryin' yourself 'bout that, old dear.

She leaves, weeping.

SCENE TWENTY-ONE

Return to interior of Church of Norwich.

THOMAS: Mighty works and miracles! True testimonies! And mark this well: he who would accuse me of stamping falsities as truths, or of dressing up facts with fiction is guilty of sin!

THOMAS allows his intimidation to sink in.

And if among you are those who still doubt, then hear this.

A young man steps forward, of subdued cockiness. He is a natural sceptic who has been cowed.

Yes! Your turn! Tell them.

WALTER: I, Walter, sometime servant of our dean at Norwich, well – me – I –

THOMAS: Tell them! Tell them! Or surely William will come at thee again!

WALTER: I doubted.

THOMAS: Only doubted?

WALTER: Doubted, mocked, made fun of all what I heard. Whenever I was told another miracle I'd imitate the sufferer.

He pauses. Frightened to continue.

THOMAS: Well show us, show us!

WALTER: *(Showing us.)* 'Cured! Cured! I be cured! Once my head was back to front an' then I give a candle to the Saint an' look! I don't need to walk backwards no more! Glory be to God and the blessed Martyr...!'

Pause.

Things like that.

Pause.

THOMAS: Yes? Go on. Tell them.

Pause.

And then...

WALTER: An' then...

Pause.

THOMAS: ...one night...

WALTER: ...one night...

THOMAS: ...as I was...

WALTER: An' then one night as I was sleepin', William come at me in a terrifying shape an' he asked me 'why do you make fun 'o me an' mock me?' An' 'corse, in the dream I were scared sick. Couldn't speak. An' when he said 'follow me' I couldn't follow. So he had to drag me, to a cave, an' he ask me 'whose cave is this?'. So I tell 'im: thaas your's, sir, your's, where you live. Well it were his, werenit? His in the wood, Thorpe Wood, where he was found? So he says to me, he says, 'enter!' Well, I thought I was goin' to drop dead in the middle o' me own dream an' that would've bin a rum thing. But howsomever I didn't, I stay alive, an' he pushed me inside his cave an' bor! he set about me. He had this great big cudgel an' he cudgelled me black an' blue an' bruised every limb. An' when I woke – an' this were the strangest part on it – when I woke I was smartin' with the pain! As though it'd actually happened, look! Well, you don't find me mockin' an' makin' fun no more, that you don't.

THOMAS: *(Prompting him.)* So everyone should learn from your dream?

WALTER: So everyone should learn from my dream.

THOMAS: Glory be to God and the blessed Martyr.

WALTER: Glory be to God and the blessed Martyr.

THOMAS: *(Triumphant.)* Mighty works and miracles!

> *Last – a YOUNG COUPLE, clinging to each other with acute shyness.*
>
> *As they speak we hear, low at first, the sound of singing.*
>
> *It grows. A hymn of praise to St William. A triumphant choral work by the end.*

COLOBERN: My name be Colobern –

ANSFRIDA: – and mine, Ansfrida –

COLOBERN: – husband and wife – wi' a son –

ANSFRIDA: – a lovely child, sweet-natured –

COLOBERN: – what were dumb.

ANSFRIDA: Dumb! Seven year!

COLOBERN: From birth.

ANSFRIDA: He understood –

COLOBERN: – but made no sounds.

ANSFRIDA: Well, it happened like this, one night –

COLOBERN: – the two on us asleep –

ANSFRIDA: – we have a dream.

COLOBERN: The *same* dream!

ANSFRIDA: Together, look!

COLOBERN: A reverend man he come to us an' he say –

ANSFRIDA: '– tomorrow you must take your son to William's sepulchre –

COLOBERN: – with a candle!

ANSFRIDA: The same dream, look!

COLOBERN: The two on us!

ANSFRIDA: So we go –

COLOBERN: – the bor with the candle in his hand –

ANSFRIDA: – and we pray.

COLOBERN: A long time.

ANSFRIDA: By the sepulchre.

COLOBERN: An' suddenly our bor he turn to us an' he say –

ANSFRIDA: – he say 'home now, let's go home now.'

COLOBERN: He were talking!

ANSFRIDA: Like he'd always been talking.

COLOBERN: An' we wept.

THOMAS: And we who stood by watching wept as well and gave praise to our Lord who had done great things by the hand of his Holy Martyr, William.

There is a tumult of voices. Many want to reach the sepulchre.

All now is spoken against the background of activity and music.

ELIAS hobbles into view.

ELIAS: *(Protesting.)* This Church was not erected to be a pilgrim's way.

THOMAS: From far and wide they come, with candles and coins.

ELIAS: It is a house of prayer, peace, reflection!

THOMAS: The decision was your's –

ELIAS: I had no idea –

THOMAS: – 'Therefore let his body be transferred into the church' you said.

ELIAS: – I could not imagine –

THOMAS: – that miracles would follow sanctification?

ELIAS: There is danger from such multitudes.

THOMAS: The Church grows rich from such multitudes. Sing! Sing out!

ELIAS: The boy William must be moved from here.

THOMAS: The boy *martyr! Saint* William.

ELIAS: He will be deemed saint when the evidence is conclusive.

THOMAS: The evidence *is* conclusive.

ELIAS: Oh, brother Thomas, your fervour is too intense for me.

THOMAS: You confuse me, brother Elias. Why do you resist? We have been blessed with a saint. Miracles have been performed. Mighty works and miracles! Listen …

ELIAS: If such miracles are listened to then I fear for the faith.

> *He falters.*

> *MONKS go to his aid.*

ELIAS: There is a chapel to the north side of the Church. It was once used specially for the worship of Holy Martyrs –

THOMAS: God be praised –

ELIAS: – transfer his body there. Pilgrims can approach without risk –

THOMAS: – sing! Sing out!

ELIAS: There must be peace inside the house of God.

THOMAS: Sing praise to the saint of Norwich. Let William hear your voices praise him, praise him, praise him!

> *THOMAS has conducted the litany of miracles, whipping up fervour and ecstasy.*

> *All loudly sing the triumphant hymn of praise as the sepulchre and coffin are raised to be translated for the last time inside the Chapel of Martyrs.*

> *The last procession moves off.*

> *The hymn ends.*

> *The stage is empty.*

> *Silence.*

SCENE TWENTY-TWO

> *The sound of WILLIAM's scream.*

> *The light.*

> 'The Jews! The Jews!'

> *The light dies.*

> *End.*

LONGITUDE

Prompted by the book *Longitude* by Dava Sobel

About this play and its production

Its feel is Hogarthian.

Its sweep is epic.

Its drive is story-telling.

Its staging convention is, let's say – loose.

The spirit is that of a group of actors who've come together to enact a story. One minute they're a character, the next a street trader crying out wares, the next they're part of a choir.

I see John Harrison's life as a series of body blows, and therefore the stage bristles with activity. Something is always happening – whether it's singing or celebration, bustling street-life or verbal conflict.

We are telling a story driven by genius and eccentricity at a time in England's history when science, medicine, engineering and manufacture are on the brink of bursting into The Industrial Revolution.

I have only occasionally indicated what the main characters maybe doing on stage while another action is taking place – John in his workshop, Elizabeth kneading dough and so on – but actions domestic or to do with work or in the form of street and tavern life will be devised by the director or actors themselves to keep the stage alive without being too fussy, too restless.

Above all, Harrison's is a constant and pervading presence throughout.

Setting

By 'Hogarthian' is meant multi-layered: streets,
alleys, Georgian shop fronts with hanging
boards, stone steps, railings...[1]

Somewhere among it all are:

Church pews in a small Lincolnshire church

A church bell

Red Lion Square – Harrison's house showing
main room, his workshop, Elizabeth's kitchen

Announcement platform

Greenwich Observatory

Graham's workshop

The Admiralty

A heaving ship's cabin

A London tavern
Richmond Observatory
Temporary observatory in Madeira
Ship's cabin

---

1. See Hogarth's 'Gin Lane' and 'Beer Street'.

Characters

Nine actors[2] will play sixteen parts. Must be able to sing.

JOHN HARRISON

ELIZABETH

WILLIAM HARRISON
their son

COMMISSIONER
reader of legal documents

DR EDWARD HALLEY
one of the Astronomer Royals

GEORGE GRAHAM
clockmaker

MARTIN FOLKES
President of the Royal Society

ROGER WILLS
master of HMS Orford

SIR KIENELM DIGBY
diplomat interested in Alchemy and Astrology

REV. NEVILLE MASKELYNE
an Astronomer Royal

LORD MORTON

LORD EGMONT

---

2. A couple of actresses to play vendors and Molls would
help create more city bustle

THOMAS KING
portrait artist

WILLIAM LUDLAM
mathematician, Fellow of St. John's College,
Cambridge.

GEORGE III

DR. DEMAINBRAY
Swiss tutor to George III, keeper of the Royal
Observatory, Richmond.

STREET TRADERS and OTHERS

Note:

about dialect. I don't know the Lincolnshire
dialect and so have only here and there hinted
at a 'northern dialect'. The right, knowledgeable
actors would no doubt change some of the
dialogue to achieve the right lilt.

Possible allotment of parts

One actor to play

Harrison

Elizabeth

William

Maskelyne

Commissioner, Folkes

Halley, Morton

Graham, Egmont

Ludlam, Kendal, George III

Digby, Wills, King (painter), Demainbray

ACT ONE

Setting in shadow

Sounds of:

a ticking clock

a growing storm

timber shattering on rock

human voices in distress

Over all this, out of the shadows, a woman's lamenting voice:

ELIZABETH: (The Litany) The Association, six hundred and fifty lives lost. The Marigold, five hundred and forty lives lost. The Eagle, four hundred and ninety lives lost. The Romney four hundred and fifty lives lost ...

Sound of choir

Lights.

CHURCH PEWS/ ELIZABETH'S KITCHEN/ THE BELL

HARRISON conducting.

ELIZABETH kneading dough.

And then - four ships of Sir Clowdesly Shovell's fleet – scuttled. Nearly two thousand lives lost. An experienced commander but he steered four prized ships on to the rocks of the Scilly Isles. Why? How came this?

Pause.

Longitude! They couldn't find longitude. Thought they were where they weren't. Disaster upon disaster. Precious lives, precious cargo, precious trade, precious wars – lost. Shook the nation, and made parliament sit up.

167

Singing continues.

So they had to pass an Act. In the reign of Queen Anne –
The Longitude Act.

HARRISON: Sing out you weavers, sing out you smithies! Sing
out you shoemakers, carpenters, ploughmen and boys.
Sing out!

He joins them.

Distress dies away leaving the singing

HARRISON: And that's how I want us always to sing – basses
in front, tenors in the pews behind, trebles behind them.
And *facing* the congregation, not with your backs to them
but facing.

The street life takes over.

Bustle. Music. Street cries.[1]

*HARRISON climbs to a church bell. He has just tuned
it, and will strike it five times.*

ELIZABETH: What's shipwrecks got to do with singing you're
wondering. Nothing really, except it was one man thought
about both. John Harrison –

Bell strike.

carpenter and joiner -

Bell strike.

tuner of bells –

Bell strike.

choirmaster and mender of clocks –

Bell strike.

helped change the world –

Bell strike.

my husband.

---

1. Street cries for distribution among actors on last page.

'Town Crier' bell takes over.

HARRISON moves to his workbench.

COMMISSIONER, ringing Town Crier's bell,[2] mounts the –

ANNOUNCEMENT PLATFORM

COMMISSIONER: The Longitude Act. An Act for providing a public reward for such person or persons as shall discover the longitude at sea.

ELIZABETH: It were such a problem that Parliament set up a committee to see what could be done. They asked advice from everyone. Even Sir Isaac Newton. It was his testimony got John going.

HARRISON: He's wrong! He's wrong! The old man is wrong!

ELIZABETH: Wrong about what, I asked him.

HARRISON: Newton says the best method to find longitude may be by a clock that keeps time exactly but that no such clock can be made.

ELIZABETH: Why does Newton say that, I ask him?

HARRISON: Because –

ELIZABETH: – says my husband – who argued with everyone as I know to my cost –

HARRISON: – because of the motion of the ship, the changes between hot and cold, between wet and dry, and because the earth's gravity pulls differently in different parts of the world. But Sir Isaac is wrong. Such a clock *can* be made. I've made clocks that go accurately on land, I'll make one goes accurately at sea.

---

2. He will do this each time an announcement or official document is read out from the ANNOUNCEMENT PLATFORM.

ELIZABETH: No arguing with a man who thinks he knows everything. Only my John didn't *think* he knew everything, he *knew* he knew everything.

Clanging bell.

Anyway the committee recommended –

COMMISSIONER: – that a reward of £20,000 be settled by Parliament upon such person or persons as shall discover a more certain and practicable method of asserting the longitude than any yet in practice, and that a Board of Longitude be set up to administer the award.

ELIZABETH: Longitude! Don't ask me to explain it. John talked, explained, talked and explained and as soon as I thought I'd understood the science of it all I'd forget it.

Reaches for a sheet.

(Reading.) 'Mean time, which can be described as the time we use, is sundial time to which a correction known as the "equation of time" has been applied, thus causing the length of each day to be the same irrespective of the season.' Get your head round that. It's possible, I'm not saying it's not possible. But then – hold it! Repeat it! Explain it to someone else! Can you? I can't, but he could. He had a *natural* understanding of numbers and mechanical things, I just had his children. Well – that's not the whole truth. He was a natural mechanic but I was naturally wise, even though it's me who says it. I mean you can't help noticing you're wise alongside a body as unworldly as John Harrison.

Wipes her hands. Punches cushion in his chair.

HARRISON, now old, shuffles to sit.

HARRISON: What were it about me?

ELIZABETH, too, is old.

ELIZABETH: They called thee strange, John Harrison.

HARRISON: 'Strange'? What were there strange? I made clocks. Taught myself to make clocks, what were strange about that?

ELIZABETH: You didn't accept payment.

HARRISON: In the beginning, no. I weren't easily content wi' what I'd done. Nowt strange about that.

ELIZABETH: They called thee obstinate, too.

HARRISON: 'Obstinate'? I saw wrong and said so and kept saying so and will always keep saying so. Wrong is wrong not obstinate. Honour is honour not obstinate. Justice is justice not obstinate. It were them were strange and obstinate. Priests and professors. Them!

Long, reflective pause.

Nay. Not them. Me. I didn't know my place. Know your place, be humble, presume nothing. I learned none of that.

Pause.

Did I presume? I built something changed men's fortunes – was that presumption?

Pause.

Nay. I presumed nothing. I earned. What I built *earned* me rights. I wanted no bestowing when I 'd earned. Bestow me no rights, I told them, favour me no favours. I earned! I used my brain and brawn, and carved myself a place. Bestow me nothing, I said. I've earned. I wanted no bestowing, and told them so.

Pause.

And lost. Didn't know my place. Wasn't humble enough for them. Stupid man!

Pause.

Be fine when I'm long dead and gone and out of trouble's way, when they don't have my bluntness and gruffness and impatience and contempt of them grinding their ears. But alive? While I'm still around to argue back and disagree and write pamphlets 'gainst their mischievousness? Difficult! Presumptuous! Troublemaker!

Pause.

Bloody priests and professors.

ELIZABETH: You liked the Professor Halley.

GREENWICH OBSERVATORY

HALLEY and a YOUNGER HARRISON.

HARRISON: Y'see, metals expand, Sir.

HALLEY: I know that.

HARRISON: But not at the same rate.

HALLEY: I know that, too.

HARRISON: And if you place brass alongside steel each expanding and contracting at different rates – as in this gridiron here – the pendulum stays the same length.

Pause.

Which means changing temperature won't distort the swing.

Pause.

Which means it'll keep time in cold climes and hot climes.

HALLEY: Congratulations, Mr Harrison. Impressive. Ingenious. But I'm a man of the heavens.

HARRISON: A star-gazer!

HALLEY: Moon-gazer. I spend my nights with her and when fathomed she'll be our guide. No more brutal smashing upon rocks and reefs, no more spilt blood, no more dangers voyaging into the unknown.

HARRISON: And where are your heavens when storms come by day or mists by night? *(Clowns.)* Pshu! Pshu! Pshu! Lost! We're all lost.

HALLEY: I don't think you understand, Mr Harrison.

HARRISON: Pshu! Pshu!

HALLEY: This observatory was built specially –

HARRISON: Pshu! Pshu!

HALLEY: My post as Astronomer Royal was created specially –

HARRISON: Pshu! Pshu!

HALLEY: Vast sums have been specially invested to chart the heavens, map the moon's movements, to pay me!

HARRISON: Lost!

HALLEY: Astronomers have to eat.

HARRISON: We're all lost!

HALLEY: Besides, sir, I know nothing of either mechanics or engineering.

HARRISON: Nothing?

HALLEY: Not enough to check your drawings and calculations. But I know a clockmaker, George Graham –

HARRISON: Him?

HALLEY: You know him?

HARRISON: *Of* him.

HALLEY: A good man.

HARRISON: Could pirate my invention.

HALLEY: Not Graham.

HARRISON: I've learned to trust no man.

HALLEY: Well unlearn it or you'll go through life seeing the devil everywhere.

HARRISON: Which is where the devil is until us root him out.

HALLEY: Mr Harrison, sir, I must alert you, The Board of
Longitude's members are astronomers, mathematicians,
navigators. They will not welcome a mechanical solution
over a lunar one. For them the only clock to be read
is in the heavens. Further more London is filled with
some of the best minds of the age who are also the most
honourable, and you are going to need their help. So take
my advice and lower your guard a little. George Graham
is a man both of honesty and integrity, and the Board of
Longitude just will not bother to meet you without his
approval of your plans.

> *The streets come alive.*

> *Bustle. Music. Street cries.*

GRAHAM'S WORKSHOP

HARRISON: Mr Graham?

GRAHAM: Sir?

HARRISON: I've come from Dr Halley. He says you must see
me.

GRAHAM: *Must,* sir?

HARRISON: Talk with me, sir.

GRAHAM: *Must,* sir?

HARRISON: Recommend.

GRAHAM: *Must,* sir?

HARRISON: If you please, sir.

GRAHAM: Please. Good. I like people to say 'please'

HARRISON: I'm not much spun on niceties, sir.

GRAHAM: Niceties are what keep us off each other's throats,
Mr – ?

HARRISON: Harrison. John Harrison. I've no design on throats, neither.

GRAHAM: I'm glad to hear it. Your business?

HARRISON: I have ideas for a clock at sea.

GRAHAM: We all have.

HARRISON: One that'll work accurately.

GRAHAM: One you *think* will work accurately.

HARRISON: One I *know* will work accurately.

GRAHAM: I've not much time for people who know things they can't know.

HARRISON: I can't help knowing what I know and I know my sea clock will work as my land clock does.

GRAHAM: You've built an *accurate* landclock?

HARRISON: Loses one second in a month.

GRAHAM: A boast indeed.

HARRISON: I boast not nor play not. I know what I know, I make what I make, and what I make I know the worth of, and I have in my house one pendulum clock that has not varied as much as a whole minute in ten years.

GRAHAM: Oil. The problem of expanding oil – how did you stop it expanding?

HARRISON: I didn't. Just stopped using metal on metal which needed the oil.

> *GRAHAM is impressed. Attentive now. Even excited.*

GRAHAM: How can a clock run without metal wheels?

HARRISON: By using wooden ones instead.

GRAHAM: Wooden wheels?

HARRISON: I'm a carpenter. I know the properties of wood. Pivots of brass move easily in hard wood. No oil.

GRAHAM: And pendulums? I've never made a pendulum that kept the rhythm of its swing because the damn things kept expanding and contracting in different weathers.

HARRISON: But not all metals expand and contract to the same degree.

GRAHAM: So?

HARRISON: So (unwraping gridiron from cloth) if you place brass alongside steel expanding and contracting at different rates you produce a gridiron.

GRAHAM: And on sea? How can you make pendulums swing evenly in high seas?

HARRISON: Don't use pendulums.

GRAHAM: What moves the seconds on if not a pendulum?

HARRISON: Springs!

GRAHAM: Springs?

HARRISON: Springs, sir. Springs dingaling.

GRAHAM: What kind of springs?

HARRISON: Spiral springs.

GRAHAM: Oh, my word. And you've structured such springs?

HARRISON: I'm working on them.

GRAHAM: Springs? Nothing else?

HARRISON: Springs and things.

GRAHAM: What things?

HARRISON: Well – bars and balances that swing on the springs.

GRAHAM: Drawings, have you got drawings?

HARRISON: It so happens –

Withdraws rolls of paper from knapsack.

GRAHAM: Oh, my word.

HARRISON: But I need help.

GRAHAM: Oh, my word, my word, my word.

> *GRAHAM is riveted by the drawings.*

HARRISON: Help?

GRAHAM: I'll make you a loan.

ELIZABETH'S KITCHEN

ELIZABETH: That's how it all began –

GRAHAM: Five hundred pounds.

ELIZABETH: – sweetly and kindly.

GRAHAM: Pay me back when you can. No interest. And I'll talk to others. We'll get you started, young man, so's you can find us longitude and save lives.

ELIZABETH: (The Litany) Too late to save The Vansittart, ninety-six lives lost, silver bullion, copper, lead, or The King George, fifty-four lives lost, iron, wool, cloth …

> *The streets come alive.*
>
> *Bustle. Music. Street cries.*

HARRISON'S WORKSHOP

> *HARRISON and ELIZABETH.*

ELIZABETH: *(To HARRISON.)* What does it mean – 'find us longitude'? Is it something us once had and lost? Is it something we know is out there and needs to be found? And why is it so difficult to find it?

> *HARRISON wheels on globe of the world.*

> *NOTE: what follows should be a kind of light show demonstrating why it is easier to identify latitude than longitude. Spectacular. Magical.[3]*

HARRISON: The world is round.

ELIZABETH: You didn't marry an ignorant woman, John Harrison.

HARRISON: But I married an argumentative one.

ELIZABETH: Pot calling the kettle black, is it?

HARRISON: And one who must have the last word.

ELIZABETH: Your globe.

HARRISON: The globe! The globe! The round earth – right!

> *Pause.*

Imagine. The sea. Vast. Empty. A ship, its captain, its crew, its cargo. A mist descends. Where are they? Are they north or south, east or west?

> *Pause.*

To find out where we are on this globe the mapmakers devised imaginary lines that go round the earth which they called latitudes; and imaginary lines that go from pole to pole which they called longitudes.

Now, Lizzie, my love, it's easy for the captain to fix his latitude, to find out how far north or south he is because nature helps him. The sun. He's got the sun, which identifies the equator. The sun dictates, the circles are drawn, the captain knows where he is north or south. He knows. Easy!

But what about east and west? What's dictates the other imaginary lines, the longitudes?

> *ELIZABETH spreads her arms, shrugs.*

---

3. We will need the assistance of someone from the Science Museum, but the light show will follow the dialogue.

Spin the globe.

She spins it.

And follow this: The earth takes twenty-four hours to spin three hundred and sixty degrees from sun back to sun – a day. It takes twenty four hours for us here in Red Lion Square to move from one high noon to the next. So, how far have we moved in an hour?

Pause.

There they are: three hundred and sixty degrees – twenty four hours.

Pause.

Divide one into the other – twenty-four into three hundred and sixty, and you get fifteen. In one hour we've moved fifteen degrees east or west.

Pause.

Am I losing you, Lizzie?

ELIZABETH: You will if you keep stopping to see if I'm breathing. In one hour we've moved 15 degrees east or west.

HARRISON: But how does the poor Captain know? There's no equator for longitude like there is for latitude. No sun to help. So what *can* help?

Long pause.

Clocks! To chart his longitude at sea a Captain needs to know, at the very same moment, the time on board and the time he left port. The difference is the distance he's travelled.

He watches her carefully.

You don't follow?

She shakes her head.

If he had two clocks the Captain would reset the ship's clock by the sun, compare it to the home port's clock, and every hour of difference would tell him he'd moved fifteen degrees east or west.

Waits and watches.

ELIZABETH: But, John my love, there are no clocks can work at sea.

HARRISON: Yet! No captain can tell if he's travelled fifteen degrees or thirty degrees. Yet!

And if he's sailing in fog no Captain knows if he's sailing into rocks or reefs or sandbanks or pirates or friendly harbours or death. Yet!

But John Harrison will tell them, he'll make them the clock they need. Yes, he will, yes. Oh will he not! Yes, yes, John Harrison will he will.

ELIZABETH: And John Harrison did he did. He made them their clock.

> *As HARRISON wheels off his globe the first clock – Clock One – is lit up in his workshop.*
>
> *The streets come alive.*
>
> *Bustle. Music. Street cries.*

HARRISON'S WORKSHOP/ ANNOUNCEMENT PLATFORM

HARRISON is at work putting the final touches to Clock One.

COMMISIONER, SIR KENELM DIGBY.

DIGBY: I have, good sir, the solution for finding longitude at sea.

COMMISSIONER: All solutions must be sifted through before The Board of Longitude considers them. I am listening.

DIGBY: I have discovered a powder with marvellous properties – it can heal at a distance. Sprinkle it on a piece of bandage from the wound and the wound will heal. Now, hear me out. Send aboard ship a wounded dog. Leave ashore a trusted individual to dip the dog's bandage into my powder every day at noon, the dog will yelp, and the captain will know the sun is at its zenith in London.

COMMISSIONER: And what when the dog's wound heals?

DIGBY: Why, the dog will have to be wounded again.

COMMISSIONER: Next one!

> *HALLEY and GRAHAM in the workshop walking round and round Clock One.*

ELIZABETH: Four years after George Graham's generosity he ups to London with Clock One. A monster. Beautiful but huge. Nothing like it had been seen before.

HALLEY: He'll get the London chinwags wagging their chins over this.

GRAHAM: When I made my clocks I was in touch with the best craftsmen of the day. *You've* worked it all out for yourself, Harrison.

HARRISON: Thank you. Yes.

HALLEY: We've got to get this before the Longitude Board.

HARRISON: Thank you. Yes. I should be most grateful.

GRAHAM: The Longitude Board? Aren't they all dead?

HALLEY: Ignore him, Harrison. He's famous for jesting.

GRAHAM: We could exhume them.

HALLEY: Be serious, George.

GRAHAM: I've given the man money to complete his lovely thing. What could be more serious, eh, Harrison?

HARRISON: I shall always be grateful.

GRAHAM: Even though bemused.

HARRISON: Confused, I think. I've never understood the point of jesting.

HALLEY: We'll show this to The Royal Society. The Board will *have* to take notice if *they* recommend, too. And we'll get the Admiralty to give the beast a practical test aboard one of its ships.

GRAHAM: I don't know why you're getting excited about all this, Halley. You're a lunar man. Never trust a lunar man, Harrison, he thinks he's in touch with God.

> *They leave.*
>
> *HARRISON returns to help ELIZABETH pull and stretch washed sheets.*

A TAVERN

HALLEY and GRAHAM.

FOLKS approaches.

FOLKS: The Royal Society has little interest in mechanical solutions to longitude. If one of the brightest minds in the land were enamoured of it we might show more enthusiasm.

HALLEY: I *am* one of the brightest minds in the land, Folks.

FOLKS: And you're a lunar man.

HALLEY: I'm also a scientist, and that means keeping an open mind.

FOLKS: I'm not denying Harrison is clever. Clever, he's clever. Can't deny that. But a carpenter! From Lincolnshire! Really! No background, no education. Who'll take him seriously? And consider it – a mechanical timekeeper competing with God's heavens. Why else give us stars if not to guide us by?

GRAHAM: To count, perhaps? Get to sleep more easily?

FOLKS: But Halley's mapped the heavens.

HALLEY: And been at it a long time, too, Folks, imagining that longitude would be known only by the intricate motion of the moon. But in the end I could see – her motions were *too* intricate, the results could only be attended with great error.

FOLKS: How can that be? Sailors have means to measure distances between sun, moon and stars.

HALLEY: But not precisely. Your study of astronomy has taught you nothing if you can't see the lunar lady is erratic and unpredictable. She defies precise measurement. She can't be pinned down.

FOLKS: But she has been! The lunar lady's subtle ways are becoming known.

HALLEY: The lunar lady's tables were calculated on land, the sailors have to make adjustments for sea levels. Their sheets become unreadable, full of rectifying calculations.

FOLKS: And doesn't all that difficulty suggest that the lunar method must be right?

Incredulous silence.

HARRISON'S WORKSHOP

HARRISON: (Old) And then – along comes a ticking thing in a box invented not by a priest or professor but by an uneducated carpenter. Born in Yorkshire, miles from London, Oxford or Cambridge. A ticking thing in a box! Ha! A clock! Oh my goodness deary me. Tick tock tick tock! A clock! Oh deary deary me. Tick tock tick tock!

Long, reflective pause.

Do I have regrets? Were there words wrong I uttered? If I'm ill-used is the fault mine? It's beholden upon me to ask – are there other ways I could have behaved?

Pause.

I've proposed laws for music and argued that a note pitched even the tiniest degree off those laws will sound ill. And I must wonder – is there in life a tone of speaking that also rings off key if not pitched according to the same laws? Perhaps I didn't tune myself sweetly enough to be listened to. I've made clocks accurate for land and sea but nothing tick tocks accurately in me. Perhaps, though time has *obsessed* me, I'm *out* of time. I must ask these things.

Considers such possibilities.

But not for long.

Nay! Nay nay nay! I began sweetly and honestly and trustingly enough until they abused my trust. They spout nonsense whereas my watch, I make bold to say, my timekeeper for longitude is the most beautiful mechanical thing in the world, and I heartily thank Almighty God that I have lived so long as in some measure to complete it. So –

Burst of Choral music.

Sing out you weavers! Sing out you Smithies! Sing out you shoemakers, ploughmen, carpenters and boys.

The streets come alive.

Bustle. Music. Street cries.

Clanging bell.

ANNOUNCEMENT PLATFORM

COMMISSIONER: *(Reading.)* John Harrison, having with great labour and expense contrived and executed a Machine for measuring time at sea, which seems to the members of

The Royal Society, to promise such a sufficient degree of exactness, that they are of the opinion it deserves public encouragement to be tried and improved.

RED LION SQUARE

ELIZABETH.

ELIZABETH: And so, clock One was given a trial on board a ship. Not to the West Indies which the Act of Queen Anne called for, but to Lisbon. Took a week to get there and four weeks to get back and my poor John was sick as a dog. But on the journey back – listen to this –

Cries of 'land ahoy'.

HEAVING SHIP'S CABIN

A sick HARRISON holding fast to Clock One.

Master of the ship, ROGER WILLS, looking down on a map.

WILLS: Well, according to my reckoning the land ahoy is the Start Point.

HARRISON: That was a dead-reckoning, with respect, Master Wills.

WILLS: Good God, man, t'is you I reckon looks dead.

HARRISON: My legs were made for dry land. The sea is for fish.

WILLS: Don't let my men hear you say that. Here –

Offers him a bottle.

good rum.

HARRISON retches.

Not here, man, for God's sake not here!

He recovers.

HARRISON: Dropping flotsam in the water and counting as you go past it to measure speed and plot course belongs to the days of Columbus.

WILLS: So you're about to tell me land ahoy is not Start Point.

HARRISON: No, Master Wills, with respect, Master Wills –

He retches again.

WILLS: Not here! Not here!

Recovers again.

HARRISON: According to my clock, and according to my observations the land ahoy is the spot known as Lizzard.

RED LION SQUARE

ELIZABETH: And he was right, and the Master writes him out a certificate of proof.

Well, you'd think after that the man would want his clock tested on the West Indies run to win the twenty thousand pound prize. Not my John.

HARRISON: I'm not satisfied. I can do better. The beast is unwieldy. Got to make it smaller. More manageable. I won't have Clock One tested again. I won't!

ELIZABETH: And when he won't he won't! Instead, he asks the Board for £500 to work on a second clock. They agree. But on conditions. £250 now, and £250 when he completes the second clock after which, now listen to this, after which he's got to hand over *both* to the nation.

HARRISON: Which is not right, I know, Lizzie love, not just. They had no hand in the making of Clock One and no right to claim it. But we need to live, don't we? And I need peace of mind to go on to the next stage.

ELIZABETH: And so you'd better agree.

HARRISON: I will, Lizzie, I will.

ELIZABETH: And I give birth to William. Don't ask me why but we all seemed to name our children William or John, Anne or Jane, or Elizabeth. John and me we had William and Elizabeth. My Elizabeth married a John and gave birth to a John. William married an Elizabeth and gave birth to a John who married a Jane and gave birth to a John. His third wife was also an Elizabeth who gave birth to an Anne who married a John and gave birth to an Elizabeth. See how time flies? Clocks one and two make John famous if not rich; Professor Halley dies; the Board of Longitude give John another £500 to work on clock three; the first is in George Graham's shop window; we move to this big house here in Red Lion Square; (proudly) William Hogarth draws clock one in a print and says: "one of the most exquisite movements ever made" he says; and John Harrison Esquire gets awarded The Copley Gold Medal.

    Clanging bell.

ANNOUNCEMENT PLATFORM

    The award ceremony. MARTIN FOLKES, President of The Royal Society, delivering award speech.

FOLKES: And so we, Honourable members of The Royal Society of which I, Martin Folkes, am proud to be president, are in no doubt therefore why the Copley Gold Medal is so deserved. A restless genius! Lived near a seaport! Heard of the importance of longitude, and became inquisitive, as genius does. What if he could construct a clock to endure the violent and irregular motions of a boisterous sea?

Amazingly he knew: two major changes must be made. Springs must replace weights, and regular motion must come from the vibrations of balances and not the swinging of pendulums. The problems were stupendous. Metal plates, screws, springs, brass weights, steel rods, wheels, cylinders – dozens of strange new parts and contrivances all had to be drawn, described, machined, tested, machined again, tested again, re-thought, re-drawn, machined again, tested again. What painstaking attention to detail. It confounds imagination.

And soon he hopes to test Clock Three in a voyage to the West Indies, as the Act requires. And although John Harrison is one of the most modest men I know yet he assures me, without doubt, that having put his timepiece through the most accurate experiments it will keep time constantly without the variation of so much as three seconds in a week. Astonishing! Stupendous!

ELIZABETH: Well, I don't know about 'the most modest of men'.

HARRISON WORKSHOP

By the time John is 64 the bulk of the work is done on the third clock. He's ready to let it be tested.

But before it was finished something else was afoot. John, mindful of the cramped quarters in a captain's cabin, was aiming at compactness. Clock three was about as small as he could get it – two feet high one foot wide. That is until –

HARRISON is dangling a pocket watch, opens it, looks at the interior through a magnifying glass.

Something is dawning on him.

HARRISON: It's small. Light. Could be, could be. Ha! Ha! Ho! Ho! Could be, could be. Let them get stiff necks gazing up at stars, let them go mad chasing the moon, and blind in one eye from measuring distance from the sun – but down here, feet on the ground, in the palm of my hand there could be the answer. Not a clock but a watch!

<u>ADMIRALTY</u>

Meeting of the Board of Longitude.

LORDS EGMONT and MORTON, and REV. MASKELYNE in attendance listening to HARRISON.

HARRISON: I'm aware, good sirs, of your patience, your indulgence and your encouraging generosity, but my third timekeeper is nigh on complete.

MORTON: Twenty years in the making, Harrison.

HARRISON: In the making, Lord Morton, *and* the designing *and* the testing *and* the redesigning *and* the making of a living meanwhile.

EGMONT: We can expect it when?

HARRISON: Soon, Lord Egmont, soon. But this time, my Lords and – er – Reverend Maskelyne, I bring other news.

MORTON: This meeting must end soon, Harrison. We live busy lives.

HARRISON: We all live busy lives, sir, and so for my own sake I won't keep you much longer. It's this.

He produces the pocket watch.

Recently made for me to my own design and specifications, and for my personal use. Beats true come hot or cold, and it doesn't stop dead when you wind it up.

Dangles it high.

Small. Compact. Not even *I* thought it possible, but now I have good reason to think that this small thing – not my huge beasts – this lovely handful could be the forerunner of such small machines as maybe of great service with respect to the longitude.

EGMONT: And you have it in mind to make such?

HARRISON: More than have it in mind, sir. My drawings are begun. I'm racing ahead.

EGMONT: What do you say to that, Maskelyne? *(To HARRISON.)* Maskelyne here is on the verge of proving the lunar method as the only sound method of finding longitude.

HARRISON: I've heard it.

MORTON: And could it be, Mr Harrison, that having heard it you're racing ahead for fear the lunar method will prove your tick-tocking clock redundant? Could it be you *fear* heaven's clock?

> *HARRISON's response stiffens the air with his contempt.*

HARRISON: Heaven has no clock! The stars are for *God* to find his way around, not men. The maker of all things made mists and storms for the confusion of mankind, and to mankind he gave the power to invent a way out of the confusion.

MORTON: Battle lines drawn, I think.

> *The streets come alive.*
>
> *Bustle. Music. Street cries.*

RED LION SQUARE

ELIZABETH in her kitchen.

HARRISON and son, WILLIAM, in workshop.

ELIZABETH: And the lines *were* for battle. Battles to break the heart of the strongest. Did you notice one man who said nothing, him that was born same year as my daughter, Elizabeth, God rest her? Rev. Neville Maskelyne,

HARRISON: Him with three chins and no hair[4].

WILLIAM: Hush now, father.

---

4. Depending upon the actor playing MASKELYNE it could be 'Him with fat lips and no chin'.

ELIZABETH: You tell him, son.

WILLIAM: *You* tell him, mother. Wives have moral authority, sons are slaves or upstarts.

HARRISON: Is that what you think I think of you?

WILLIAM: I jest, father. I jest.

HARRISON: Why does everyone jest?

WILLIAM: It's city life.

HARRISON: It's not healthy. Listen to the nonsense of his prattling.

ELIZABETH: Whose?

WILLIAM & HARRISON: *(Together.)* Him with three chins and no hair.

ADMIRALTY/RED LION SQUARE

Meeting of the Board of Longitude.

MASKELYNE, MORTON, EGMONT.

HARRISON barracks with 'asides' to the amusement of his son and wife.

MASKELYNE: The lunar method for finding longitude is both simple and complicated.

HARRISON: Both at once! The man lives in a fog.

MASKELYNE: Simple because it merely requires looking at the moon –

HARRISON: If the night sky is not covered with clouds, that is.

MASKELYNE: – which moves in relationship to the stars which are fixed.

HARRISON: And can only be seen if the night sky isn't covered by clouds, that is.

MASKELYNE: And it's complicated because the path of the moon is so erratic –

HARRISON: And often covered by clouds, that is.

MASKELYNE: – so that it was considered impossible to record and tabulate its position.

HARRISON: Because the bloody thing was covered by clouds, that is.

MASKELYNE: However, in recent years lunar tables have been produced which will enable our navigators to find longitude with the sextant which is replacing the quadrant –

HARRISON: – and doesn't make a ha'peth of difference because our navigators can't see through the bloody clouds.

> *Great laughter from WILLIAM and ELIZABETH over which –*
>
> *CHOIR breaks into choral song.*

That's right, my lads. Drown his nonsense with singing. Harmony over chaos!

ELIZABETH: *(Over the singing.)* And now clock three is ready to be tested at sea. John is too old to make the journey. And so – who else but his son, our son, William, loyal, devoted, hardworking.

WILLIAM: Though I'd sooner live the life of a city gentleman. But no! Clock Three, and soon the watch will take over my life, and I will admire my father for his brilliance, love him for his kindness, fear him for his acerbic view of men and matters, and resent him for chaining my life to his marvellous obsession – a timepiece!

ELIZABETH: The Board gave him £250 to kit himself out, sent him to Portsmouth to await further instructions, and left him there for five months!

WILLIAM: Five months! In Portsmouth!

HARRISON: Oh, worthy powers that be! Oh, worthy authority! Oh, eminent men of science who can make or break.

WILLIAM: Making me wait! Playing for time while Maskelyne checks his lunar tables and men die.

> *Sounds of shipwreck at sea.*
>
> *Timber shattering on rock.*
>
> *Human voices in distress.*

ELIZABETH'S KITCHEN

> *She is laying a table. As she does so she chants.*

ELIZABETH: (The Litany) The Sussex, ten lives, tea, silk, chinaware, lacquer ware. The Grantham, ninety– six lives, cotton, a hundred tons of pepper, twenty tons of cloves, mace, nutmeg…

> *The crying dies away.*
>
> *HARRISON and WILLIAM take their place round the table. All is mimed.*

It's always the kitchen. We have a lovely dining room but we always gather in the kitchen.

WILLIAM: All families do, mother.

ELIZABETH: And get in your way.

WILLIAM: But you love it.

ELIZABETH: Chatter when you're cooking, pick at food with their fingers –

WILLIAM: That were Elizabeth not me.

ELIZABETH: – complain that its lamb when its pork, and pork when its lamb.

WILLIAM: You wouldn't have it any other way.

ELIZABETH: Oh, I wouldn't wouldn't I?

WILLIAM: *(Mimicking her.)* 'You'll miss me when I'm gone.'

Kisses her.

ELIZABETH: No! *I'll* miss me when I'm gone! *(Beat.)* What's wrong with your father?

WILLIAM: Father, what's wrong with you?

HARRISON: Nothing's wrong. I'm thinking.

WILLIAM: He's thinking.

ELIZABETH: No he's not. I know when he's thinking – he looks up at the ceiling.

WILLIAM: Well he's looking down now.

ELIZABETH: Which means he's decided.

HARRISON: Not the clock!

ELIZABETH: What 'not the clock'?

HARRISON: I'm not sending Clock Three for the West Indies trial.

ELIZABETH: You must send the clock for trial.

WILLIAM: We've told the Board we would.

HARRISON: The watch must go instead.

WILLIAM: The watch?

HARRISON: We must offer the watch for trial.

WILLIAM: But it's not ready, father.

HARRISON: It'll be ready.

WILLIAM: If we fail this trial we fail for all time.

HARRISON: The watch won't fail.

WILLIAM: All your years wasted.

HARRISON: I am not letting those Priests and Professors take a foothold with their daft lunar theories. Heads like balloons, empty of aught but air. They're only happy in the clouds, star gazing to no avail, thinking they're in communion with God. I'll not let them deprive me of a fair trial.

ELIZABETH: I'm glad we're all together – father, mother and son –

WILLIAM: Even though we're in the kitchen!

ELIZABETH: Be serious now for I want something explained. There's some of it I understand and some of it I don't understand; and some of it I don't care to understand and some of it I *want* to understand.

HARRISON: Get on with it, woman.

ELIZABETH: Don't you be impatient with me, John Harrison, save that for –

HARRISON: – for me priests and professors. I will, Lizzie, I will.

ELIZABETH: Two things. First, before the ship leaves you must take a reading of equal altitudes. What's that?

WILLIAM: It's a method for checking time, mother. You set up instruments to measure the altitude of the sun as it rises towards noon, and then you check it with your clock.

HARRISON: And if you check it at eleven a.m., one hour before noon, then you must check it again when the sun is dropping one hour after noon.

WILLIAM: When it's one p.m.

They wait for a sign that she's understood.

ELIZABETH: You check the hour that the sun tells you it is and then check that your clock says the same thing.

HARRISON: Correct.

Pause.

ELIZABETH: Why?

WILLIAM: So that when I arrive in Jamaica I can make the same measurements of equal altitude and calculate how much the clock has gained or lost.

HARRISON: Only it'll be the watch.

ELIZABETH: To see if it's running accurately as you're telling the world it can.

HARRISON: Correct.

Pause.

ELIZABETH: Second question: what's 'the rate'?

WILLIAM: The 'rate' is what we tell the Board of Longitude we think the watch will lose by each day.

They wait for a sign that she's understood.

ELIZABETH: Ah!

Pause.

Why?

WILLIAM: Because if our watch loses the same amount each day and not wildly differing amounts each day then it can be depended upon to help us find longitude.

They wait for a sign that she's understood.

ELIZABETH: You mean if it loses half a second one day and fourteen seconds the next day you'll be all at sea?

HARRISON: Correct.

Long pause.

ELIZABETH: How do you know what rate to tell them?

WILLIAM: That's why father has been locked away in his workshop – testing and adjusting.

ELIZABETH: Testing and adjusting. Ah!

WILLIAM: Fine tuning.

ELIZABETH: Fine tuning. Ah!

> *HARRISON sweeps up his wife in a kind of jig, singing –*

HARRISON: Ah! Ah! Tick a leary
Tick tock tick my dearie.
Ah! Ah! Tick a leary
Tick tock tick my dearies.

> *Over which come the sounds of wind and waves. Not a storm, just a ship at sea.*
>
> *Clanging bell.*

ANNOUNCEMENT PLATFORM

COMMISSIONER reads an official letter.

COMMISSIONER: The plans for the trial of the Harrison watch at sea in HMS Deptford are clear-cut. One: The box containing the watch to be fitted with four different locks. Two: The keys to be retained by travellers on the boat. Three: Mr Robertson – Master of the Portsmouth Royal Academy will calculate local time and record corresponding time of the watch in the presence of Captain Hughes, Captain Digges, and William Harrison. Four: Prior to sailing, Mr Robertson in the presence of same witnesses to set watch to local time. Five: Mr Robertson, on landing in Jamaica, will ascertain local time there and compare it with time of watch – all to be witnessed and the results sealed and forwarded to the Admiralty.

> *Sound of wind and sea rise to storm level, beginning half way through previous speech and finally taking over.*

SHIP'S CABIN

WILLIAM, wrapped and struggling to stand in a cabin heaving and wet, enacting what he's describing.

WILLIAM: That was a voyage I feared would end my days. The return was hell. A sea of monsters with gaping jaws, and a great marvel to me that our timepiece kept going at all. I placed it in the Captain's cabin. Driest place, he said. But when the sea struck, the water flowed in through every joint. Sometimes two feet of water on deck and five inches deep in the cabin. Six weeks and never a dry inch. How did I keep the watch box dry in all that you're wondering? Kept it wrapped in a blanket; and when that became soaked I squeezed it out and covered it with another and another and another. And when I ran out of dry blankets I slept in one so that my body heat dried it some, which led to me being racked with a fever. Add that to seasickness, and I was left ill as I never hope to be again. But the watch ticked on. Amazing! and lost only one minute 54 ½ seconds in 147 days. One minute 54 ½ seconds in 147 days! The £20,000 prize was ours! A watch to find longitude the world over! Who could dispute it?

Storm dies away.

ELIZABETH: The Board of Longitude, that's who.

HARRISON: Priests and professors!

ELIZABETH: They met and called William to account. The procedures laid down had not, they said, been followed.

ADMIRALTY

WILLIAM, EGMONT, MORTON.

EGMONT: First, the instrument for measuring equal altitude at Portsmouth was set up in one place for the morning measurement and in another for the afternoon measurement, and therefore we feel the results obtained must be erroneous.

WILLIAM: Not so, Lord Egmont, sir. Moving the measuring instrument is normal and legitimate. The need to *level* the instrument is fundamental. No one who is responsible would ever proceed to measure the altitude of the sun with an instrument that wasn't very precisely level, and –

MORTON: But our most urgent objection is –

WILLIAM: You have a *more* urgent objection?

MORTON: – is to do with the rate of loss. The return journey from Jamaica in The Merlin was not conducted under supervision. Without supervision we cannot eliminate the possibility of tampering.

WILLIAM: The Act doesn't say the return journey is part of the official test.

MORTON: No matter. You're claiming the watch lost one minute 54 ½ seconds in 147 days there and back.

WILLIAM: Forget the return journey. Look to the journey just from Portsmouth to Jamaica. In 81 days our timekeeper lost only 5.1 seconds.

MORTON: Yes, if you take into account an *agreed* daily rate of loss.

WILLIAM: We *have* taken into account a daily rate of loss – 2.66 seconds a day.

MORTON: A loss that was not agreed upon in advance.

HARRISON: Priests and professors!

WILLIAM: It wasn't asked for in advance.

The streets come alive.

HARRISON: Priests and professors! They keep moving the damn target.

Bustle. Music. Street cries.

RED LION SQUARE

WILLIAM, HARRISON, ELIZABETH.

WILLIAM: It seems like this, father. The Board is not seriously questioning my procedure for securing equal altitudes – they've accepted my explanations. Their real worries are with the rate. We claim that the calculations should be based on a losing rate of 2.66 seconds a day; they say we should have declared that rate before leaving.

HARRISON: Maskelyne. Him. The Reverend bastard Maskelyne.

WILLIAM: He's not on the Board, father. Forget the man.

HARRISON: Not *on* the Board maybe but he knows the Board. Everyone of them. They know each other.

ELIZABETH: Forget the man.

HARRISON: Priests and Professors!

ELIZABETH: You'll drive yourself mad.

HARRISON: Talk among themselves.

ELIZABETH: Forget them.

HARRISON: Tittle tattle tittle tattle!

WILLIAM: Father! I'm none too certain myself.

HARRISON: Thee! Not certain!

Pause.

WILLIAM: We *should* have declared the rate of loss beforehand, and I'm not sure that the rate of loss we decided on *after* the voyage was any but rough and ready.

HARRISON: So what do us do now?

WILLIAM: The commissioners have decided that to clear up the doubts and differences of opinion there should be another trial run to the West Indies.

ELIZABETH: Another?

HARRISON: I'll agree to that.

ELIZABETH: Risk his life and your timekeeper?

HARRISON: If it will end all disputes, I'll agree.

ELIZABETH: Your son's life and your life's work?

ADMIRALTY/WORKSHOP

EGMONT, MORTON and WILLIAM.

EGMONT: Our problem is we need it explained *before* it goes back to sea for a second trial run. None of the astronomers or admirals on the Board knows anything about the mechanism of the watch. We don't really understand what makes it run so regularly.

MORTON: After all, what if you and the watch sank in a disaster?

> *HARRISON barracks from his workshop where he's planning wood.*

HARRISON: And who will protect my rights when all is known? Ask them that.

EGMONT: Tell your father that of course we will protect his rights.

HARRISON: Ask them how?

WILLIAM: Will you award us five thousand pounds in support of your promise to protect our rights?

MORTON: *Not* five thousand! Fifteen hundred now and a further one thousand after the second sea trial.

EGMONT: Though we don't feel the watch to be of such great use for discovering longitude at sea we nevertheless recognise it as an invention of considerable utility to the public.

WILLIAM: We don't understand, sirs. If the watch is of no great use for discovering longitude how can it be an invention of considerable utility to the public?

EGMONT: As an invention it is impressive. As an invention capable of being reproduced for public utility we have yet to be impressed.

MORTON: The Act demands that we shall determine how far the invention is practical.

WILLIAM: 'Practical'. Not 'reproducable'.

EGMONT: Do not you and your father want your timekeeper to be 'reproducable'?

MORTON: Would you have us award twenty thousand pounds to an invention that only your father can make and no one else?

> *Pause.*

> *The question has hit home.*

WILLIAM: What, sirs, would you have us do?

> *Clanging bell. Over it –*

> *ELIZABETH brings drink and food to HARRISON in his workshop.*

HARRISON: Don't they know that if they give me my due I'll build workshops and train men to reproduce the damn things?

ELIZABETH: You get in the way of yourself.

HARRISON: Can't they see ahead?

ELIZABETH: They would see more if you were less bullish.

HARRISON: I'm not bullish, I'm just right.

ELIZABETH: Of course you're right, John. You're just the wrong person to be right.

ANNOUNCEMENT PLATFORM

COMMISSIONER.

COMMISSIONER: 31ˢᵗ March 1763. Act Three in the reign of His Majesty King George III lays down:

One: That when John Harrison fully and clearly discloses the principles of watch four and reveals the true manner and method in which the same may be constructed then he should be awarded five thousand pounds.

Two: This sum will be deducted from any longitude prize the watch might subsequently win.

Three: John Harrison's rights will be safeguarded, and no other person may claim an award for finding longitude based by means of a Timekeeper.

Four: A decision on the efficiency of the watch must be reached within four years.

Five: A special sub-committee of twelve persons of high standing including professional watchmakers, scholars, and scientists will be appointed to receive the technical information that Mr Harrison shall lay before them.

ADMIRALTY

HARRISON joins the other three.

EGMONT: What we want, Mr Harrison, are examples of the tools you used –

HARRISON: Oh, yes?

EGMONT: – so that craftsmen can reproduce them for making copies of the watch.

HARRISON: Oh, yes, yes?

EGMONT: Then we want you to dismantle the watch piece by piece –

HARRISON: Yes, yes.

EGMONT: – and explain what each piece does.

HARRISON: Oh? Really?

EGMONT: We will further require you to supervise the making of two more watches.

HARRISON: Just two? Not four? Not six? Not ten?

EGMONT: And finally we will need to test those watches to see if, when made by other workmen, they'll work with equal efficiency.

HARRISON: To make two more will take years. I'm seventy for heaven's sake. What good is money to me in the grave? Mean little minds you have. You make me ashamed to be English and I'll say no no no no as long as I have a drop of English blood in my body.

EGMONT: Sir, I have not heard talk like that before, never!

HARRISON: Then, sir, it's about time you did hear talk like that, for if this goes on, you, your professors and your priests will find reasons and more reasons for not awarding me my due, or you'll prevaricate and find tasks and seek guarantees and safeguards – none of which is required in the first Act of Queen Anne of fifty years ago.

EGMONT: Sir, you –

HARRISON: And ships will wreck themselves upon rocks and women and children made widows and orphans.

EGMONT: Mr Harrison, you are the strangest and most obstinate creature –

HARRISON: Me? Obstinate? Have none of you any idea how long it will take to prepare written descriptions and working drawings of the mechanisms and then, *then* make two watches?

EGMONT: Mr Harrison, sir –

HARRISON: Sir sir sir!

EGMONT: – if you would but do what we want you to do, and which is in your power to do, I will give you my word to give you the money if you will but do it.

HARRISON: And I know too well *why* you want me to do it. Yes, sir, I do, sir. Indeed I do, sir.

MORTON: Why, tell us, sir, what evil, underhand connivances do you suppose this illustrious body of men are up to? Eh? What dastardly schemes, pray, are you imputing?

HARRISON: That while my timekeeper is dismantled and out of function your priest and professor the very very oh so reverend Neville Maskelyne will seek a trial of the lunartic method with its mad and cumbersome measurements between fixed stars and a crazy moon. And you'll love that, all of you. Your little heads will look up and gaze at the magnificence of the heavens and you'll imagine God is speaking to you, telling you the way, and it won't matter if there's a cloud or two or three or four you'll wait till they're passed and waste time calculating when all you need is my little piece of machinery. But no! Oh no! Too vulgar for you. What's a little metal, a few springs, and tiny wheels compared to the stars? Good Lord and little fishes! Who is this upstart from up north with his tick tocking cogs and balances?

Well I'll tell you who I am. I'm John Harrison from Barrow-on-Humber, and I'm seventy years old, and I've given half my life to solving the one problem could make this country the greatest maritime nation in the world, and you little men with your tawdry conditions for this to be done first and that to be done first and everything to be done first before I receive my just rewards, you little men of theory – you're squeezing the blood out of my last years. Oh, yes. I know only too well why you want my timekeeper dismantled.

MORTON: And we know only too well why dismantle it you will not.

HARRISON: Which is?

MORTON: You fear your timekeeper is not ready.

HARRISON: Let the second sea trial be judge of that, shall we Lord Morton?

EGMONT: And let us hope all will proceed simply from here on.

BARBADOS/HARRISON WORKSHOP/ ELIZABETH'S KITCHEN

A temporary OBSERVATORY is being erected on the Madeira sands by MASKELYNE and his assistant.

The HARRISONS are in their workshop.

ELIZABETH in her KITCHEN.

ELIZABETH: And did it proceed simply? Nothing to do with my John could ever be simple. Up came pen and paper again – he reached for his quill as some reach for their sword – and off he wrote at once to the Board of Longitude requesting that new conditions for the second trial at sea be clearly stated.

The biggest problem was the rate. What should it be? It was a matter of such importance that, Mr Bliss, the Astronomer Royal himself, suggested the watch be sent to Greenwich to ascertain the rate. But would the Harrison men leave the watch out of their sight?

HARRISON: Never. What, leave it to Reverend Maskelyne to check how many seconds a day our timekeeper loses? Him so biased against us?

ELIZABETH: So it was agreed, after much unpleasant argument, that just before sailing to Barbados William should send the Admiralty his own estimate of the timekeeper's rate. But then came the big row. When William arrived in Barbados who did he find but the Reverend Maskelyne who'd been sent ahead in order to determine the exact moment of noon, and compare it to the hour on our timekeeper. But on the way to their makeshift observatory, now listen to this, William heard someone saying "here comes the other competitor for the prize!"

OBSERVATORY IN BARBADOS

MASKELYNE and WILLIAM.

MASKELYNE: No matter what you heard, sir, there was nothing of ill intent on my part.

WILLIAM: No ill intent? Who talked to people here about his work on the lunar solutions and his hope that it would gain the prize?

MASKELYNE: And if so?

WILLIAM: And if so then how could you be impartial in your astronomical observations since they might favour an alternative to your lunar solutions.

MASKELYNE: You should have made known your qualms to the Board before I left.

WILLIAM: We did.

MASKELYNE: And were assured of my integrity.

WILLIAM: And assured, too, that your instructions were to do everything to ensure the proper execution of this test.

MASKELYNE: Which I have done, am doing, and will continue to do.

WILLIAM: Then what business was it of yours to lord your lunar theories all over the place?

MASKELYNE: Please, Mr Harrison, lower your voice, do. In six months here is it to be imagined I would not talk of work that has occupied me all these years? There had never been any secret about my interest and support of the lunar method. In fact the Board themselves instructed me to test the accuracy of the new lunar tables which I have done, and was able to predict the longitude of Barbados to within half a degree. Would you deny me sharing my enthusiasms? Was I to remain silent about my own experiments because the Harrison timekeeper was on its way? I have been a man of science since my youth and what matters to me are my integrity and scientific truth. You have no reason to doubt either, sir. And I bid you good day.

RED LION SQUARE

ELIZABETH and HARRISON.

ELIZABETH: Their quarrels died away as quarrels do between rational men. Maskelyne took his readings, thoroughly checked the timekeeper, and everything was sent back to the Admiralty for the next stage. And do you hear how I can now talk with ease about scientific matters?

When the Board met in January my men were not invited. Four mathematicians were called instead, and each declared that the watch had an accuracy three times better than that required to win the full £20,000. Success! A lifetime of endeavour was about to be crowned with fame and fortune. But was it?

HARRISON: No! Was the fortune placed in my bank? No! Was the crown of fame placed on my head? No! Was glory and honour bestowed? No, no, no! Now why? Ask me why?

ADMIRALITY

*EGMONT, MORTON, MASKELYNE, WILLIAM &
HARRISON.*

MORTON: Can I remind the Board that a section of the Act Three of King George the Third is still operative?

HARRISON: Oh? And which one is that my ever so lordly Lord Morton?

MORTON: You lack respect, sir. Your nature is intemperate.

HARRISON: My nature is blunt.

MORTON: Blunt natures do not by nature command the truth.

HARRISON: What has my nature to do with the truth? Truth resides in facts. The facts are simple. There was a problem – longitude. There was a prize for solving the problem – I solved the problem. The prize is in all honour mine.

EGMONT: If only the world were that black and white, Mr Harrison.

HARRISON: It is, my Lord Egmont. Black and white. Good and evil. Right and wrong. If you see it muddy it's because your priests and professors muddy clear waters.

EGMONT: It is not that clear waters are muddied, but that human motivation renders the human condition grey. Grey, Mr Harrison, grey. Which means nothing is simple.

HARRISON: The results of the mathematician's calculations were favourable to the watch. Simple! I wrote to the Board requesting humbly ever so humbly that they grant me the authority to claim the prize. Simple!

EGMONT: Not simple. We couldn't grant you that authority because not all the Board members were present at that meeting. One man in particular had to be party to any such decision.

HARRISON: Let me guess who that man was.

EGMONT: You know very well who that man was. While your son was in Barbados Doctor Bliss, the Astronomer Royal, died, and it was my pleasure to inform the Board that the King had approved the appointment of the Reverend Neville Maskelyne.

HARRISON: Another reverend in command!

MASKELYNE: You misjudge me, Mr Harrison, as your son misjudged me, as indeed you misjudge everyone and all things. I've called this Board meeting just twenty-one days after my appointment because I consider the issue of great importance.

HARRISON: Important not to me alone but the nation, sir.

MASKELYNE: Yes, yes! The nation, sir.

HARRISON: The poor damned sailors of His Majesty's navy who have to sail blindfold while you fart around my invention which anyone can see –

WILLIAM: Father, be quiet. This is a time for reason not anger.

HARRISON: Then you be reasonable with them. I give you my blessing.

MASKELYNE: We are all agreed that your timekeeper kept its time with sufficient correctness in the voyage from Portsmouth to Barbados.

WILLIAM: It did better than that.

MASKELYNE: Yes, the minutes will record it did better than that.

WILLIAM: It kept time with correctness beyond the limits laid down by the Act of Queen Anne.

MASKELYNE: Correct, even *considerably* beyond the limits laid down by the Act of Queen Anne.

HARRISON: But? But? Don't we hear a 'but' in your tone of voice?

EGMONT: Quiet, Mr Harrison. It's time for quiet now.

MORTON: Yes he does hear a 'but' – let's stop pussy-footing around the man. Act Three of King George the Third is still operative and calls for the invention to be practical and useful at sea, and the only way we can ascertain this is for the man to dismantle his watch as he agreed in '63 and prove it is a mechanism easy to replicate.

HARRISON: I agreed on conditions.

MASKELYNE: And those conditions were accepted and written into the new act – your invention to be protected, and no other person allowed to claim a reward for a timekeeper until judgement had been passed on the merits of your watch.

MORTON: And the time has come to judge its merits. It is not enough that your timekeeper found longitude, it must also be capable of easy manufacture in sufficient quantity.

HARRISON: The target! The Target! You keep moving the target.

EGMONT: You must disclose on oath the mechanism of your watch and explain to us how duplicates may be constructed. When this is done we will award an amount which, together with monies already advanced, will total £10,000.

HARRISON: *Ten* thousand? The prize is for twenty. The Act of Queen Anne states clearly –

EGMONT: The remaining £10,000 can only be paid on proof being made to the satisfaction of this Board that the construction of your timekeeper will provide a method of common and general utility in finding the longitude at sea.

WILLIAM: What in God's name does such gibberish mean?

MASKELYNE: It is perfectly clear, Mr Harrison.

WILLIAM: No it is not perfectly clear, Mr Harrison. 'Provide a method of common and general utility in finding the longitude at sea'? My father has provided such a method – his timekeeper. It has made two sea voyages and each time has proven accurate to within seconds. What more do you want?

MORTON: We've told you, man. We keep telling you. We need to know *how* it works and we need to assure ourselves it is not too complicated to be reproduced.

HARRISON: Grant me my just prize, and I will refine the watch to make it so.

MORTON: We go round in circles. Let's call this meeting to an end.

HARRISON: It *can* be reproduced! I'm telling you! It can be! Will *no* one listen to me? Is everyone a nincompoop?

EGMONT: MISTER HARRISON! SIR! Curtail your rudeness and answer me this – can any seaman purchase your invention as an aid to navigation?

HARRISON: Of course not! The machine has only just been invented for God's sake.

EGMONT: Correct! Just so! And therefore we need to spend time satisfying ourselves it can be reproduced. Extraordinary though the Barbados trial was we need to reassure ourselves that it was not owing to chance.

HARRISON: Chance? Do I hear you right? Chance? Have you no understanding of the simplest mechanism? Does the wheel turn without collapsing by 'chance'? Does the arch not cave in by 'chance'? Do your buildings stand erect by 'chance'? Laws govern the movement and structure of things. My timekeeper kept time because it was constructed according to the laws of motion and balance and the laws applying to hot and cold. Even your elusive moon keeps its distance because of laws of gravity – or do you imagine it's a button on God's jacket which he might chance to pull off in a fit of pique?

MORTON: I think, gentlemen, we have an impasse.

> *HARRISON and WILLIAM return to RED LION SQUARE.*
>
> *ELIZABETH is polishing her husband's boots. He takes them from her.*

HARRISON: How many times have I told you – I'll polish my own boots.

ELIZABETH: Has he rubbed them up the wrong way again?

WILLIAM: We both did, mother.

The ADMIRALTY meeting continues.

HARRISON 'barracks'.

MASKELYNE: And now, gentlemen, I would like to remind the Board of the very persuasive evidence I presented to the honourable members from my recent voyage to the West Indies. I was able to predict the longitude of Barbados to within one half degree, and, on my return, to forecast the longitude of the Isle of Wight to within ten miles of its true position – both by means of the lunars.

HARRISON: The lunars! Hurrah – the lunars!

MASKELYNE: In a very short time I will produce nautical tables –

HARRISON: Nautical headaches.

MASKELYNE: – purchasable for mere pounds rather than the hundreds a watch will cost.

HARRISON: And listen. There's more.

MASKELYNE: However, I further recommend that we propose John Harrison be elected a Fellow of the Royal Society.

HARRISON: Confer honours and withhold the prize! How's that for deviousness?

ELIZABETH: What's devious about honours?

HARRISON: Confer honours and silence the noise mongers.

ELIZABETH: That's perverse reasoning, John, and I hope you told them 'yes'.

HARRISON: I told them – not me.

ELIZABETH: You told them 'no'?

HARRISON: What about my son instead, I told them?

Pause.

You'll accept it won't you, William?

WILLIAM: Of course I will, father.

HARRISON: And the silence they intend they won't achieve, right, son?

WILLIAM: Father, they've already achieved what they want to achieve.

Resigned silence.

We must do it.

HARRISON: I know.

WILLIAM: And when you receive the ten thousand you must hand over all four timekeepers.

HARRISON: I know, I know.

ELIZABETH: You've unleashed their spites.

WILLIAM: And for the remaining £10,000 father must make two more watches, which again must needs be tested at sea.

HARRISON: To prove what?

ELIZABETH: They're asking no more than that you dismantle your timekeeper and demonstrate what you claim, John.

HARRISON: How much more do I have to give, how much longer to fight?

WILLIAM: I'll talk for us, father.

HARRISON: You'd better, my son. Thee must take over. I'm too old to stand before nitwits and explain the perfectness of my watch and argue my case and defend my rights. When a right is so obviously a right I can't find words to say why it's right. I'm contemptuous where I should be patient and arrogant where I should be humble, I know it. But I can do nothing about it. Thee must take over, William, and be the wise mouthpiece for your father.

WILLIAM: Be father to the son's father?

HARRISON: Aye, that.

WILLIAM: Slap his wrists, scold his sins?

HARRISON: Aye, that and that.

WILLIAM: Tell him to shut up, urge him to hold back, suggest he thinks twice before putting pen to paper to make the world see the world as he sees the world?

HARRISON: Aye, you can try that, too.

Takes father in his arms.

WILLIAM: Comfort him in bleak times?

Hold.

HARRISON: *(Pushing him away.)* As long as tha doesn't sing to me. Tha's not got a right note in thy throat. Since childhood tha's chased notes like butterflies, never quite able to grasp one and hold it.[5]

WILLIAM: So you'll make known the construction of the watch?

HARRISON: Aye, I will.

WILLIAM: Good, father.

Long pause.

HARRISON: On conditions.

ELIZABETH groans.

HARRISON embraces her by way of apology.

---

5. If the actor playing WILLIAM is also one of the singers the line could read: '*As long as tha does na kiss me. Tha slobbers as though lips were nipples.*'

ADMIRALTY

WILLIAM addresses the BOARD MEMBERS –
MORTON, EGMONT, MASKELYNE.

HARRISON in attendance.

WILLIAM: My father proposes, if it is acceptable to the honourable gentlemen, to explain the mechanism of his watch by handing over the drawings from which it is made together with his explanations in writing –

MORTON: *(Viciously interrupting.)* No, sir. Not good enough, sir. Not acceptable at all. Yes, your father must hand over the drawings and written explanations, but he must also dismantle the watch in front of the Board's representatives and must answer on oath any questions put to him

HARRISON: Hark them! I must this and I must that. I hear you talk of 'musts' but do I hear you talk of needs? Of the nation's needs? I hear you talk of 'musts' but do I hear you talk of concerns? Concern for sailors lost at sea along with untold wealth all sunk to Davy's bosom? No – just Harrison must do as he's told. Well Harrison won't, and you can all rot in hell for your damned dishonesty.

FATHER and SON leave.

EGMONT: I think we can assume that there's an end to the matter.

MASKELYNE: No, Lord Egmont. We are dealing with a stubborn man but not a stupid one. He wants the prize, and if we remain firm in our resolve that he reveals the mechanism of his watch to the world I believe he will relent.

EGMONT: However, I confess sympathy for Harrison's fear of pirating. May I propose that every member of the committee we select to hear the disclosures of the watch's mechanism be enjoined not to disclose them to any but the Board?

MORTON: Agreed! And let me be honest – I dislike the man. Uncouth. The manners of a pig. No sense of his place –

EGMONT: Because, Morton, he senses his place to be among the great scientists of the land rather than the greats lords of the realm.

MORTON: Don't spell it out for me, Egmont, it'll only make me angrier. What do you propose, Maskelyne?

MASKELYNE: He imagines we will relent. We must find a way to let him know unequivocally that we will not. The man is impressed with the power of print, and so –

Clanging bell.

– I propose we print the minutes of all the meetings of May and June stating our position as well as John Harrison's so that the public can know –

ANNOUNCEMENT PLATFORM

COMMISSIONER: – that it is the opinion of this Board, that the terms which have been proposed to Mr Harrison for the discovery of the principles and construction of his timekeeper, are reasonable and proper; and that, as he has so peremptorily refused to comply therewith, they do not think themselves authorised to give him any certificate, or that it is to any purpose to treat with him any further on the matter till he alters his present sentiments.

Sounds as at beginning:

A ticking clock

A growing storm

Timber shattering on rock

Human voices in distress.

Slow dimming of light

ELIZABETH: (The litany) The Newcastle, ninety-six lives lost.
  Cloves, cardamom, saffron, ginger. The Doddington.
  Seventy-six lives lost. Bamboo reeds, elephants' tusks,
  mother of pearl shells, opium...

End of Act One.

ACT TWO

Bustle. Music. Street cries.

HARRISON'S WORKSHOP

WILLIAM: I think they have us, father.

HARRISON: Schemers!

WILLIAM: I think we must sign the oath.

HARRISON: Must must must!

> *Projections one after the other of HARRISON's drawings for the watch. We marvel at the incredible draughtsmanship.*
>
> *The final projection is of the watch itself.*
>
> *The SEVEN NOMINATED MEN gathered round a table studying drawings we see projected.*
>
> *Throughout, the seven are frozen until –*
>
> *Clanging bell.*

ANNOUNCEMENT PLATFORM

COMMISSIONER: *(Reading.)* We whose names are hereunto subscribed do certify that Mr John Harrison has taken his timekeeper to pieces in the presence of us, and explained the principles and construction thereof and that we have compared the drawings of the same with the parts, and do find that they do perfectly correspond.

RED LION SQUARE

ELIZABETH: Hip hip horray! Another declaration of approval.

HARRISON: We collect approvals, wife, but no silver.

ELIZABETH: 'Wife'? 'Wife'? What happened to Lizzie? Where's she?

> *Streets come alive.*
>
> *Bustle. Music. Street cries.*
>
> *HARRISON sitting for his portrait by THOMAS KING.*

ELIZABETH: Look at him – my uneducated genius from up north. Relax your face, husband. Don't look so stern for those to come.

HARRISON: 'Husband'? You calling me 'husband'?

ELIZABETH: As you're calling me 'wife'.

HARRISON: 'Cos wife you are.

ELIZABETH: As husband you are. *(To KING.)* Marriage! Beware! From love and wild nights in the loft to dried up indifference. Haranguing is all he cares about these days.

ADMIRALTY

> *BOARD MEMBERS in attendance.*
>
> *HARRISON harangues from his portrait sitting.*

MASKELYNE: Gentlemen of the Board, I must bring to your attention other problems to do with the Harrison timekeeper. Reverend Ludlam, please.

HARRISON: More bloody reverends, more bloody problems!

LUDLAM: Good sirs. As you know, the Reverend John Michell, a Cambridge Professor of Geology, and myself, a mathematician and Fellow of St John's College Cambridge, were two of the seven nominated to receive John Harrison's disclosures of his watch.

HARRISON: Of which they understood little you can be sure.

LUDLAM: Let me say from the outset that our doubts have nothing to do with the candour and proud delight with

which this engineering genius dismantled and revealed his machine. There can be no doubt that, however cantankerous –

HARRISON: Cantankerous, that's me!.

LUDLAM: – and we all know how the best minds range from the eccentric to the cantankerous – however cantankerous, our carpenter and joiner from the backwaters of Lincolnshire is *more* than a carpenter and joiner. He is an extraordinary, sharp minded and original inventor.

ELIZABETH: Approvals, John, more approvals! No need to be stern, see!

HARRISON: Wait! They're not done yet.

LUDLAM: No, our misgivings are not only to do with the questionable efficiency of some of the devices fitted to the watch –

HARRISON: I knew I shouldn't have explained anything to them. They don't understand how the bloody wheel works!

LUDLUM: – but with doubts that satisfactory copies can be made by other workmen using everyday methods.

HARRISON: Targets! Targets! They're shifting the targets again.

LUDLAM: Mr Harrison outlined his improvements but could offer no rules for arriving at those improvements. He says he adjusted the parts by repeated trials, and that he knows no other method.

HARRISON: Of course I adjusted the parts by repeated trials. But having done it once I can do it next time with fewer trials. And next time with even fewer trials. And then with no trials at all. It's called 'experience'.

LUDLAM: Now it may be that such experience can be gained by other workmen but this means that it will be some time before many such watches can be constructed with the same degree of accuracy as that obtained under Mr Harrison's capable hands.

MASKELYNE: Nevertheless – I move that we authorise Mr Harrison to apply for ten thousand pounds – or to be more exact, seven thousand five hundred pounds since two thousand five hundred pounds was allocated him at the conclusion of the first trial to Jamaica.

HARRISON: Authorise? They authorised what was mine by right? Lunatics! And even then it took another six weeks before I got my money.

ELIZABETH: But you got it, John. Be fair.

HARRISON: Fair! Fair! Only half the prize – fair? And what must I do in return? Construct another two, look! Without the original to help me! And where are the drawings? The scrupulous Reverend Maskelyne wants them, him with three chins and no hair. And to do what? To have them copied and sold to the public, that's what. Said it was now theirs, they'd paid ten thousand pounds for it.

ELIZABETH: Forgive me saying, Mr Harrison – *(To KING)* I have to challenge him now and then to keep him alert – forgive me, Mr Harrison, but ten thousand pounds *is* a lot of money.

HARRISON: My timekeeper has fulfilled all the requirements for the *full* amount of money.

ELIZABETH: Good God, man. There is no pleasing you.

HARRISON: Oh yes there is. Justice pleases me. And honesty. And straight dealing and hard work and rewards for hard work, and what's good for mankind and my fellow creatures – that pleases me. And my timekeeper pleases me.

ELIZABETH: You will have the last word.

HARRISON: Nay! *You* will.

At which both laugh.

He kisses her.

ELIZABETH: Why look! A glimmer of past times.

Streets come alive.

Bustle. Music. Street cries.

RED LION SQUARE.

HARRISON is dictating a letter to his son.

HARRISON: '...and in return for the sum of £800 I will construct two duplicates of the watch, which will become the property of the nation, on condition that at the same time as I be given the £800 I humbly beg the Board to allow me to claim the second award of £10,000, which I would swear on oath would be devoted to the setting up of a manufactory in which workmen and apprentices would be instructed by myself in the construction of further watches for this is the only way my invention will go into the world. And so I humbly urge that my watch be returned to me in order to facilitate and speed up production.'

There! What could be fairer than that? More than fair – what could be more practical? Can they deny me that?

Clanging bell.

Can they possibly have arguments against that?

ANNOUNCEMENT PLATFORM

COMMISSIONER: 26 April 1766. As Secretary of the Board I am instructed to acquaint you with the following decisions in regard to Mr John Harrison and his proposals as outlined in his letter of the 25th March. That if there is any neglect in the prosecution of his invention it is his own. And that only when he shall have made other timekeepers of the same kind as the watch now in possession of the Board, and when such timekeepers have been proven at sea only then will he be entitled to the remaining £10,000.

WILLIAM: Rejected!

COMMISSIONER: Further, the Board remains anxious that duplicates of watch four cannot be made successfully by a workman other than John Harrison who appears to possess special gifts enabling him and him alone to adjust the intricate mechanism of the watch, and so for this reason the Board proposes that an exact replica of the Harrison watch be constructed by the renowned clock-maker, Larcum Kendall, for the sum of £450 –

HARRISON: Took him two and half years.

COMMISSIONER: And Mr Harrison's drawings to be reproduced by an engraver working under the supervision of the Astronomer Royal –

HARRISON: – him with three chins and no hair –

COMMISSIONER: – who shall further ensure that these engravings together with the notes taken by himself and others during the explanations made by John Harrison, shall be printed, and five hundred copies put on sale to the public.

HARRISON: Useful enough to be made public but not useful enough to earn me the full prize. Are these good men and true? I ask you – just, wise, good men and true?

COMMISSIONER: It is further proposed that –

HARRISON: More! Nothing will please them but my death.

COMMISSIONER: – that because certain members of the Board fear that the undeniably impressive results of the Barbados trial might be a fluke of circumstance, the watch should be sent to the Royal Observatory at Greenwich and there be given rigorous tests over a period of ten months under the personal supervision of the Astronomer Royal.

WILLIAM: You're a thorn in their side, father. They want thee dead.

HARRISON: Well die I won't. I'll hell not die. I know all about them as glory in the end of things, the passing of this and that. *He's* had his day, they say with sadness in their voice and glee in their dried up hearts. Expect no more from him. His days are ended, done! Well pass I won't and end I won't and more there is, and they can *choke* with glee for I've got oak and God and cleverness where they've got naught but three chins and a shiny arse. Oh, yes, I know such men. Beware of them, William lad. They'll drain joy from a nightingale, dampen your sun, and lay waste the best in you. But not in this carpenter, not in this clock-maker, not in this bell-ringer. Don't ask from whence but I've got energies and fires in me to last ten lives and ring them all to hell.

> *Streets come alive.*

> *Bustle. Music. Street cries.*

RED LION SQUARE

MASKELYNE arrives.

HARRISON: You, sir!

MASKELYNE: Mr Harrison. I have a letter for you from the Board.

> *HARRISON accepts it, reads.*

> *Clanging bell.*

ANNOUNCEMENT PLATFORM

COMMISSIONER: We the under mentioned, being part of the commissioners appointed by the Acts of Parliament for the discovery of the Longitude at Sea, do hereby require you to deliver up to the Reverend Mr Neville Maskelyne, Astronomer Royal at Greenwich, the three several

Machines or Timekeepers, now remaining in your hands, which are become the property of the public. Given under our hand at the Admiralty, the 26th of August 1766…

HARRISON: They could find no one else to come for them?

MASKELYNE: Mr Harrison, permit me to remind you that the Royal Observatory was founded for the express purpose of finding longitude by lunar observation –

HARRISON: Did they send you to lecture me, too?

MASKELYNE: – but since becoming Astronomer Royal, to show my impartiality, I have fostered timekeepers no less than I have attended to the motions of the moon. And further –

HARRISON: Spare me!

MASKELYNE: – and further, I know you see me as the demon in your life but I assure you as I assured your son in Barbados – I have been a man of science all my life and what matters to me are my integrity and scientific truth.

HARRISON: While what matters to me is that I have spent thirty years of *my* life engineering these three clocks. What matters to me is that they were never entered for the longitude prize yet they must leave my sight is what matters to me.

MASKELYNE: To which you agreed let it not be forgotten.

HARRISON: Forgotten is what I most certainly will not let it be, and shall hold you responsible till I die for prevarications, delays and the barriers put before me.

MASKELYNE: Come, Mr Harrison, you exaggerate.

HARRISON: Oh I do, do I? Exaggerate do I? Shall I list them all, those barriers and delays?

MASKELYNE: Sir! The problem of longitude is central to the nation's prosperity, the prize of £20,000 is a vast sum. And the task of recognising the solution and deciding who has won such a vast sum is a solemn task, and the men chosen to supervise that task are solemn men. What you call barriers we call caution; what you call prevarication we call investigation; what you say is delay we name as trial. Caution, trial and investigation is what an honest nation requires of its honest guardians. Now sir, inform me how best we may carry your precious cargo to the Greenwich Observatory.

HARRISON: First I shall need a receipt for them.

MASKELYNE: Of course. You shall have it.

HARRISON: And it must state they're in perfect order.

MASKELYNE: That I cannot do sir.

HARRISON: Why not, sir? For they are, sir.

MASKELYNE: I'm not able to judge that to be the case.

HARRISON: You don't have to. I'm telling you.

MASKELYNE: If I am to say so then I must know so.

HARRISON: Then you must look at them so, and watch their movements so, and see how like clockwork my clocks go so.

MASKELYNE: And what if when they arrive at the Observatory they function differently from when they were here?

HARRISON: Then you can be sure damage was done on the way, sir.

MASKELYNE: You are an impossible man to deal with, Mr Harrison, do you know that?

HARRISON: No sir, I don't know that.

MASKELYNE: Well I'm telling you that.

HARRISON: And that you tell me that, I should accept that? Is that what that 'that' is about?

MASKELYNE: I really can't stand here battling words with you, sir. I am, let me remind you –

HARRISON: – the Astronomer Royal. I know it. The Very Reverend Astronomer Royal who can't tell if a clock works because his head skips in the clouds with the moon and the stars.

MASKELYNE: Enough, Mr Harrison.

HARRISON: No, not enough, Reverend Maskelyne, sir. Never enough.

MASKELYNE: We must arrive at a wording acceptable to us both.

HARRISON: Till my last days it won't be enough.

MASKELYNE: I propose the following: 'The timekeepers were by appearances in order'.

HARRISON: 'The timekeepers were by *all* appearances in order.'

MASKELYNE: I accept.

HARRISON: 'The timekeepers were by all appearances in *perfect* order.'

MASKELYNE: I accept, I accept. Now, your advice on how to transport them.

HARRISON: Oh, no, sir. You don't catch me like that. I'll not be trapped in giving advice for their transport, for if they be found damaged the blame will be mine.

MASKELYNE: Mr Harrison, this is perverse in the extreme.

HARRISON: Not so. The Board has empowered you to transport my timekeepers, then it must be you who instructs his men how to do so.

MASKELYNE: This is childish.

HARRISON: Childish? Did *I* want them gone?

MASKELYNE: Childish and petulant.

HARRISON: Oh deary me. Childish and petulant.

MASKELYNE: You do not endear yourself to the world, Mr Harrison.

HARRISON: The truth of things needs no endearings, Reverend Sir, though I know it be the way of your world.

MASKELYNE: Do you want your darlings cared for?

HARRISON: Indeed I do.

MASKELYNE: Then instruct us for heaven's sake.

HARRISON: And be blamed when all goes wrong?

MASKELYNE: You will not be blamed, I vow.

HARRISON: Vow on.

MASKELYNE: I take full responsibility.

HARRISON: Vow on, vow on!

MASKELYNE: *(Furious.)* I will vow no more, talk no more, quarrel no more. You will respect, through me, the Board set up by Parliament or I will advise the Board no further dealings with –

HARRISON: *(Interrupting.)* Then do this. Take clocks one and two in pieces. Even you, sir, with your head on the moon will find the sections identifiable. But clock three can be moved in one piece. And that's all I have to say to this meeting that was both unannounced and uninvited. Good day, sir.

> *HARRISON leaves for his workshop.*
>
> *MASKELYNE nods to TWO WORKMEN standing by.*
>
> *Between them they lift clock one. After a few steps it slips out of the hands of one of them and cracks to the ground.*
>
> *An electrifying moment.*
>
> *The streets come alive.*
>
> *Bustle. Music. Street cries.*

ELIZABETH: *(Over the bustle.)* Broke some of the movements!
But that was not the half of it. The man was so determined
to put John out of the race that all three machines were
transported to the boat waiting on the Thames not in a
chairman's horse – a frame in which all fragile articles are
transported – but in an unsprung cart. An unsprung cart!
On the cobbled streets! Imagine!

> *A chairman's horse moves across the stage as the clocks*
> *are bundled onto an unsprung cart.*
>
> *We watch with horror as they are bounced along.*

And that man was entrusted with John's life and our future!

ADMIRALTY

MASKELYNE, HARRISON, WILLIAM, EGMONT,
MORTON.

MASKELYNE: Gentlemen, the Board of Longitude laid down
very detailed instructions for the ten-month trial of the
watch which I conducted. All actions were to be witnessed
by retired officers of the Royal Greenwich Hospital –

ELIZABETH: – who were decrepit old naval cast-offs unable
to see what they're witnessing – those that could climb the
hill that is.

MASKELYNE: I was to keep daily records which the
Commissioners authorised me to make public.

ELIZABETH: And what a record of lies they were.

MASKELYNE: My summing up was fair and just. I divided the
ten months into seven sea voyages of six weeks each, and
for each except the last, the errors were of such variation as
not to warrant the Queen Anne Prize.

HARRISON: Not our errors, reverend sir. Your distortions.

MASKELYNE: I concluded that Mr Harrison's watch cannot be
depended upon to keep the longitude within a degree in a

West India voyage of six weeks. Nevertheless this fourth of his timepieces is a useful and valuable invention, and –

ELIZABETH: Wait! Here it comes!

MASKELYNE: – and in conjunction with lunar observations may be of considerable advantage to navigation.

HARRISON: Humbug! If my watch can't be depended upon to keep the longitude then how can it be 'of considerable advantage to navigation'? Humbug! Hypocrite!

MORTON: Mr Harrison, sir, I will not have you constantly imputing the Astronomer Royal's integrity.

HARRISON: *(To his son.)* You explain it to them, William. I'm tired.

WILLIAM: It is too complicated, father. These are laymen.

HARRISON: Professors and Priests, I know. Try!

WILLIAM: *(Trying.)* No clock runs accurately to the split second.

MORTON: Don't tell us what we already know!

WILLIAM: All clocks gain or lose seconds each day. If it loses or gains erratically –

MORTON: Nor do I want to be spoken to like a child.

WILLIAM: I must tell you what you know in preparation for what you don't know. If the watch loses or gains erratically – twenty seconds lost one day, three seconds gained the next day – then it becomes impossible to gauge longitude. If, on the other hand it loses or gains the same or similar amounts each day then an average daily allowance can be made in the calculating of longitude. Reverend Maskelyne failed to make such an allowance during his ten-month trial of our timepiece.

MASKELYNE: The rate was too irregular.

WILLIAM: The rate was irregular when the watch was laid down on its back –

MASKELYNE: Which is what the Board stipulated.

WILLIAM: No, sir. The Board stipulated that the trials should be for the watch laying at different angles.

MASKELYNE: And that I did, too, sir.

WILLIAM: But for only the last forty-five days in the ten month trial.

MASKELYNE: And recorded the results fairly.

WILLIAM: But you did not calculate the *entire* ten months making any allowance for gain.

MASKELYNE: The gains were too various.

WILLIAM: Not according to your own records they weren't. According to your own records you should have applied a gain of nineteen point five one in all your calculations.

MASKELYNE: I could not imagine you would want that when on your trip to Barbados you requested a gaining rate of only one second a day to be allowed.

WILLIAM: Had you spoken to us first we'd have told you that we'd not yet adjusted the watch satisfactorily.

MASKELYNE: And whose fault was that?

WILLIAM: We were not given time or opportunity.

EGMONT: Because everyone was so heartily sick of the quarrels that erupted whenever you were around.

MORTON: And had father and son not sulked they could have sent word that the watch was not in a perfect state.

WILLIAM: You might have guessed the watch could not be in a perfect state after it had been taken apart.

HARRISON: Should've taken the reverend apart, see how well he functioned after being reassembled.

WILLIAM: And had you applied the gaining rate of nineteen point five one seconds overall, then voyage one and voyage four in your ten month trial would each have won us £20,000.

HARRISON: What do you say to that?

MASKELYNE: I say to that that I will print my report and let the world know what's what.

HARRISON: And to that I say I, too, will let the world know what's what.

MASKELYNE: And what, precisely, *is* it that you'll let the world know?

HARRISON: How the Board behaved illegally, that is what I'll let the world know.

MORTON: Damn it, Mr Harrison, I won't have the Board insulted in this way.

HARRISON: Then deny it.

MORTON: Deny what, precisely? Precisely how did the Board behave illegally?

HARRISON: You allowed my devices to be publicly exposed when you swore they would be kept private.

MASKELYNE: It didn't matter! Your beautiful watch was too complicated for your contemporaries to copy, anyway.

HARRISON: I had plans for constructing other watches at a price within the reach of ordinary seamen.

MASKELYNE: A feat you failed to accomplish!

HARRISON: It's in construction. A fifth watch is in construction.

WILLIAM: – which you now want on trial at the Royal Observatory for the space of another ten successive months –

HARRISON: – another ten months to wait –

WILLIAM: You keep changing the rules.

HARRISON: *That's* how the Board behaves illegally!

WILLIAM: You keep changing the bloody rules!

HARRISON: And look! You've made my son swear!

The streets come alive.

Bustle. Music. Street cries.

ELIZABETH: Meanwhile Larcum Kendal completed his replica of John's watch for £450, which the Board were so pleased with they gave him another £50.

WILLIAM: And it's beautifully made. It has to be said. Very fine.

ADMIRALTY

MASKELYNE, EGMONT, MORTON, KENDALL.

MASKELYNE: Gentlemen. We have subjected Mr Kendall's replica of the Harrison watch to the same tests, and now they've proved satisfactory we've asked Mr Kendall to tell us the terms under which he would instruct other workmen to make further copies.

KENDALL: And I've declined so to do, sirs. In my view the Board will be disappointed to rely on watches like the Harrison watch ever coming into general use at sea unless the expensive parts of the watch can be reduced in costs and a simpler method be contrived to adjust the mechanism. To achieve all this will take many years, if ever, before such watches could be afforded for £200.

EGMONT: Can you construct such a watch?

KENDALL: I can, my Lord.

EGMONT: Leaving out the expensive parts?

KENDALL: I can, my Lord.

EGMONT: Making the adjustments simpler?

KENDALL: All that, my Lord, and thus they will come into general use at sea.

MORTON: Let the man do it, I say.

EGMONT: It's not so easy, Morton. The King George Act protects the Harrisons.

MORTON: Criminal mistake if you ask me. Look at the difference in time. The Harrisons have been working on their fifth watch for four years while Kendall here produced his in two and a half.

EGMONT: We must ask Parliament to legislate that Harrison forfeits his rights to the remaining £10,000 unless two more watches are completed within five years.

MORTON: That'll send him into print again!

Bring in RED LION SQUARE

HARRISON: They can laugh and scoff all they want – it only further proves what damned rapscallions they are. That prize is mine! The Barbados trial proved it and the world knows it!

MORTON: The world also knows the damned watch has to do more than function at sea – it has to be manufacturable so that every damned seaman can purchase the damn thing.

EGMONT: And Kendall here can solve the problem but we can't ask him to because we're tied to the Harrisons by old legislation.

HARRISON: Ungrateful bastards!

MORTON: And he calls us ungrateful. Ungrateful? John Harrision – *that's* who's ungrateful. In four years he's not produced new watches, and the legislation we're proposing gives him another five for God's sake.

HARRISON: By which time I'll be eighty-two!

MORTON: And if by then nothing is produced then it never will be, and he'll have earned from the nation £10,000 and a luxurious old age the old battleaxe! I never liked the man.

The street comes alive.

Bustle. Music. Street cries.

HARRISON: But we beat them. Ha! Ha! The rapscallions! Ho! Ho! Parliament wouldn't pass the legislation they wanted, and I've finished my new watch! A fifth timepiece! Bloody lovely! Bloody ingenious. Bloody, bloody, bloody serves them right. I've done it.

WILLIAM: Only half true, father. Done it all bar the final adjustments.

HARRISON: Half truths are not lies, my son, they're just the truth waiting to be completed.

Long, contemplative pause.

WILLIAM: And now you must make a sixth timepiece, father.

HARRISON: I know it.

WILLIAM: No second ten thousand, else.

HARRISON: I know it, I know it!

WILLIAM: The Board stipulated and we agreed – new watches, news tests.

HARRISON: And the years are passing.

ELIZABETH: And we don't dance any more, and you don't call me 'my love' any more.

HARRISON: I can't do it, William.

ELIZABETH: (The Litany) The Lincoln, ninety-six lives lost. Cinnamon, cashew nuts, tamarinds, vermilion …

HARRISON: I can't.

WILLIAM: I know it.

ELIZABETH: The Resolution, ninety-nine lives lost. Saltpetre, rice, tigers' teeth, chintz…

HARRISON: Too old, too weary.

ELIZABETH: Too bitter, my love.

HARRISON: Fight's gone.

ELIZABETH: The Phoenix. Eighty lives lost. Muslins, calicoes, nankeen, sugar candy…

WILLIAM: I have one last thought, father. *(Beat.)* King George. *(Beat.)* A letter to him. I hear he has sympathy for our case.

RICHMOND OBSERVATORY

KING GEORGE III and DR. DEMAINBRAY, his Swiss philosophy tutor.

DEMAINBRAY: *(Reading.)* 'Man is only a reed, the weakest in nature, but he is a thinking reed. Even if the universe were to crush him, man would still be nobler than his slayer, because he knows that he is dying and the advantage the universe has over him. The universe knows none of this. Thus all our dignity consists in thought.' Who said this?

GEORGE: I know who should have said it.

DEMAINBRAY: Who?

GEORGE: Me! I should have said it 'cos then I'd be a wise king. *(Beat.)* Pascal.

DEMAINBRAY: I'm impressed, sire.

GEORGE: You should be. It's why I engaged you as my tutor. Not simply to teach me philosophy but to be impressed by me and keep telling me you're impressed by me.

DEMAINBRAY: Died young, Pascal.

GEORGE: I like clever young men. The future of the nation.

DEMAINBRAY: What about clever old ones, sire?

GEORGE: The Harrison saga. Not good. Not good at all. Not just. And as for my Lords Morton and Egmont – well, I'm not sure what *they're* going to bequeath the nation.

DEMAINBRAY: Egmont is charmingly eccentric.

GEORGE: But dissipated. He'll be dead in a trice.

DEMAINBRAY: Morton is a clever astronomer.

GEORGE: But a tight-arsed amateur, and we all know what bullies tight arsed amateurs are. The Harrison letter says they had a good relationship with the Board –

DEMAINBRAY: – friendly, helpful –

GEORGE: – up until the trial of the timepiece to Jamaica –

DEMAINBRAY: – which was a success –

GEORGE: – but after which, the help and friendliness disappeared, and now we – what?

DEMAINBRAY: *(Reading.)* ' – and now we find ourselves brow beaten by one set of men and betrayed by another.'

GEORGE: Not good. Not good at all. These people have been badly treated. Read me their last paragraph again.

DEMAINBRAY: *(Reading.)* 'If his Majesty would be so graciously pleased to suffer our new made watch, to be lodged for a certain time in the Observatory at Richmond, in order to ascertain and manifest its degree of excellence, I should hope that the prejudices of many might thereby be vanquished, and that it would be easy to obtain redress'.

GEORGE: We'll do it. A six week trial of the new watch, Mr Demainbray. By God, Harrison, I will see you righted.

DEMAINBRAY: Here, in your own Observatory, sire?

GEORGE: Of course here, of course. Where else? I shall enjoy that. I'm getting excited just thinking about it.

The streets come alive.

Bustle. Music. Street cries.

GEORGE III, DEMAINBRAY, WILLIAM confront the box.

GEORGE: Now, gentlemen, the procedure is simple. Like the other tests. To ensure the fifth Harrison watch won't be tampered with I've had three locks fitted to the outer box here containing the watch. I'll hold one set of keys, Dr Demainbray a second, and you, Mr Harrison, the third set. We'll meet here every day at noon, check the temperature, check the watch with the regulator clock, and rewind it. The good doctor will keep a record, which we'll each initial, and in the end we'll see what's what and who's who and the next to be done. Oh, I am *so* excited.

The THREE MEN separate.

The bustling street takes over.

The MEN come together again. Three locks unlocked. Times compared.

GEORGE: Well! What do we say to this? Your timekeeper is so different from the regulator clock it's not good from here to the city never mind from Portsmouth to Barbados.

DEMAINBRAY: Perhaps the watch needs to settle, sire.

WILLIAM: Shouldn't need settling. Should be going from the start.

GEORGE: We'll give it a few days.

The THREE MEN separate.

The bustling street takes over.

They come together again. Three locks unlocked. Times compared.

GEORGE: Well this is no good, Mr Harrison. Your timekeeper is way out.

WILLIAM: I don't understand it, sire. I'm looking and looking and can see nothing to cause such erratic behaviour.

GEORGE: Right! We'll lock it up, then. Try again tomorrow, then.

The THREE MEN separate.

The bustling street takes over.

They come together again with much intrepidation.

GEORGE: I'm almost frightened to unlock the wretched thing. I do have a reputation to think of, Harrison. I hope you and your father aren't going to let me down?

They unlock the case.

Check the time.

GEORGE: Out! Out again!

WILLIAM: I'm at a loss, sire. I can only assure you there is absolutely no reason, no reason at all why this watch shouldn't function.

GEORGE: Demainbray?

DEMAINBRAY: I'm astounded. I have every faith in John Harrison's skills but –

GEORGE: But what? *You* didn't steal back here to tamper with it. *I* certainly didn't. So – what?

WILLIAM: I ask for a full week, sire. And then I'll take it back to my father who is so distressed, *so* distressed it can't be imagined.

GEORGE: Oh yes it can! I'm also feeling sick and anxious – for whom more I can't tell, your father or myself. *You* don't look too good, either, young Harrison. Rewind it, sir, and we'll be on our ways.

As WILLIAM winds.

I've got all these dratted children to play father to. I don't
know what's wrong with Charlotte. She keeps having these
babies. And they all turn out to be cleverer than me by the
age of five. I couldn't read till the age of eleven you know.
Did you know that? Now I've got Demainbray here to talk
philosophy to me. Keep me sharp, so's I can answer back
my ten-year old. You done?

WILLIAM: Wound, sir.

GEORGE: Don't look so glum, man. Alls for the best in
this best of all possible worlds. Or is that inappropriate,
Demainbray?

DEMAINBRAY: Excellent, sire, excellent! I'm impressed.

> *They separate.*

> *But before they're apart GEORGE cries out.*

GEORGE: Oh ye Gods and little fishes! The cupboard. Go to
the cupboard.

> *The other two are mesmerised by his agitation.*

> *He must move himself, throw open the cupboard,
> and retrieve three small rocks.*

Lode stones! Of course your watch wouldn't function.
Powerful magnetic lode stones! Using them for my own
daft experiments. Pulling your timekeeper all over the
place. Scatterbrain! Cretin! Run home, William. Tell your
father. We'll test it for more than six weeks. We'll test it for
eight. Nay, ten. Nay, twelve weeks to prevent any cavilling.
Tell him – his watch will work. Hallelujah!

> *Handel's triumphant 'Hallelujah Chorus'.*

> *The MEN separate.*

> *Street bustle adds to the excitement of the moment.*

> *Dies away.*

RED LION SQUARE

HARRISON: Never did like Mr Handel. The man refused to tune his instruments to suit the voice, so the voice went one way and the instrument another. Don't much care for Mr Shakespeare, either. Too many thoughts contradicting each other. If my timekeeper is driven by mechanical laws so music and writing must be. Can't abide the ornate. Made the first watch ornate. A mistake. Changed all that with the next watch. Plain. Simple. Practical. To hell with flowery Shakespeare. Less is more. Give me a simple Psalm. 'The Lord is my shepherd, I shall not want.' Practical, simple, plain.

ELIZABETH: But – nothing is plain and simple about my plain and simple husband. Not content with the King's support he commissioned another pamphlet to be written because of course the one he wrote can't be understood, it had sentences so long you lost your way before meaning could dawn; and this commissioned pamphlet he sent to every member of parliament: 'The Case Of John Harrison'.

And then came an event we'll remember till our dying day, which, truth be told, can't be far off now. Unannounced, no warning, the king knocked on our door. George himself!

GEORGE III appears.

Comically embarrassed responses from HARRISON and ELIZABETH.

I didn't know what to do, bow or curtsey or go down on my knees. I think I did all three. He called for port, stopped us fussing, and made himself at home like an old friend.

Close, intimate, late night atmosphere.

GEORGE: I understand you, Mr Harrison, believe me. But the time for haranguing is past. It has led nowhere and it *will* lead nowhere. Be quiet now. Still your anger, select your friends, and listen to me. You think that because the King tested your timekeeper the Board must relent and award you the second part of the £20,000 prize. They can't. They've been given a task by Parliament who've made them the sole authority to help find longitude at sea. Any test must be an official one controlled by them. Listen to me. I know the Board – austere men, unyielding, a bit bloodless, not even the King can go against them, and that, dear man, is the way of the world, which I suspect you and your son have never really understood. Bit unworldly, both of you, if you'll forgive my saying. But – and this, too, is the way of the world – the King appointed Lord North as Prime Minister and therefore Lord North, who between you and me is a bit of a nitwit but quite capable, is in the King's debt. The Board will not award money – they must save face, and we mustn't stop them saving face, but – Parliament can reward achievement. I'll arrange that with North, and North will arrange it with the powers that be. Trust me on that.

HARRISON: *(Quoting.)* 'He hath led me and brought me into darkness but not into light. Surely against me is he turned; he turneth his hand against me all the day.'

GEORGE: No, Mr Harrison, sir. No, no, no! The world tires of lamentations – even Jeremiah's. Leave off printing your pamphlets and telling your story over and over again. I urge you. Remember – young men are coming up from behind. See this ring on my finger – it's a watch. John Arnold made it – a brilliant young watchmaker who has already made two watches for sailors at a fraction of what it has cost you. The Board is no longer interested in your complaints to them. Listen hard to me, Mr Harrison, sir – the young are clambering for attention. Forget the Board, appeal to the Prime Minister. I'll prepare the way for you.

CHURCH PEWS

As HARRISON moves to the scene of his young manhood he intones.

HARRISON: 'My flesh and my skin hath he made old; he hath broken my bones. He hath set me in dark places as they that be dead of old.'

A YOUNG HARRISON is now before his CHOIR OF MEN in church who shuffle uncertainly.

Come on now, you ploughmen. You don't walk backwards when you plough. And you tailors, you don't sew behind your backs. Nor none of you shoemakers, carpenters, smithies, weavers – you don't work not facing your work. So why should you sing with your backs to the congregation? Face them. Remember that stranger who'd been told about our choir up here in Barrow – he'd not heard the like, he said, neither in St. Paul's nor the King's Chapel Cambridge. So stop shuffling and arrange yourselves. Basses in front, tenors in the pews behind, and trebles behind them. We've got more strangers today, sing out for them. Sing out.

He conducts. They sing.

Clanging bell.

Against the choral background ELIZABETH mounts the –

ANNOUNCEMENT PLATFORM

ELIZABETH: Listen to this, my curmudgeonly husband. *(Reading.)* 'Because John Harrison of Red Lion Square, having for forty-eight years applied himself with unremitting industry to the making of a timekeeper for ascertaining the longitude at sea; and having discovered the principles of constructing the same by which other timekeepers have already been made, and from which great benefit will arise to the trade and navigation of these kingdoms, he is highly deserving of public reward. Be it therefore enacted that the Treasurer of His Majesty's navy shall cause to be paid to the said John Harrison a sum not exceeding eight thousand seven hundred and fifty pounds…'

RED LION SQUARE

WILLIAM helps his father from church to his chair at home, which is now centre stage.

Singing continues.

HARRISON: It should have come from the Board not Parliament.

WILLIAM: No matter, father, it's come.

HARRISON: And it should have been £10,000.

ELIZABETH: Well it wasn't, old man, not unless you add the £4000 you received over forty-eight years.

HARRISON: In which case – ha ha! hee hee! ho ho! – it becomes £22,750.

ELIZABETH: Oh, good God! Will he never relent?

HARRISON: £2,750 more than the offered prize!

ELIZABETH: You mischievous old bugger, you.

HARRISON: Still, small consolation for the soured joy of it all.

WILLIAM: Let's console ourselves this way, father. Not merely with the knowledge that we deserved better treatment but with the knowledge that our fame is in the hands of impartial posterity.

HARRISON is seated.

HARRISON: I wish, William, upon every father a son like thee.

ELIZABETH: Amen to that.

WILLIAM leaves.

Singing still in the background.

Lone unstoppable, unquenchable figure centre stage.

HARRISON: And now let me treat of another matter that has come my way and must be of worth if rightly thought about as I have done, namely this: because in nature there is no such thing as major or minor tones, therefore as the diameter and radius of a circle is to its circumference, so, too, is the sharp third to the octave. And I have constructed a musical scale based on this principle.

> *ELIZABETH is at some domestic chore. Polishing a brass tray?*

ELIZABETH: What's musical scales got to do with watch-making you're wondering? Nothing, really, except it was one man thought about both.

HARRISON: The chief consequence of my musical scale is the creation of intervals of melody truly sweet and mathematically perfect in a way never before thought possible.

> *Next two speeches delivered together, a duet.*

ELIZABETH: John Harrison...carpenter and joiner...tuner of bells...choirmaster...mender of clocks...

HARRISON: Away with your non-sensical chromatic and enharmonic scale – all buzzed and blazed about the world through ignorance. Only one true scale of music exists and it is stupendously obvious because so well grounded in *my* explanations.

ELIZABETH: Helped change the world.

HARRISON: But who listened?

ELIZABETH: My curmudgeon.

HARRISON: And thus I conclude: spite and poison runs through malicious minds that object to what is proven and true.

ELIZABETH: My husband.

HARRISON: Neither my musical scales nor my longitude will ever be proven or completed until such minds resign or die.

Singing swells.

ELIZABETH: My curmudgeon, my husband.

HARRISON rises. The YOUNG HARRISON now.

HARRISON: Sing out you weavers and smithies! Sing out you shoemakers, carpenters, ploughmen and boys.

Sing out!

Singing swells and swells.

The End.

STREET CRIES[6]

Pretty maids, pretty pins, pretty women!

Buy a fine singing bird, a fine singing bird.

Buy any wax or wafers? Fine writing ink?

Old shoes for some broomes! Old shoes for some broomes!

Chimney sweep! Chimney sweep!

Old cloaks, old suits, any old coats!

Lilly white vinegar! Vinegar light as Lillies!

Old chairs to mend! Old chairs to mend!

Twelve pence a peck, Oysters. Twelve Pence a peck.

Old Satten, Old Taffety, or Velvet!

Buy a new Almanack! Buy a new Almanack!

Buy my singing glasses, singing glasses, buy my singing glasses.

Any kitchen stuff have you, maids? Knives, combs, or inkhorns?

Four for sixpence, Mack-er-el. Four for sixpence, Mack-er-el.

Any work for the Cooper? Cooper, Cooper, any work for the Cooper?

Four pair for a shilling, Holland socks! Holland socks! Four pair for a shilling.

Colly Molly Puffe Patries, Colly, Molly Puffe!

'Ere's yer toys for girls an' boys!

Who's for mutton pie, or an eel pie?

Sand, ho! Buy my nice white sand, ho!

Any new river water, water here?

Fine ripe duke cherries, a ha'penny a stick and a penny a stick, ripe duke cherries!

Shrimps like prawns, a ha'penny a pot!

---

6. A selection. Many more.

CARITAS

a play

in two acts without an interval

Dedicated with love and hope to my nephew Jake

Author's Note

I would like to thank the touring theatres of Norway and Sweden and Det Danske Teater of Denmark for generously commissioning this play.

I should also like to thank Professor Paul Levitt of the English Department of the University of Colorado for urging me to look into the world of anchoresses and in particular the scant story of Christine Carpenter.

The historical Christine Carpenter lived in the Surrey village of Shere. She became an anchoress in 1329. Document have recently come to light revealing that the original Christine was immured, broke out three years later and then seems to have been persuaded by the authorities to re-enter her cell.

Note for translators

The dialect, as in *Roots* and *The Wedding Feast*, is from Norfolk. I have not rendered everything in dialect. Simply, 'ing' is *in*; 'and' is *an*; 'that' is *thaas*; and the rest is peppered with the occasional *hev* and *hed* for 'have' and 'had'; *bein't* for 'be not'; *on* for 'of'; *ent* for 'is not' and 'am not'.

Note for Directors

This is a relatively short play, but the first and second acts must run together.

The lighting for the first act dictates itself. For the second act, although I haven't indicated it, the 'parts' being in the main very short, they need to be divided by 'puffs' of lights fading in and out with sufficient darkness in between to allow Christine to move into a new framed position.

Caritas is about the pursuit of the ideal through dogmas which lead to the destruction of things human.

There are two stories. They are not related narratively but it is hoped that through their juxtaposition the play will make a poetic impact, as a parable does.

One story relates the simple stages of the abortive English peasant uprising of 1381. It records that injustice existed which the peasants fought against, and that in the process they became intoxicated with blood-letting, and perpetrated other injustices.

The parallel story tells of a young girl's pursuit of an ideal state of mind through dogmas which lead to another kind of injustice. She becomes imprisoned by her dogmas; her pursuit of the ideal has led her to a denial of the life she thought would be divinely liberated.

The play is not contrived to prove a theory. The incident happened. I have attempted to extract meaning from the experience.

All dogma is anti-human because it presumes the way life *must* be lived, which kills spontaneous creativity. The human spirit must be given room to grow, enjoy, to innovate. Anything that suppresses this spirit, whether it is a capitalist or socialist or religious dogma, is anti-human.

Injustice cannot be tolerated but that does not mean the ideal is ever attainable.

It is right not to tolerate injustice, but it is foolish to expect people ever to be perfect.

Caritas is about the anti-human quality of dogmas which presumes to dictate the way life must be lived.

A.W., 24 October 1981

One cause of disillusionment among certain types of young people is the new materialism which is sweeping Chinese society in the wake of the post-Mao leadership's emphasis on raising living standards and incomes. A Peking author who published the story about a young girl still under the influence of Maoist ideas received the following letter from one of his reader, describing her own dead sister:

All year round she would only wear black, white, grey and blue. She berated me for getting a special hairdo. She only read the *People's Daily* and the *Red Flag* [the Party's theoretical journal]. She thought everything else was decadent or pornographic or reactionary, feudal, capitalist, or revisionist. After the Gang of Four was overthrown she still persisted in her attitude. She worked in a factory and came home angry, saying the other workers were all reactionary; the younger ones would talk only about clothes, while the older ones would only talk about housekeeping and shopping for food. Why didn't they want to talk about global and national affairs? When it was payday, she didn't want to take any, saying, 'What do I want with stinking money?' She was living off her father, but couldn't even grasp what that meant. When bonuses began to be paid, she called it revisionist restorationism. She said people were trying to corrupt her with money. She kept a diary, but it was just full of Mao quotes. She had a few friends she had met during the Red Guard period, and she wrote to them. Their letters were always the same: first a bit about the 'excellent situation prevailing', then something on the latest slogans in the press, like 'plant the country with green trees'; then she would criticise a few people who were backward, and not revolutionary, and say, 'We are the only revolutionaries, we have the friendship of comrades in struggle' – and end up with some revolutionary salute. She wanted to go to university, but wasn't good at her courses because she didn't think it important to study culture. But she wanted to be a teacher, feeling this was 'noble and lofty' – not thinking that teachers have to accept wages too. She was madly revising for the exam, when Father offered her some watermelon and advised her to go to bed. She said, 'You want to corrupt me with melon, but I won't eat it.' Father said, 'You've lived this long, and you still don't understand a thing.' Then she ran into her room, to poison, and hanged herself.

from David Bonavia,
The Chinese (Penguin, revised edition, 1989)

Characters

CHRISTINE CARPENTER   a young anchoress, between sixteen and twenty-one years old.

AGNES CARPENTER   her mother, aged around forty.

WILLIAM CARPENTER   her father, a carpenter, aged around forty-two.

ROBERT LONLE   Christine's ex-fiancé, apprentice to William, aged about twenty.

MATILDE   an old woman, in her sixties.

HENRY   Lord Bishop of Norwich, aged fifty.

MATHEW DE REDEMAN   Rector of St Jame's Chapel, Pulham St Mary, aged about thirty.

RICHARD LONLE   Robert's father.

VILLAGER/ TRAVELLING PRIEST/ BAILIFF

    to be played by one actor

BISHOP'S CLERK/ TAX COLLECTOR

    to be played by one actor

Time

July 1377 to July 1381

Settings

Act one   a composite set to include: the wall,
altar and circular window of the chapel;
part of the anchored cell wall and its
grill window; a carpenter's workshop

Act Two   interior of anchoress's cell

Caritas was first performed by the National Theatre Company at the Cottesloe Theatre, London, on 7 October 1981. The cast was as follows:

CHRISTINE CARPENTER	Patti Love
AGNES CARPENTER	Sheila Reid
WILLIAM CARPENTER:	Roger Lloyd Pack
ROBERT LONLE	Martyn Hesford
MATILE	Elizabeth Bradley
HENRY	Frederick Treves
MATHEW DE REDEMAN/ RICHARD LONLE	Patrick Drury
VILLAGER/ TRAVELLING PRIEST/ BAILIFF	
	Paul Benthall
BISHOP'S CLERK/ TAX COLLECTOR	
	James Taylor

DIRECTOR	John Madden
DESIGNER	Andrew Jackness
LIGHTING DESIGNER	Rory Dempster

A pre-production version of the text was published by Jonathan Cape in 1981. Substantial changes were made during rehearsals; further changes were made after the author had worked on the libretto for the opera during the summer of 1988.

ACT ONE

SCENE ONE

JULY 1377.

The interior of the church in St. James in the village of Pulham St Mary, Norfolk; a carpenter's workshop; the window and part of the wall of the anchoress's cell anchored to the church.

CHRISTINE, daughter of William the carpenter, is about to be immured in the cell.

Sound of 'Alleluia te martyrum'.

Light slowly touches the opening in the wall. This is the first thing we see. Huge stones alongside, waiting to be put in place.

Light then touches the solitary figure of CHRISTINE, who stands before the altar, her back to us.

Light next touches the carpenter's workshop where stand three rough but solid pieces of furniture: a small table, a chair, a hard wooden bed. They are for Christine's cell, made by her father. The bed is not complete. One side is down and needs to be dovetailed to complete the frame, after which the boards must be hammered into position.

Note: What follows is based upon the recorded ceremony for enclosing anchoresses. Poetic licence is taken. But scene I must be performed in full, as a real church service, so that an audience is saturated in an intense religious atmosphere and feels itself witness to the ceremony of immurement. All the words of the service have relevance to what's happening and should be delivered as text, not mumbled.

HENRY, Lord Bishop of Norwich, enters, followed, by MATHEW DE REDEMAN, Rector of the church, and then Christine's parents, WILLIAM and AGNES, followed by Christine's ex-fiancé, ROBERT LONLE, followed by an old villager, MATILDE, and two others, a VILLAGER and the BISHOP's CLERK. A strong smell of incense is in the air.

Bishop HENRY begins the service.

HENRY: *(Intoning.)* Psalm 6, which is David's: O Lord, rebuke me not in thine anger, neither chasten me in thy hot displeasure.

Have mercy upon me, O Lord; for I am weak: O Lord, heal me; for my bones are vexed.

My soul is also sore vexed: but thou, O Lord, how long?

Return, O Lord, deliver my soul: O save me for thy mercies' sake.

For in death there is no remembrance of thee: in the grave who shall give thee thanks?

I am weary with my groaning: all the night make I my bed to swim; I water my couch with my tears.

Mine eye is consumed because of grief, it waxeth old because of all mine enemies.

Depart from me, all ye workers of iniquity, for the Lord hath heard the voice of my weeping.

The Lord hath heard my supplication; the Lord will receive my prayer.

Let all mine enemies be ashamed and sore vexed: let them return and be ashamed suddenly.

> *During this beginning AGNES stands before her daughter rand begins to unbutton her dress. She is so distressed that she cannot complete the task. Sobbing, she is taken aside by her husband, WILLIAM. MATILDE, the old villager, takes over and soon the girl is in a white chemise. Another VILLAGER stands by with Christine's habit in his arms. The service is continuing meanwhile. Everyone responds to the psalm.*

ALL: *(Intoned.)* Glory be the father, and to the Son, and to the Holy Ghost; as it was in the beginning, is now, and ever shall be, world without end. Amen.

> *CHRISTINE prostrates herself. HENRY and MATHEW stand before her. HENRY holds a cross in front of her. MATHEW sprinkles her three times with holy water, then three times with incense. HENRY raises her up. Two lighted tapers are placed in her hands.*

MATHEW: This is the Gospel of the Lord.

HENRY: O God, who dost cleanse the wicked and willest not the death of a sinner, we humbly beseech thy majesty that in thy goodness thou wilt guard thy servant, Christine, who trusteth in thy heavenly aid, that she may 'ever serve' thee and no trials may part her from thee. Through out Lord Jesus Christ.

ALL: Amen.

> *CHRISTINE moves forward, places her candles before the altar, steps back, reads her profession from a document.*

CHRISTINE: I, Sister Christine, offer an' present myself to the goodness of God to serve in the order of an anchoress, an' according to the rule of that order I promise to remain henceforward in the service of God through the grace of God and the guidance of the church an' to render canonical obedience to my spiritual fathers.

> *A pen is handed to her. She scratches the sign of the cross upon it. Returns to stand before the altar. She is helped on with the rough habit as HENRY intones:*

HENRY: May God put off from thee the old woman with all her works, and may God clothe thee with the new woman, for you who yearn passionately for union with her God are created in righteousness and true holiness.

ALL: Amen.

CHRISTINE prostrates herself before the altar. HENRY and the congregation continue in subdued tones to chant the hymn of Pentecost in Latin, Veni Creator.

Veni, Creator Spiritus,
Mentes tuorum visita,
Imple superna gratia
Quae tu creasti pectoral.
Qui diceris Paraclitus,
Altissimi donum Dei,
Fons vivus, ignis, caritas
Et spiritalis unction.
Tu rite promissum Patris,
Sermone ditans guttural.
Accende lumen sensibus,
Infunde amorem cordibus,
Infirma nostril corporis
Virtute firmans perpeti.
Hostem repellas longius,
Pacemque dones protinus:
Ductore sic te praevio
Vitemus omne noxium.
Per te sciamus da Patrem,
Noscamus atque Filium,
Teque utriusque Spiritum
Credamus omni tempore.
Deo Patri sit Gloria
Et Filio qui a mortuis
Surrexit, ac Paraclito
In saeculorum saecula.
Amen.

(WILLIAM, AGNES and ROBERT break away to the workshop; she to finish the last stitches on a tablecloth, they to finish making the bed.)

ROBERT: I know her passions. They have more to do with her than heaven.

AGNES: Why, why, why? I ask her, she tell me, but I understand narthin',

WILLIAM: An' it's just you who should!

AGNES: *(Ignoring that.)* 'All right,' I say. 'You want to retreat? Retreat! But fastin'? Beatin'? Prayin'? Weave!' I tell her. 'Mend the Church's clothes, collect for the poor, minister the sick, comfort the grievin'! But this?' An' she tell me, she say – with a scorn she get from I don't know who but I guess *(Looking at her husband.)* – she say, 'Mother,' she say, 'there's weakness in good deeds.' So I yell at her –

WILLIAM: Tryin' to be the right mother at the wrong time!

AGNES: *(Ignoring that too.)* I yell at her: 'But where be the virtue in sufferin'? The divine spark is offended by sufferin'. Offendeth by it!' 'Nay, Mother,' she say. '*Life* offended the divine spark, which can only be found in heaven, an' thaas what I prepare myself for.' 'Narthin'! Narthin'! I yell at her. 'That reveal narthin'! 'Heaven! Heaven!' she yell back. 'The truth is revealed in heaven.' 'Huh!' I say. 'Huh! Huh! If heaven is where all truth is revealed then it must be hell!'

ROBERT: It were me to blame, me! 'Wanna marry Christ,' she say. 'Not you. Christ! Not you!'

AGNES: *(Meaning WILLIAM.)* It's him! He's to blame. Had her taught words and grammar.

WILLIAM: Which she nagged for.

AGNES: Which *you* encouraged.

WILLIAM: An' who made her grow strange? Who took her from the love of fairs an' runnin' an' dancin' which rightly belongs to young girls? Who talked her silly about angels an' heaven an' hell an' the suffering of the Lord Jesus Christ?

AGNES: Which mother does different?

WILLIAM: Which mother has a daughter lock herself up in small rooms for months on end? Too much piety in the house! More passion than a child should take.

AGNES: But I warned against books.

WILLIAM: Too late, woman, the child was called.

AGNES: By the devil, called.

WILLIAM: She'll miss them fairs.

AGNES: An' the tumblin' an' the wrestlin'. Blust! She loved all that.

WILLIAM: There! A table an' chair for I don't know what.

AGNES: *(Mumbling on and quoting her daughter.)* 'Change, change! There must be change!'

WILLIAM: And a hard bed to prevent her sleepin' too well.

ROBERT: Suppose we must be thankful she didn't ask for a coffin to sleep in.

> *They place the chair and table on the bed and carry all to and through the hole in the wall. Soon they return as the intoning of the hymn comes to an end. The ceremony continues over the prostrate CHRISTINE. MATHEW goes to the altar, plucks up one of Christine's candles.*

MATHEW: O God, who willest not the death of a sinner, but rather that she should repent and be cleansed, we humbly beseech thy mercy for this thy servant who has forsaken the life of the world, that thou wouldst pour upon her the help of thy great goodness that, enrolled among thy chaste ones, she may so run the course of this present life that she may receive at thy hand the reward of an eternal inheritance. Through Christ our Lord.

ALL: Amen.

> *CHRISTINE rises. MATHEW turns, hands the taper to her. HENRY takes her hand; the others form a*

procession behind. They move towards the hole. A litany, 'Invocation to Christ', is sung. The procession moves through the family. Against the singing, AGNES, WILLIAM and ROBERT talk as though from afar.

AGNES: How will she wash when she sweat and she bleed? She'll die of her own smells, mad gal.

WILLIAM: No more games for you, my gal. Your runnin', dancin' days is done, all your fleet, sweet days, sweet daughter.

ROBERT: *(Angry.)* She've seen blue skies, she won't forget that. She've seen mares mate, she won't forget that. She've seen lambs skip, the calves suck, the settin' sun, the rivers run, and once she've seen me naked, touched me once, an' she won't forget that.

CHRISTINE stands before her cell. HENRY intones his prayer.

HENRY: Bless, O Lord, this house *(Signs the cross.)* and this place, that in it may dwell health, holiness, chastity, power, victory, devotion, humility, gentleness, meekness, fulfilment of the law and obedience to God, Father, Son, and the Holy Ghost. And let a full measure of thy blessing *(Signs the cross.)* rest upon this place and upon all who dwell therein in thee, that, dwelling in all sobriety in these temples made with hands, they may ever be temples of thy Spirit. Through our Lord Jesus Christ thy Son, who with thee liveth and reigneth in the unity of the Holy Spirit one God.

HENRY takes CHRISTINE into the cell.

The Kingdom of the world –

CHRISTINE enters.

ALL: – and all the glory of it have I despised for the love of my
  Lord Jesus Christ, whom I have seen, whom I have loved,
  on whom I have believed, whom I have chosen for myself.

HENRY: Go, my people, enter into thy chamber, shut thy
  doors upon thee, hide thyself a little, for a moment, until
  the indignation pass away. *In nomine patris, filii et spiritu
  sancti.*

> *HENRY leads the procession off to the Gregorian
> chant which began the ceremony: 'Alleluia te
> martyrum'. Two VILLAGERS now slowly block
> up the entrance. It is a chilling sight. The cell is
> walled up. Empty. Silence. Then – a song is heard.
> CHRISTINE is singing to herself, very sweetly, calmly.*

CHRISTINE: I will forsake all that I see,
  Father and friend, and follow thee,
  Gold and goods, riches and rent,
  Town and tower and tenement,
  Playing and prosperity,
  In poverty for to be one with thee.

> *Between many of the scenes – as though to comment
> on a scene – will be heard the chanting of children:
> loud or soft, vicous or sympathetic, like a styreet game.
> Now we hear it tenderly.*

CHILDREN'S VOICES: *(Off.)* Christ-ine, Christ-ine, had a
  revelation yet? Had a vision, had a word, had a revelation
  yet? Christ-ine, Christ-ine, had a revelation yet? Had a
  vision, had a word, had a revelation yet?

SCENE TWO

Loud scream from a man. RICHARD LONLE is dragged into the centre space by a BAILIFF. His hands are tied behind his back. He kneels with his back to us. The BAILIFF carries a brazier of hot coals with an iron poking from it.

HENRY and MATHEW appear. It is some months later.

HENRY: You know what's to happen, Richard Lonle?

RICHARD: Hypocrites! You preach labourers should be freed from all estates except your own!

HENRY: We think it's better it takes place here, before the Church, as warning to others.

RICHARD: The law says if I live in a town for a year an' a day I've earned my freedom.

HENRY: You were caught before then.

RICHARD: Three days! Three more days!

HENRY: And why *should* you have wanted to leave? The manor made you, fed you, rented you land, guarded you in sick times. Was I a bad lord? Was my bailiff here unfair? And in these times! When labour is desperately needed on the estate! You run away. *You* behaved unfair. And for why? To claim freedom! Freedom! No man's free! We're all bound by duties and responsibilities. So *(Brandishing branding iron.)* I want you to understand the justice of this punishment.

MATHEW: *(Reads from the manorial roll, his heart not in it.)* Richard Lonle, bondsman to the Manor of Henry, Lord Bishop of Norwich, you did hold twenty-four acres of land for which rent of four pence an acre was due, also three hens at Christmas and fifteen eggs at Easter. Further, you were bound to perform two days' ploughing in the year, four half-days mowing grass, two half-days for hoeing, six days in autumn for reaping, and one day for your horse and cart to carry corn. You were charged with absconding from your local place of work and domicile, withdrawing your services, and dispersing your family, for which a right and proper jury found you guilty. By grace of his Lordship the Bishop Henry of Norwich, you have been granted the return of your house and land on condition of renewed service but that you be branded with hot iron upon the forehead as sign to your neighbours and before God that you have broken your bond.

HENRY: Bailiff.

> *MATHEW holds the victim, and turns away in horror. The BAILIFF plucks the hot iron and brands RICHARD on the forehead. He screams, faints. The BAILIFF drags him away. HENRY and MATHEW move up into the church.*

They wanted him hung but I wasn't having any blood-letting, besides we're short of labour. *You* think I shouldn't even have had him branded, don't you?

MATHEW: The times change and the Church should follow, my Lord Bishop.

HENRY: The Church will decide if times change.

MATHEW: With respect, the Church called not for plague to decimate the population, robbing labour from the land.

MATHEW: God's plagues are God's affairs, God's Church is ours, to be obeyed, no matter what John Wyclif says. John Wyclif! Huh! An intellectual! *(Contemptuously.)* 'Each man holding dominion from God!' The man doesn't know what he's talking about! Wants to do away with the power of the priests. Wants to do away with you, Rector, what d'you say to that? You! A Wyclif man! Individual conscience! Pah! Have every man according to his own dictates and you'll have chaos. First thing God did he made order out of chaos and then divinely fired Paul to build his Church that

order be preserved. Order out of chaos! God's Church! To
be obeyed! And I will see it is! Forgive me, Rector. Talk
too loud. Unsettled times. I wasn't made for them. Not
intellectual like you and old John Wyclif. I worked hard,
learnt words, pursued my duty and – developed passions
for the land. 'Divinely inspired are you not, Henry,' I said.
'Leave that to those imagining they are. Acknowledge your
limitations and administer. Enough! You love the earth
and its seasons like a mother her child and its tempers.
Administer what you love. Enough!' And let me tell you
something else. I don't approve of them! How is she?

MATHEW: She says her prayers, eats little, advises from her
window, confesses through her quatrefoil. In the beginning
her confessions were full of guilts for small sins. Now, she
confesses to anger that the 'old life' still clings to her and
she hasn't found the new one yet.

HENRY: After six months? Huh! Tantrums and fervours – not
always easy to distinguish between them and the real thing.
But you insisted. 'She's called, my Lord Bishop, it's her
vocation, my Lord Bishop. She's in communication with
the angels, my Lord Bishop.' Pah! *(Grumbling as he goes off.)*
I've always warned – some can't bear the touch of God so
they scream loud hymns and prayers to drown him out.
Fervours! Fervours! Tantrums and fervours!

SCENE THREE

*Light up on the cell and window. ROBERT outside
CHRISTINE's cell.*

ROBERT: It's not God's call you're serving, more a private
devil.

CHRISTINE: There's things you say, young Lonle, I don't hear.

ROBERT: That's not what I say, that's what the Bible say. God
didn't make you for that hole, he made you for the world
which he made for you.

CHRISTINE: In here's the world. Out there is clutter.

ROBERT: There's cruelty, p'rhaps, unreason, killin'. But is that God callin' you or man a drivin' you?

CHRISTINE: Don't taunt me, Robert Lonle, pray for me. You love me? Pray for me!

ROBERT: You explain this, an' you explain that, black meanin' white an' white meanin' black! Your words is wind an' mist.

CHRISTINE: I don't have no other words.

ROBERT: Try village words, an' fairground words.

CHRISTINE: Them's for villages an' fairgrounds!

ROBERT: Then I'll keep askin'. Again an' again an' again.

CHRISTINE: Love, Robert, love! I can't say more than that. Love, Robert, love! I'm filled with love for him what took upon hisself great sufferin' an' torment an' death. To redeem us to God's grace. He suffered. For *us*. Can't you see the powerful pity thaas there? That make me weep. An' when I weep I know I got to share a tiny part on it.

ROBERT: In the silence an' the dark?

CHRISTINE: In a silence what is speakin' an' a dark what is light.

ROBERT: There you go! Wind an' mist an' black is white! You make no sense.

CHRISTINE: If I make no sense don't come no more. Don't taunt me! Don't taunt me! Don't! Don't taunt me!

ROBERT: Sorry, then. Sorry, sorry!

Long pause.

CHRISTINE: I hear tell a story, once. Mother and son. Lived at the foot of high mountains. And the son was drawn to them. He had to climb. The spirit of the mountains drew him. 'No!' his mother begged. She feared for him. 'No!'

she begged. But come the day he knew his strength and he climbed. He climbed and he climbed. His mother watched and feared for him, and watched and feared. The long days passed. She suffered anguish but she marvelled and were proud. But oh the ache, the helpless ache. Until one day she made a resolution. She would trace his steps. For what was life without her son, without her lovely loving son? She needed to be with him, tread the road he travelled on, share the pain, the fate. Adored him, see? There were no other way.

Sounds of taunting children.

CHILDREN'S VOICES: *(Off.)* Christ-ine, Christ-ine, had a revelation yet, had a vision, had a word, had a revelation yet?

ROBERT: Get off! Get away with you! Get off! Off!

But we hear them again, at a distance.

CHILDREN'S VOICES: *(Off.)* Christ-ine, Christ-ine, had a revelation yet, had a vision, had a word, had a revelation yet?

SCENE FOUR

Carpenter's workshop.

WILLIAM and ROBERT are answering the questions of the TAX COLLECTOR, who's writing on sheets propped on a sawn tree trunk.

TAX COLLECTOR: Name and age?

WILLIAM: William. Forty-two.

TAX COLLECTOR: *(Writing.)* Willelmus. Wife?

WILLIAM: Agnes. Forty.

TAX COLLECTOR: Agneta. Children?

WILLIAM: One. Christine.

TAX COLLECTOR: Christina. How old is she?

WILLIAM: The Crown will get no tax from her, she give her all to God.

TAX COLLECTOR: *(Sceptically.)* Is that so?

WILLIAM: You've not been told of her? She've made these parts famous enough.

TAX COLLECTOR: Ah! The anchoress! A rebuke to rudeness and self-indulgence. Very chastening. But I confess, I am a mortal man of sins and shames. Some temptations I control; other have a power I'm not built to control. What's to be done? Nothing, I say, but guard against excesses and be what of a good man I can, and God can spit wrath and indignation as he will, I am what I am an' there's an end, for I can do no more.

WILLIAM: There speaks someone from the city.

TAX COLLECTOR: Right! The solitary life is not one *I'd* be fit or excited for, but I'm full of reverence and awe, full of it. You must be proud.

> *His tone is casual. The men are silent. The TAX COLLECTOR looks around, then at WILLIAM for confirmation.*

WILLIAM: Aye, carpenter.

TAX COLLECTOR: Carpentarius.

ROBERT: He say one thing you write another.

TAX COLLCTOR: Latin, young man. They may preach sermons in English these days but tax returns must still be recorded in Latin. And who are you?

WILLIAM: My apprentice.

ROBERT: You'll know me from my father, Richard Lonle. You were there yesterday.

TAX COLLECTOR: *(Looking through sheets.)* Lonle, Lonle. Ah. Ricardo, Agricola, Alicia, Edmundo, Henrico, Johanna and Claricia. And you must be Roberto. *(Smiles.)* Latin! And you're all bondsmen to the Bishop's Manor.

ROBERT: Now. But next year us'll buy our liberty.

TAX COLLECTOR: Is that so? Now, possessions? And I want to hear everything. You know the penalty for hoarding. Although – arrangements can be made, eyes closed, this and that ignored.

He smiles.

WILLIAM: *(Coldly ignoring the invitation of a bribe.)* Three saws, two axes, a spokeshave, two adzes, two hammers, four oxen, seven steers, two cows, two and a half quarters of winter wheat, five quarters of oats…

SCENE FIVE

WILLIAM's voice dies away as CHRISTINE's voice from the cell takes over.

CHRISTINE: There was a oneness time. I search that. When I were with my soul, an' my soul were with my body, an' my body were with me, an' we was all one with God an' his lovely nature an' there were oh such peace an' rightness an' a knowing of my place. That really were a oneness time that were. An' I search that, Lord Jesus.

Old MATILDE, the busybody and gossip, enters, places her stool beneath the window, cards her wool, and chatters.

MATILDE: You crossed your mouth?

CHRISTINE grunts her replies.

Good! An' your eyes an' ears an' your breasts? Good! For as the advice goes – an anchoress must love her window as little as possible, especially a young'un. There's men in this village with lewd eyes an' soft tongues, an' there's boys with taunts, an' old women with useless prattlin'. Your mother bring you your food? Good! Now here's a story about a Belgie saint called Yvetta, tell me by a smithy who heard it from a nun who heard it on a pilgrimage to Rome which is how I get all my stories being a collector of stories 'bout saints which you'll be one day if you work hard at it. Yes! Get them from all over. Pilgrims. Vagabonds. Ole cooks at the fairs who I growed up with but them's also old an' widows now. Full o' stories. So, Yvetta. Sweet and pretty thing she were, an' happy, but, poor gal, she had to marry. Howsomever, when her husband die she renounce the world and go to serve in a leper colony where she so much wanted to be a leper herself that she eat an' drink with them, look, an' even wash in their bath water! Blust! You shouldn't catch *me* doin' that! An' all her day an' nights were spent in prayers, tears, genuflexions an' striking of the breast, an' when she sleep that were on sharp pointed stones. An' she die exactly on the day she say she were goin' to die. Hands outstretched an' eyes raised to heaven. Seventy she was. An' they say that even though it were the middle of winter wi' a great storm of wind an' hail an' snow, yet the birds gathered round her cell an' sang as if it were a summer day. An' her face was all a brilliant glow, they say.

SCENE SIX

Inside the church.

MATHEW by the quatrefoil taking confession from CHRISTINE.

CHRISTINE: …O all you blessed angels an' saints of God! Pray for me, a most miserable sinner, that I may now turn away from my evil ways, that my heart may henceforward be forever united with yours in eternal love, an' never more go astray. Amen. I've sinned, father.

MATHEW: What sins, daughter?

CHRISTINE: I find pleasure in my cell.

MATHEW: Who told you pleasure was a sin?

CHRISTINE: Time pass quickly. I look forward to each day.

MATHEW: That is a joy. God has rewarded you with joy.

CHRISTINE: I feel my suffering is false. I feel a fraudulence, deceit. I feel an emptiness.

MATHEW: Be patient, child –

CHRISTINE: I don't suffer.

MATHEW: Patience –

CHRISTINE: I do not suffer.

MATHEW: Patience, patience –

CHRISTINE: Not to suffer is a sin.

MATHEW: What are you saying, child!

CHRISTINE: My chains! My haircloth! I want my chains, I want my haircloth!

MATHEW: You will enfeeble your body.

CHRISTINE: My chains! My haircloth!

MATHEW: Enfeebled bodies cannot sing the praise of God.

CHRISTINE: Enfeebled bodies come from comfort, too much ease. You do not understand. My body needs the pain to help me concentrate on him.

MATHEW: No! No! Pain will intrude!

CHRISTINE: My chains! My haircloth!

MATHEW: What harmony can be known through torn flesh?

CHRISTINE: The torn flesh of our Lord brought harmony to the world. His suffering brought peace.

MATHEW: Suffering brings suffering.

CHRISTINE: I want my chains! I want my haircloth!

MATHEW: You *want*, you *want!* *Those* are the sins.

CHRISTINE: I'm dirtied! Unclean! Selfish! Wilful! I must destroy that selfish will.

MATHEW: To which end you apply the most extraordinary power of will.

> *He stops suddenly, realising he's arguing against the entire concept of the solitary pursuit which the Church has sanctioned. He's caught in a moment of doubt which Christine senses. She's a powerful personality of which he is afraid.*

CHRISTINE: Are you a priest or not? Do I have God or Satan here?

MATHEW: Beware, Christine. Into a life of solitude creep many evil beasts. The serpent of venomous envy, the bear of sloth, the fox of covetousness...

CHRISTINE: – the swine of gluttony, the scorpion with the tail of stinkin' lechery!

MATHEW: And the lion of pride, and the unicorn of wrath!

CHRISTINE: I know them!

MATHEW: I will come another time. You sound out of temper today.

> *(He leaves. She calls after him.)*

CHRISTINE: Bring me my chains an' haircloth, father. Bring them!

CHILDREN'S VOICES: *(Off, taunting.)* Christ-ine! Christ-ine! Had a revelation yet? Had a vision, had a word? Had a revelation yet? Christ-ine, Christ-ine. Had a revelation yet? Had a vision, had a word? Had a revelation yet?

SCENE SEVEN

Carpenter's workshop.

WILLIAM and ROBERT at work on a wheel. AGNES and MATHEW alongside.

AGNES: Here's your bread an' some meat from the fair, an' some bean and bacon soup which is good for you. *(Pause.)* And here's the Bishop's priest. *(Meaning: who is not good for you. Pause.)* No! I aren't leavin'!

> *Awkward silence. The men don't know whether to eat or not. AGNES decides for them.*

Eat up, look. That'll be cold presently.

WILLIAM: Worried about our daughter are you? Speak to *(Pointing to AGNES.) her*, then.

MATHEW: I urged the Bishop, it's true. Even against his doubts. But I believe she was called.

AGNES: You believe your church looks better with an anchoress to boast of.

MATHEW: *(Attempting sternness.)* My church is your church and you remember I'm the Vatican's choice for this parish, granted me by Pope Urban himself –

> *But his feeble authority touches their stony defiance not one bit. He relents. He's a good man really.*

(Gentler.) She asked for haircloth and chains.

AGNES: An' she'll get them. Somehow. An' go on to crueller things. I know her.

MATHEW: There's such a powerful hold on her mind.

ROBERT: Ent that what you want?

MATHEW: The solitary life is a search for union with God, it should bring freedom.

AGNES: Instead of imprisonment by stubborn love, you mean?

MATHEW: *(Dismissively.)* Love's an intoxicant. It clouds the truth of things. It makes you feel great good is done to you as hate can make you feel great harm is done when neither is the case.

WILLIAM: *(Curious about him now.)* An' *you* approved of her goin' in, father?

> *MATHEW is troubled. Every time he speaks he seems to surprise himself. Is he moving away from the faith? Is he a Wyclif man? He is fearful he will say too much to the wrong people.*

MATHEW: *(Leaving.)* I promise I'll keep close to her.

ROBERT: Well, *he* didn't stay long!

AGNES: I should've offered him food.

> *Now moonlight falls on CHRISTINE's cell as she whispers desperately to herself.)*

CHRISTINE: A showing! A showing! Give me Jesu Lord my lovely Christ a showing1 Touch me with your passion. That crucifix before me. Bleed! Weep! Smile! Whisper to me! I crave a showing, to stay with me every dark day of my dark life in this dark cell!

SCENE EIGHT

CHRISTINE's cell.

MATILDE arrives, places her stool, cards her wool, and chatters.

MATILDE: You crossed your mouth? Good! An' your eyes an' ears an' breasts? Good! Your mother brought your food? Good! Now here's a story. Saint Veridiana. Born two hundred years ago they tell me, place called Siena in Italy. This one fasted even as a child, an' wore a chain an' hairshirt. *Her* cell were ten feet long an' only three an' a half wide. No furniture, narthin', just a ledge in the wall an' two snakes for company. She tell her bishop they were sent in answer to a prayer that she be allowed to suffer similar to what St Anthony did, cos you know *he* were tormented by devils in the form of wild beasts. They say them snakes sometimes lashed her insensible with their tails. They killed one just before she died, the other never returned. In summer she slept on the ground, an' in winter on a plank with a piece of wood for a pillow, an' now she wore an iron girdle an' a hairshirt. Only one meal a day she had, sometimes bread and water, sometimes boiled beans, most times narthin' cos she give it away to the poor what used to come beggin' every night. Course she don't talk to no one but the poor an' afflicted, you know. An' she live like that for thirty-four years. Till she were sixty. Then she die. She also knew exactly *when* she were goin' to die cos she sent for her confessor, an' closed her windows. An' at the very moment she die all the church bells began ringin' by theirselves, look. An' when they pulled down the wall there she was, dead on her knees, with her psalter open at the Miserer! *(Pause.)* Is that another comin' to your window? *(Shouting.)* Go off there! That ent the right time o' day to be callin'. *(To CHRISTINE.)* My, they do come, don't they? All wonder an' excitement an' reverence. Think cos you cut yourself off from life you can explain life's mysteries. *(Shouting to CHILDREN.)* Get away, I say! *(To CHRISTINE.)* Your solitary life make folk uneasy. Your fastin' make them feel their greed. Your gentle ways make folk reflect upon their violence. The Church may be your anchor, gal, but ha!, she needs you, that she do. *(Calling.)* You're persistent. What's your question then? *(Pause. She listens. Then, to CHRISTINE.)* It's a young gal. No more'n about twelve. Says she wants to know how this life begin for you.

> *Long pause.*

CHRISTINE: I hear rumours, little gal. My soul hear rumours. Rumours like whispers. Not in words but in feelin's, feelin's whispered that another place up there existed. I don't talk of heaven, not rumours of heaven but *(Struggling.)* rumour

of another kind of knowin'. Oh, how shall I describe it
for you? I couldn't make things fit together, rumour come
and say it could. I couldn't walk beside myself, rumour
come and say I could. I couldn't ever love myself but
rumour come and whispered I was loved. Where did them
whispered rumours come from? They must come from
somewhere, little gal, I say, and so I listen hard, follow
sound, hope for the truth. Sometimes I think I hear the
truth. I get excited, eager but – thaas not the truth. Only
an echo of the truth, an' so I rage an' weep an' have to
start again. *(Beat.)* Rumours, rumours, little gal, beware the
echoes but wait for the rumours.

MATILDE: *(Collecting herself, speaks to 'gal'.)* There! You got that?
Rumours! Rumours! Wait for the rumours. Beware the
echoes, but wait for the rumours.

> *MATILDE leaves, shrugging, utterly lost.*

SCENE NINE

Carpenter's workshop. February 1379.

*WILLIAM, AGNES, ROBERT and the TAX
COLLECTOR.*

TAX COLLECTOR: Be sensible! This new tax must be paid by
everyone.

AGNES: The King had tax from us two years ago.

TAX COLLECTOR: Twelve pence from you but, look!, the rich
have twenty shillings each to pay, the clergy six and eight.
But you? Twelve pence!

> *He's becoming increasingly fearful of their mood.*

You know my policy: six in the family, I count five, we
split twelve pence. *(Pause.)* Not to be sneezed at. *(Pause.)* If
you don't work with me the King's men will send officers
with greater powers and it'll be imprisonment for all of
you.

Silence. He tries authority.

Right! My good nature's at an end. This money's needed for the safety of the realm and to support the army in its wars abroad.

WILLIAM: The wars in France.

TAX COLLECTOR: Yes, them!

WILLIAM: Disastrous wars. Losin' wars. Costly, disastrous, losin' wars.

TAX COLLECTOR: They pay me to collect the tax not judge how it's spent.

WILLIAM: *(Threateningly.)* We hear from Kent a tax collector raped a farmer's gal.

TAX COLLECTOR: *(Frightened.)* Well, that's in Kent and that was him, and this is Norfolk, this is me.

ROBERT: The farmers hung him.

AGNES: Why! I do believe the tax collector's shit hisself!

SCENE TEN

Interior of the church.

MATHEW at silent prayer. We hear CHRISTINE at her prayers.

CHRISTINE: …We adore thee, O Christ, an' we bless thee, because of thy holy cross thou hast redeemed the world. We adore thy cross, O Lord. We commemorate thy glorious passion. Have mercy on us, thou didst suffer for us. Hail' O holy cross, worthy tree, whose precious wood bore the ransom of the world. Hail O –

She stops abruptly. Ecstatic joy enters her voice.

Oh! Oh! A showing!

She can hardly believe it.

A showing! A showing! I have a showing! There before me!

MATHEW raises his head.

I see the world's shape. God shows me the world's shape. I see its joins, I see its links, I see what claps and holds it together. There's the hole and there's the dowel, there's the dovetail, mortise, tenon. Oh! Oh! I hear the flower blossom, see the harvest grow, I know the colour of the wind, the dark in light. Oh! Oh! It joins and locks and fits and rhymes. That be no echo this time, Lord, I see the shape. There is no mystery for Christine now. Oh, blessed Jesus Christ, I begged and prayed and prayed. The cross! The tree! The precious wood! And you have give to me a showing, you have give to me a showing!

MATHEW: Beware, Christine, beware of the vision. Awake, asleep, dreaming, beware the vision. They could be illusions. Satan's stratagems. Once he made a man believe he was an angel and his father was a devil, and he made him kill his father. Beware, Christine, beware the vision.

Long pause.

CHRISTINE: The dark in the light? I said 'the dark in the light'. I *did* say 'the dark in the light', didn't I? *(Pause.)* That were no showing, then. *(Pause.)* Though it did make sense. Gone. An' I nearly named the parts. *(Pause.)* There's a foul stench in my cell. Arrgh! Who'll rid my cell of its foul stench?

Long pause.

MATHEW: Christine? Christine? Are you all right, Christine? Shall I confess you?

CHRISTINE: *(Hissing.)* Go away.

Sad, taunting voices of the CHILDREN.

CHILDREN'S VOICES: *(Off.)* Christ-ine! Christ-ine! Had a revelation yet? Had a vision, had a word, had a revelation

yet? Christ-ine! Christ-ine! Had a revelation yet? Had a
vision, had a word, had a revelation yet?

SCENE ELEVEN

Carpenter's workshop. May 1381.

*WILLIAM, AGNES and ROBERT. It's evening, dim.
They sit over a pint of ale, animated by the events
they discuss.*

AGNES: I hear plans an' plottin's in the villages around.

WILLIAM: Are you surprised? Our grazin' places gone, forbid
to hunt an' fish which we have done for years, look!

ROBERT: A third tax comin'.

AGNES: Plans an' plottin's to set fire to the Manor documents.

WILLIAM: Burn them an' they won't have record of who's tied
to who, for what, nor where.

ROBERT: Good rid on 'em, too.

AGNES: The documents an' rolls of Carrow Priory first. The
Manor House at Methwold next.

WILLIAM: You know a lot.

AGNES: If I depended on your ear to know the world we'd all
be lost.

ROBERT: Then tell us all you know, missus.

AGNES: I don't know, I just guess. There'll be killin's.

WILLIAM: What's the sense in that?

AGNES: You sit on people, you squash sense out, don't you?

ROBERT: A third tax! Want their heads examined!

MATHEW enters.

WILLIAM: Come to share some ale, father?

AGNES: *(Fussing.)* Sit you there, look. I'll see to him.

ARNOLD WESKER

She pours.

ROBERT: I know why he've come.

MATHEW: The Bishop has refused.

WILLIAM: Refused him what?

ROBERT: To study grammar.

WILLIAM: Even though his father's got the money?

ROBERT: No matters how much money my father've got, the Bishop ont take it. The yearly levy, thaas what he'll take. Ploughin' his lands, shearin' his sheep. maltin' his grain – thaas what he'll take. An' when we grind our corn in his mill an' must leave some, he'll take that! An' when we brew ale in his brewery an' must leave some, he'll take that! An' when we bake break in his ovens an' must leave some he'll take that! Course he ont let me study grammar. Us study, us'll leave!

AGNES: An' be branded with hot irons on your forehead like your father.

ROBERT: That was then. Now my dad is saving hard to buy his freedom and he wants his son to read. He sees my talent for the word, my mother sees, my brothers, sisters see, and now they tell us English will replace the French in church and court and school and parliament I must command the word, and if Christine had not retreated to a hole then she'd've been my teacher of the word!

They all sit in silence for a while.

MATHEW: It's not in her to be solitary.

ROBERT: I could've told you that.

MATHEW: She sits demanding visions. Now! At once! After only three years! When there's some have waited sixty and not been graced.

AGNES: I know my daughter's ritual well. The dawn appears, she rises, genuflects and kneels upon that bed you made, and with bowed body prays and prays and prays some more. And prayin' still and mublin' still she dresses into God knows what. Because you know I took her once a day a shift until she said 'each week' and now 'each month' and soon she'll live a year in one foul dress and, oh!, the filfth, the smell, the misery and pain – for what? I ask myself for what? *(Weeps.)* My gal, my gal, my own poor gal.

MATHEW: To give up now she knows there's only excommunication, fire and hell.

WILLIAM: It's not in her to be solitary nor in you, it seems, to be a priest.

MATHEW: For this Church –no!

SCENE TWELVE

CHRISTINE's cell.

MATILDE arrives, places her stool, cards her wool and chatters. But now a distressed and wild CHRISTINE mocks and mimics her familiar opening sentences.

MATILDE: You crossed your mouth?

CHRISTINE: *(Mimicking.)* 'You crossed your mouth?'

MATILDE: *(Surprised but impervious.)* Good! An' your eyes – ?

CHRISTINE: 'An' your eyes?'

MATILDE: An' your ears?

CHRISTINE: 'An' your ears?'

MATILDE: An' your breasts?

CHRISTINE: 'An' your breasts?'

MATILDE: Good!

CHRISTINE and MATILDE: *(Together.)* Your mother brought your food?

MATILDE: Good!

> *But she does a double-take. Something is wrong.*
> *Waits. Will CHRISTINE continue to mock her?*

Now here's a story.

> *But she is uncertain what is wrong or what to do.*
> *She'll risk what she's always done, however.*

My favourite. You'll like this one. St Christina. Another
Belgie, an' she weren't an anchoress or narthin', she were
just – well, holy! A spirit! A real spirit who could climb
trees an' church towers an' was so thin an' light from livin'
in the wilderness that she could sit on the thinnest branches
of trees, look, and sing psalms! There were three sisters,
three on 'em, an' she were given the job o' lookin' after the
cows. But did she mind? Course she didn't. She'd sit out
there contemplatin', an' contemplatin' an contemplatin'
so much that she put herself into a trance. Yes, a trance!
An' that were so deep they all thought she was dead so
they took her to church to be buried. But halfway through
she was dead so they took her to church to be buried. But
halfway through Mass she got off her bier an' clamber
up the walls to the roof, look!, an' she don't come down
till her Mass is finished an' the priest promise to absolve
her. An' when she *do* come down she tell 'em all how
when she were dead she were shown purgatory, hell an'
then paradise, an' they give her the choice o' remainin' in
heaven or sufferin' on earth for the conversion o' sinners.
She come back! Cor, that congregation fled! 'Cept for
her eldest sister who was too terrified to move. Glorious
life she had. In an' out o' the wilderness, livin' on herbs,
prayin', comtemplatin', prophesysin', hevin' ecstasies. Like
a sparrow she was, very weird and wonderful.

> *CHRISTINE shrieks loudly. Three times.*

SCENE THIRTEEN

Inside the church. 17 June 1381.

*A TRAVELLING PRIEST is giving a 'sermon'. But **not**
to the audience, rather from a pulpit to a congregation
of our characters and 'extras'.*

TRAVELLING PRIEST: 'Blow ye the trumpet in Zion, and
sound an alarm on my holy mountain.' Thus saith the
prophet Joel. New sermons are being preached in our land,
beloved. Here's one for you: to each man hath God given
conscience! Dominion over himself! Therefore turn to your
priests and tell them this: one vicar cannot be upon the
earth, for each is vicar to himself.

'Beat your ploughshares into swords, and your pruning
hooks into spears: let the weak say I am strong.' Thus saith
the prophet Joel. One hundred thousand men are gathered
under Wat Tyler, brothers. Canterbury opens her gates, the
manor records burn and they have snatched the mad John
Ball from gaol to sing his lovely sermons to us all. Have
you ever heard John sing, beloved?

'Good people,' sings John Ball, 'good people, things
will never go well in England as long as goods be not in
common held. By what right', sings he, 'are they who are
called lords greater folk than we? Clothed in velvet, warm
in furs and ermines, while we are covered with rags! Tell
me', sings John Ball, 'when Adam delved and Eve span,
who was *then* the gentleman?' D'you like those songs,
brothers and sisters? They sing them from the coast of
Kent up to the Wash.

'And it shall come to pass afterwards that I will pour
out my spirit on all your flesh; and your sons and your
daughters shall prophesy, your old men shall dream
dreams, your young men shall see visions.' Thus saith the
prophet Joel. And –

Bishop HENRY storms in.

HENRY: In my church? Blasphemy and treason in my church?

> *Comic chase. The TRAVELLING PRIEST dodges here and there with confident fun, throwing out slogans and rhymes of the day.*

TRAVELLING PRIEST: 'Help truth and truth shall help you!'

HENRY: Who gave him permission? Who let him in? *(Calling.)* Bailiff! Rector! Who opens God's house to the wandering blasphemer?

TRAVELLING PRIEST: 'Now reigneth pride in price

And covertise is counted wise

And lechery withouten shame

And gluttony withouten blame.'

HENRY: I'll have you hung, drawn and quartered! You'll burn in hell!

TRAVELLING PRIEST: *(Fleeing.)* 'God do bote, for now is tyme!'

> *HENRY strides after him. CHRISTINE screams again. Three times.*

CHRISTINE: *(A voice of dread.)* I do not have the vocation! Release me! I do not have it!

SCENE FOURTEEN

Inside the church. Lit away from the cell wall.

HENRY and MATHEW.

HENRY: Knew it! From the start! Wrong! I felt it, warned it! But you insisted. 'She's called, my Lord Bishop, it's her vocation, my Lord Bishop!' And now, on top of everything else, farmers and knights and Wyclif's mad Lollard priests on the rampage. They're burning records in the manor houses, d'you know that? How can we know who's bonded to who, now? And in the midst of all a mad girl raves to be absolved from that most sacred vow. You satisfied?

MATHEW: There must be a hearing, my lord.

HENRY: Who says so? I'll say what must and must not be.

MATHEW: We *must* be seen to be considering the pleas.

HENRY: I've considered them. She took the vows of poverty, chastity and obedience. A vow is a vow! It must be kept!

MATHEW: Perhaps she can be moved, share a life with another anchoress.

HENRY: She wanted unity with God? The perfect state? Upon her head the perfect state! A vow is a vow!

MATHEW: *(Persistent.)* Her parents and the apprentice Robert Lonle are waiting to see you.

HENRY: Well, send them away! I trust not her, not him, not any of them. Their heads are full of discontent, confusion, and their tempers are insolent.

MATHEW: But what shall I tell them?

HENRY: Tell them! Tell them! Tell them they neglected to plough and harrow my lands in the spring. Tell them God's granted my corn to grow and they owe it to God and me and the land to reap and make hay and grind. Tell them that! A struggle, why is everything a struggle?

MATHEW: I'll call them in, my lord.

> *MATHEW leaves. HENRY glares in the direction of CHRISTINE's cell. MATHEW returns with AGNES, WILLIAM and ROBERT.*

HENRY: And was she an aggravation for you, too? Did she have tantrums as a child which you thought were visions? Thought you had a special little girl, so you indulged her? Fanned her fervours, inflamed her imagination?

WILLIAM: It were her mother made her pious.

AGNES: It was her father had her taught the word.

HENRY: *(Exploding.)* The word? The word? She learned to read? And did you ask permission? Was the levy paid? And *you (To ROBERT.)* want my permission to learn the word! *(Pointing to the cell.)* See where reading leads? To notions that take power of minds too weak to contradict them. Notions have a life of their own to chain you, grab you, bind you, hold you! *(Pauses to collect his temper.)* What have you come to ask of me?

AGNES: She's our only child, Bishop, sir. No sons to help our work, look after our old age, and bring us heirs. Thaas a hard life on earth, an' the promise o' heaven then an' a family now – them's the only relief in it. She give our Lord three precious years. She've tried to please God an' the Church. Let them be pleased enough, Lord Bishop, sir, your reverend. Let her go.

WILLIAM: What's to be gained from a reluctant solitary, my lord? You want your folk to take strength an' example from your anchoresses, don't you, sir? To give courage, light, set a standard? What standard can my poor daughter set? She've gone in there to fill her head an' heart but look – she've emptied them instead. No light, no standard, lord, no use to God or Church, or Bishop Henry. Let her go.

ROBERT: She were betrothed to me for love of me, an' I to her for love of her. There ent a week passed in these three years I've not sat with her, an' she talk an' talk an' talk an' talk, and I know she love me still. Let her go, sir. Let her go an' we'll be married. You'll hear narthin' of us more if you relent and let her go.

Pause.

HENRY: We will think on it.

(HENRY and MATHEW leave, followed by the other three. Now a red glow slowly grows, like a house burning, as we hear the children's voices.)

CHILDREN'S VOICES: *(Off.)* Christ-ine, Christ-ine, had a revelation yet, had a vision, had a word, had a revelation yet? Christ-ine, Christ-ine, had a revelation yet, had a vision, had a word, had a revelation yet? Christ-ine, Christ-ine…

CHRISTINE: Not fit! Not fit! Christine not fit! You have hell anchored to your church, Bishop Henry. Break down its walls, break them, break them. IN THE NAME OF God, BREAK THEM DOWN!

Sound of drums and marching feet. They grow louder and louder, topped by the cry of a man being slaughtered. The red glow lingers. Light shifts from church to carpenter's workshop.

SCENE FIFTEEN

CARPENTER'S WORKSHOP

AGNES seems anxiously to be waiting for someone.

The TRAVELLING PRIEST enters carrying the dead ROBERT in his arms. Lays him gently in the wood shavings. The PRIEST is himself in tatters and blood.

AGNES gasps, bends to wipe away the blood, her low moaning continues throughout.

TRAVELLING PRIEST: London, the Friday after the feast of Corpus Christi, the boy King meets Wat Tyler at Mile End, agrees to his demands. I watch it happen. Watch the King bow to his people, listen to the roar, the cheer go up. Shivers down my spine. Exhilarating.

Then the mood changes. People become intoxicated with their gains and powers. A peoples' court behead Sudbury and Hales and at the Tower the King's physician, which intoxicates their passions more. Then the crude and rough ones surface. Scum arising to the top to pay off ancient scores and murder aliens.

I shout and warn but there are quick and easy tongues to call me traitor. Oh, those quick and easy tongues! We come to Smithfield where we give the King a second paper of demands. 'Come talk to us' he says. Again I warn but oh the tongues were quick and easy. Wat the Tyler goaded by the quick and easy mob steps to the other side where – swish! The Mayor of London kills him quick and easy. That was that!

The Freedom Charters are withdrawn. John Ball sings his last sermon and is hung, drawn and quartered at St Albans, and the rest come home. *(Looking at ROBERT.)* One way or another.

> *CHRISTINE is heard singing her song, but sadly now.*

CHRISTINE: I will forsake all that I see,
Father and friend, and follow thee,
Gold and goods, riches and rent,
Town and tower and tenement,
Playing and prosperity,
In poverty for to be one with thee.

> *Light transfers to inside the church.*

SCENE SIXTEEN

Inside the church. Lit away from the cell wall.

HENRY and MATHEW confront WILLIAM who is on his knees before them awaiting the verdict.

HENRY: We cannot. It is not in our power to sanction the breaking of a vow, nor can we bless an adulteress to Christ. She cannot leave the cell.

The cell wall revolves slowly. We see the inside of the cell. Backed against the wall is CHRISTINE. The sight of her is shocking. She is dirty, unkempt and terrified as her eyes take in what she now realises is to be her cell for ever.

CHILDREN'S VOICES: *(Distant.)* Christ-ine, Christ-ine! Had a revelation yet? Had a vision, had a word, had a revelation yet? Christ-ine, Christ-ine! Had a revelation yet? Had a vision, had a word, had a revelation yet?

And on the chanting the lights slowly fade.

ACT TWO

One continues scene – in eleven parts. The interior of CHRISTINE's cell.

PART ONE

CHRISTINE in the corner of her cell, terrified.

CHRISTINE: I ent narthin', I hev narthin' I desire narthin', save the love of Jesus only. I ent narthin', I hev narthin', I desire narthin' save the love of Jesus only. I ent narthin' …

PART TWO

CHRISTINE on her knees before her crucifix.

CHRISTINE: O Jesus Christ whose flesh were torn and into which you bid us creep for comfort – comfort me. Comfort me, deliver me an' show me mercy, Lord. Have mercy an' deliver me from here. I ent no saint nor martyr but a little thing afeared wi' timid soul an' helpless heart an' no strong body like I thought. I tried, my Lord, wi' all I got. I give, my Lord, wi' what I had. But what I had and what I got was not what you and me imagined, Lord. I thought I heard you speak to me, sign me a path, but that were Satan, Lord, the devil givin' me ideas my feeble head weren't made to take. Your father made me, Jesus Lord. He know me what I am an' fit for. Speak to him, Lord. Tell him make a sign to Henry. Tell him what you see, Lord Jesus. Look at me and tell him how this little gal ent made for solitary life. I ent, Lord, I ent, Lord, I ent, Lord, I ent, I ent, I ent, I ent, I ent, I ent…

PART THREE

CHRISTINE in the corner of her cell.

CHRISTINE: I ent narthin', I hev narthin', I desire narthin'
save the love of Jesus only. I ent narthin', I hev narthin', I
desire narthin' save the love of Jesus only. I ent narthin', I
hev narthin', I desire narthin' save the love of Jesus only. I
ent narthin'...

> *Sounds of taunting children outside the grille window
> of the cell. Their hands come through, hoping to touch
> her. She ignores them, sits on in her corner. Their
> chanting takes over from hers.*

CHILDREN'S VOICES: Christ-ine, Christ-ine, had a revelation
yet? Had a vision, had a word, had a revelation yet?
Christ-ine, Christ-ine, had a revelation yet? Had a vision,
had a word, had a revelation yet, Christ-ine, Christ-ine...

PART FOUR

CHRISTINE by the quatrefoil.

CHRISTINE: I know, father, yes, I know, I begged to be a
solitary, yes, I did. But now I must return to people. Live
among the living, see? Thaas like this here. Alone, in the
silence, in the dark, I see the truth – thaas noisy, truth. 'Tis!
People pullin', pushin' different ways – 'I'm this, I'm that,
here's right, there's right, I want this, I want that, do that,
do this!' screamin', screamin'! I can't stop 'em, I can't blot
'em, rub 'em out. But, thinks I, put me *among* 'em, *with* 'em,
look, I'll only see a few, hear a few, believe me. Stands
to reason, father. Honest. Anchoresses hear the truth an'
it's more'n they can bear. You show me anyone who's
born to carry *all* the truth? So help me, father, please, or
I'll go mad with the noise. What good'll Christine be to
God, then, poor little mad gal? Eh, father? God don't want
no poor little mad gals, do 'ee? So help me, father, help
deliver me from here. Please, father, help me, help me,
help me, help me...

PART FIVE

CHRISTINE in the corner of her cell.

CHRISTINE: I ent narthin', I hev narthin', I desire narthin'
save the love of Jesus only. I ent narthin' I hev narthin', I
desire narthin' save the love of Jesus only. I ent narthin', I
hev narthin' I desire narthin' save the love of Jesus only. I
ent narthin'…

PART SIX

*CHRISTINE is lying flat on her back on her bed. After
many, many seconds she sits bolt upright, swivels
round, her face alight with a new thought.*

CHRISTINE: There ent one God, there's two! Why would
one God make livin' difficult by putting good *and* evil in
the world? There *must* be two! Both made the world! One
shovelled earth from out a hole the other shovelled earth
back again. One shovelled out, one shovelled in! one
shovelled out, one shovelled in.

She's incredulous at the thought, then panics.

O Lord! O Lord! To which one do I pray? To which? To
which one do I pray?

*She moves to the crucifix, then away from it, then
to it, then away, uncertain which end of the cell to
go to. Finally she chooses the one she knows, and
desperately kneels before crucifix.*

Hail Mary, full of grace! The Lord is with thee, blessed art
thou amongst women, an' blessed is the fruit of thy womb,
Jesus. Hail Mary, full of grace! The Lord is with thee,
blessed art thou amongst women, an' blessed is the fruit
of thy womb, Jesus. Hail Mary, full of grace! The Lord is
with thee, blessed art thou amongst women, an' blessed is
the fruit of thy womb, Jesus. Hail Mary… *(Stops suddenly.)*
Thaas a blasphemous thought, Christine Carpenter. Two
Gods! Where'd a thought like that come from?

*She returns to lying flat on her bed. Long silence.
Then –*

Two Gods, two Gods. One shovelled out, one shovelled
in. two Gods, two Gods. One shovelled out, one shovelled
in…

PART SEVEN

*CHRISTINE paces up and down her cell. HENRY and
MATHEW are talking with her through the quatrefoil.
They can't be seen by the audience.*

CHRISTINE: Two Gods, two Gods! One shovelled out, one
shovelled in! Two Gods, two Gods! One shovelled out, one
shovelled in.

HENRY: Be still, child. Sit. Take hold. You are a bride of
Christ. Trust him. Now, are you sitting on your stool? The
one your father made specially for you with his loving
hands? You're loved, Christine. Loved and admired.

CHRISTINE: *(Sitting on the stool.)* Not fit, not fit!

MATHEW: The villagers look up to you.

CHRISTINE: Not fit, not fit!

MATHEW: They're proud of you, their anchoress, their very
own.

CHRISTINE: Not fit, not fit!

HENRY: Control yourself, be calm. I have some questions
for you. Answer carefully. Have you told people of your
vision?

CHRISTINE: Yes.

MATHEW: 'Yes, my lord.'

CHRISTINE: 'Yes, my lord.'

HENRY: And it's your own vision, no one put it to you?

CHRISTINE: No, my lord.

HENRY: Have you had fevers recently, sickness?

CHRISTINE: No, my lord.

HENRY: You don't have to *keep* saying 'my lord'. Only the first time.

CHRISTINE: The vision's mine! All burnin' bright and fresh and mine alone! *For* me! For the *world!* There be two Gods!

HENRY: That's heresy!

CHRISTINE: *(Hardly restraining her glee.)* Not fit, not fit! Let Christine go, she is not fit!

HENRY: Do you still love Christ?

CHRISTINE: Yes! Yes!

HENRY: Still long for union with God?

CHRISTINE: Not fit, not fit!

HENRY: And it was not a temptation of the devil?

CHRISTINE: No, no! The Lord tell me. There's a God of Love an' a God of hate. The good one shovelled out, he say, the evil shovelled in. I am the good God's son, he say, the evil God had Satan. All what you see an' all what's been, an' all that ever will be seen, the two on 'em created, look! An' thaas the truth, he say.

HENRY: That cannot be!

CHRISTINE: It is! It is! It is! It is!

MATHEW: Christine. Listen to me. It's Mathew talking to you. Calm yourself and listen. How can you be so certain it was Christ you saw?

CHRISTINE: Because, because, because –

MATHEW: Because?

CHRISTINE: *(Inspired.)* Because beside him stood the other son.

MATHEW: The two together?

CHRISTINE: To prove, to prove, to prove.

MATHEW: Saying?

(Long pause. She cannot answer.)

HENRY: Convenience thoughts! She's seen two Gods? Possible, but conveniently for her, unprovable. It's as good a a way of describing the workings of this damned life as any.

MATHEW: Just like the teaching of our Church?

HENRY: Except that it *is* our Church and the one in power with responsibility, and I want that Church obeyed, respected and strong. Order is order, duty is duty, a vow is a vow! And I think you'd do well to find another parish.

MATHEW: Or another Church!

> *CHRISTINE realises her stratagem has failed. Desperation turns to fury. The doubter emerges at last.*

CHRISTINE: *(Viciously.)* There are no Gods, there are no sons. For, look you, would a God of *love* put *evil* in your heart, would he? Would he? Do you believe a God so careless? Answer me. A careless God?

You have hell anchored to your Church, father. Break down its walls, break them, break them, break them. In the name of God BREAK THEM DOWN!

PART EIGHT

CHRISTINE is by the windowgrille.

CHRISTINE: Thaas no good comin' to me for advice, little gal.
What advice can a miserable sinner like me give anybody?
Go to the Bishop Henry, or the Rector, or my mother
an' father. They'll give you good advice. *(Pause.)* Oh no,
because I live here don't mean –

> *She thinks. Then changes her mind and decides to
> offer advice.*

Hear me then. When you die your soul goes to the terrors
you've been afeared of all your life. You had no terrors
then your soul's left in peace. You hev them – they go with
you! So you live that you should have no terrors, little gal,
you live like that, look.

> *Pause. The taunting voices of CHILDREN return.
> Their hands poking through the grille, close to her
> face. She stands, wild-eyed, listening to the words,
> transfixed by the waving hands, her teeth clenched
> tight.*

CHILDREN'S VOICES: Christ-ine, Christ-ine, had a revelation
yet? Had a vision, had a word, had a revelation yet?
Christ-ine, Christ-ine, had a revelation yet, had a vision,
had a word, have a revelation yet? Christ-ine, Christ-ine…

> *They give up. She relaxes a little. Struggles to collect
> herself.*

CHRISTINE: Well, thaas an improvement. I give advice to
somebody. Didn't know what I was talkin' about but I
spoke, leastways. So there, now. *(Pause.)* So there, now.
(Pause. Looks left and right.) So there, now.

> *She must establish a routine. She runs to kneel before
> the crucifix and begins fast praying.*

Hail O cross, dedicated to the body of Christ, and adorned
with his limbs as with pearls, save the sound an' heal the

sick. *(Striking her breast hard.)* Let what cannot be done by human power be done in thy name. *(Crossing herself each time.)* We adore thee. We adore thee. We adore thee.

> *With her thumb she makes the sign of the cross on the ground and kisses it.*

Hail Mary, full of grace! The Lord is with thee; blessed art thou amongst women, an' blessed is the fruit of thy womb, Jesus. Hail Mary, full of grace! The Lord is with thee; blessed art thou amongst women, an' blessed is the fruit of thy womb, Jesus. Hail Mary, full of grace! The Lord is with thee, blessed art thou amongst women, an' blessed is the fruit of thy womb, Jesus. Amen. *(Pause.)* What next?

> *She rises quickly and sits on her stool. Pause.*

What next?

> *She rises. With the end of her dress she dusts the table, then the stool, then the bed, then the stool again. Pause.*

What next?

> *She places the stool in a different position. Then another position,. Then in another position. Pause.*

What next?

> *There is a hairbrush in her cell, under her bed. She reaches for that and begins furiously to bring order to her unkempt hair.*

It's because you don't look after yourself, gal. Thaas why they don't trust you. They look through them holes an' they see dirt an' filth an' there's smells an' goodness knows what, and they think they see a mad woman. So comb your hair and bring back the runnin' gal, the dancin' gal, the gal-at-the-fair gal what made the village proud. They didn't mind you then, your prayers for all them an' preachin' them an' lockin'-yourself-up-to-suffer-for-them. So comb your hair and pull your old self together, there's folk at your window for words of advice. *(Moves to the window.)* Yes, little gal, I'll answer your questions. *(To herself.)* You crossed your mouth? *(Crosses her mouth.)* Good! *(To the window.)* Now, ask away. *(Pauses. Listens. Laughs.)* Ha, ha! Ho,ho! 'The meanin' of life'? Thaas big! You're bold! *(Gaily.)* There *ent* no meanin', little girl. None! But – ha, ha! There's purpose! To do good. In a word, a deed, a chair made, a tree planted, the poor fed, a wrong forgiven, in love...in love...in love... For, as' it's written: 'An' God said, "Let there be light", an' there *was* light. An' God saw the light, that it was good...an' God saw everything that he made, an' behold, it was very good.' Love, little gal, the purpose is to love. Cos the Lord Jesus Christ loved you so much, look, that he suffer an' die for you. Love, little gal. There en narthin' more powerful than that!

> *She is jubilant. Continues brushing her hair.*

There! That weren't bad! I did well then. You did very well, Christine. Narthin' mad about that. She'll go away and tell people that the gal Christine Carpenter give her good words of advice, an' people'll start coming again, and the word'll spread, an' get to the Bishop's ears, an' he'll write to the Pope, an' you'll see, gal, you'll see, you'll see, you'll see, and then...you'll see...

What next?

> *Pause. She runs to kneel before the crucifix and recites three Aves.*

Hail Mary, full of grace! The Lord is with thee. Blessed art thou amongst women, an' blessed is the fruit of thy womb, Jesus. Hail Mary, full of grace! The Lord is with thee. Blessed art thou amongst women, an' blessed is the fruit of thy womb, Jesus. Hail Mary, full of grace! The Lord is with thee. Blessed art thou amongst women, an' blessed is the fruit of thy womb, Jesus. Amen.

What next?

Pause. She rises. Sits on stool. Intones.

The remedy for pride is humility. The remedy for envy is love. The remedy for anger is patience. The remedy for sloth is work. The remedy for covetousness is contempt for earthly things. The remedy for avarice is a generous heart. The remedy for lust is mortification of the flesh. *(Beats her breast, hard.)* The remedy for lust is mortification of the flesh. The remedy for lust is mortification of the flesh. The remedy for lust is mortification of the flesh. The remedy for lust is mortification of the fle-e-e-e-esh!

> *She shrieks the last word. Rises, bangs her head against the stone wall, calling out at the same time.*

Flesh flesh flesh flesh help help help help mercy mercy mercy mercy O mother! Tell them, Mother, tell them tell them, Mother, Mother, I have no vocation I am not fit I am not fit I AM NOT FIT!

> *Stops abruptly.*

What next?

> *Pause. She sits on her stool. Defeated. Intones.*

The remedy for pride is humility. The remedy for envy is love. The remedy for anger is patience. The remedy for sloth is work. The remedy for covetousness is contempt for earthly things. The remedy for avarice is a generous heart. The remedy for lust is mortification of the flesh. *(Beats her breast, hard.)* The remedy for lust is mortification of the flesh. The remedy for lust is mortification of the flesh.

What next?

> *Pause. She rises, moves to a corner of the cell, hoists her dress, urinates, all hope draining from her.*

PART NINE

CHRISTINE in the corner of her cell. She cradles the heavy crucifix in her arms. Laments and rocks backwards and forwards.

CHRISTINE: The poor wail, the orphan sighs, the widow is desolate, the pilgrim needs water, there's danger for the voyager, hardship for the soldier, cares for the bishop. Come to me, come to me, come, come, come, come.

Pause.

I've loved him from cradle-time. No smile like my baby's. See, they humiliate him now. *I* can't comfort him, though. I've loved him from his first falls. No cry like my baby's. See, there are thorns on his head. *I* can't comfort him though. Was anything so tender? The smell of oil on his skin, the trust in his eyes as I wrapped him up warm. See, they've given his poor body a cross to bear. Why don't *my* bones crack instead? I can't comfort him though. And that first word he spoke! Such cleverness. How swift he learnt. See, they nail him now. My lovely boy, my own, my flesh, my blood. An' did I feed an' watch you grow an' guard you 'gainst the plagues for this? An' did we look at blue skies, the matin' mare, the suckin' lamb, the settin' sun, an' watch the rivers runnin' – for this? *(Cries out.)* Put nails through me! Through my hands, my feet. Me! Me! Oh, the ache, the ache, the helpless ache. I can't bear it! Can't bear it! Cannot. Oh, oh…

Pause.

The poor wail, the orphan sighs, the widow is desolate, the pilgrim needs water, there's danger for the voyager, hardship for the soldier, cares for the bishop. Come to me, come to me, come, come, come, come…

PART TEN

CHRISTINE in the corner of her cell. She is squeezing one bare breast, part a caress, part a maternal longing, intoning.

CHRISTINE: The poor wail, the orphan sighs, the widow is desolate, the pilgrim needs water, there's danger for the voyager, hardship for the soldier, cares for the bishop. Come to me, come to me, come, come, come, come, come, come, come, come…

PART ELEVEN

CHRISTINE, by the quatrefoil, her back to the wall.

CHRISTINE: It's my thoughts, father, I can't put my thoughts on *him*. I see him on the cross, I see that sweet face sufferin', I see that poor body hangin' limp on its nails, an' I feel the pain here an' here an' here an' here' an' here, an' I stand with my back to the wall, my arms outstretched *(Her movements follow her words.)* my eyes closed, an' I cry out, 'Lord Jesus, sweet lord, I'm with you, here I stand, I feel the pain, I'm with you.' An' then, an' then – Oh forgive me, father, forgive me! – but as I stand, my arms outstretched, my eyes closed – I think new thoughts which I can't deny. *(Her legs move apart now.)* Cos, oh, they're sweet, so sweet. I'm naked. My body open to the sky, my skin in the grass, sun on my breasts. I feel cool winds bring me the smell of hawthorn and the wild mint. An' I see the birds sweep high an' singin'. An', oh, those clouds, those glorious, rollin' shapes, that sweet scent, that soft air – thaas not the devil's forms. An' I'm torn between shame and delirium. The spring, father, the spring! I am crucified upon the spring!

> *The taunting chants of CHILDREN are heard. Their hands wave through the grille.*

CHILDREN'S VOICES: Christ-ine, Christ-ine, had a revelation yet, had a vision, had a word, had a revelation yet? Christ-ine, Christ-ine, had a revelation yet, had a vision, had a word, had a revelation yet? Christ-ine, Christ-ine...

> *She stands with her back to the wall, arms outstretched, listening, watching the waving hands. Slowly she moves towards them. Watches. Then – she grabs one and plunges her teeth into it. There is a terrible scream. She releases the hand. The voices, screaming, move and die away.*

What next?

> *Long pause. She looks around her cell. She turns to a wall, places her hand on it, mumbles to herself, turning her head slowly around the cell.*

CHRISTINE: This is a wall, an' this is a wall, an' this is a wall, an' this is a wall, an' this is a wall, an' this is...

> *On which poor, mad, imprisoned figure the lights slowly fade till only a faint light comes through her grille. Then – darkness.*

OTHER ARNOLD WESKER TITLES

WESKER'S DOMESTIC PLAYS
9781849431606

WESKER'S COMEDIES
9781849431286

WESKER'S LOVE PLAYS
9781840027914

WESKER'S MONOLOGUES
9781840027921

WESKER'S POLITICAL PLAYS
9781840029543

WESKER'S SOCIAL PLAYS
9781840028898

WESKER ON THEATRE
9781840029864

GROUPIE
9781840029550

JOY AND TYRANNY
9781849431088

THE KITCHEN
9781849430272

AMBIVALENCES: A PORTRAIT OF ARNOLD WESKER FROM A TO W
CHIARA MONTENERO AND ARNOLD WESKER
9781849431323

www.ingramcontent.com/pod-product-compliance
Ingram Content Group UK Ltd.
Pitfield, Milton Keynes, MK11 3LW, UK
UKHW020720280225
455688UK00012B/443